Flourishing in Community

Flourishing in Community

A Theology of Togetherness

JOEL A. KIME

WIPF & STOCK · Eugene, Oregon

FLOURISHING IN COMMUNITY
A Theology of Togetherness

Copyright © 2024 Joel A. Kime. All rights reserved. Except for brief quotations in critical publications or reviews, no part of this book may be reproduced in any manner without prior written permission from the publisher. Write: Permissions, Wipf and Stock Publishers, 199 W. 8th Ave., Suite 3, Eugene, OR 97401.

Wipf & Stock
An Imprint of Wipf and Stock Publishers
199 W. 8th Ave., Suite 3
Eugene, OR 97401

www.wipfandstock.com

PAPERBACK ISBN: 979-8-3852-2232-2
HARDCOVER ISBN: 979-8-3852-2233-9
EBOOK ISBN: 979-8-3852-2234-6

VERSION NUMBER 121824

Unless otherwise indicated, Scripture quotations are taken from the Holy Bible, New International Version®, NIV®. Copyright © 1973, 1978, 1984, 2011 by Biblica, Inc.™ Used by permission of Zondervan. All rights reserved worldwide. www.zondervan.com The "NIV" and "New International Version" are trademarks registered in the United States Patent and Trademark Office by Biblica, Inc.™

Where indicated, Scripture quotations are taken from New American Standard Bible®, Copyright © 1960, 1971, 1977, 1995, 2020 by The Lockman Foundation. All rights reserved.

Where indicated, Scripture quotations are taken from The Holy Bible, English Standard Version. ESV® Text Edition: 2016. Copyright © 2001 by Crossway Bibles, a publishing ministry of Good News Publishers.

Where indicated, Scripture quotations are taken from New Revised Standard Version Bible: Catholic Edition, copyright © 1989, 1993 the Division of Christian Education of the National Council of the Churches of Christ in the United States of America. Used by permission. All rights reserved.

Contents

Acknowledgments | vii

Introduction: Just Getting People Together Is Not the Point | 1

PART 1: Defining Human Flourishing and Togetherness
1. Flourishing | 13
2. Individualism | 24
3. Christian Faith as Individual and Together | 39

PART 2: Theology and Togetherness for Flourishing
4. What Is a Theology of Togetherness? | 61
5. God as Trinitarian Community | 67
6. Sin as Selfishness | 72
7. Salvation as Selfless Emancipation | 80
8. Covenant for Community Flourishing | 90
9. A Kingdom of Loving Togetherness | 94
10. Union with Christ Together | 100
11. Solidarity with Others | 115

PART 3: Practices of Togetherness in Christian Communities
12. How a Theology of Togetherness Leads to Practices of Togetherness | 123
13. Practicing Ritual Together for Flourishing | 126
14. Purple Church: Practicing Togetherness to Bring Political Unity in the Church | 133
15. Beloved Community: Practicing Togetherness to Bring Racial Unity in the Church | 150

16 Practicing Repentance Together as a Prerequisite for Flourishing | 178

17 Creating Culture Together for Flourishing | 196

Conclusion: A Vision of Flourishing Together | 217

Appendix 1: Additional Suggestions for Practicing Ritual, Habits, and Disciplines Together | 229

Appendix 2: Questions Asked of Ministerium Churches Regarding Diversity | 233

Bibliography | 235

Acknowledgments

Throughout the process of writing, I have felt what other authors have sometimes expressed, that writing can be a lonely pursuit. An author is one person by themselves wrestling with ideas, attempting to sort out those ideas with words on a page. *But there are so many other people involved.* In fact, the community of people required to publish this book is an illustration of its topic: togetherness. Therefore, I have so many people to thank, for so many worked together to produce flourishing in my life while I wrote.

The book's genesis occurred during my doctoral studies. I am grateful for my fellow members in my organizational theology track of the doctor of theology cohort at Evangelical Seminary, from 2018–2021—Allen Bingham, Tony Blair, Jeff Byerly, Amin Flowers, Kenneth Gates, and Shawn Keener. I thank these men for their laughter, their support, and their input. I learned so much from each of you.

Likewise, I thank each member of my dissertation committee, Tony Blair, Doug Jacobsen, Brian Leander, and Kim Shatzer. Their constant kindness and guidance encouraged me as I wrote the dissertation that would eventually become this book. Their feedback shaped the dissertation in a multitude of important ways, so much so that it was, and thus this book is, a product of togetherness, start to finish. It was Tony who, after reading an early draft of my dissertation, which was supposed to be a theology of organizations, said, "I think you have a theology of togetherness." My initial reaction when I first read Tony's comment was, "Oh no . . . did I just spend two years writing for naught?" I hadn't lost two years. I just needed to refocus.

I am grateful for the family of Faith Church and their support of my doctoral studies, the dissertation, and this book. You provided prayer, finances, accountability, insightful feedback, and even two personal writing retreats, all of which helped me greatly. Talk about togetherness! You also supported me when I traveled to India in March 2023, where I taught this book as a course to master of arts in ministry students at Evangelical College of Theology in Churachandpur, Manipur. Thanks to Lalrosiem Songate, Principal of ECT, for that amazing opportunity. Thanks to my class of six students for graciously engaging with this Westerner and helping me think much more holistically. I am so grateful to George Callihan and the team at Wipf & Stock for publishing my book and graciously guiding me through your process. I am astounded at the eagle eye of my copyeditor, Brittany McComb. Thank you, Brittany, for your thorough, winsome work. Your edits improved the manuscript and fixed errors on nearly every page.

Most of all I thank my amazing family and friends for their support and encouragement. Thanks to Chris Readinger, who, other than my parents and siblings, is the person in this acknowledgments section that I have been in relationship with the longest. I am grateful for all our meals, phone calls, texts, and prayer times. Don and Ang Bentley, thank you for your constant encouragement, guidance, and wisdom; and Don, thank you for your advice, as a writer who has gone before. More, I'm grateful for your friendship. Though we live twenty-five driving hours apart, I appreciate your practice of togetherness on WhatsApp, on Zoom, and those many vacations. To the Tribe—Jeff and Tasha Byerly, Kirk and Debbie Marks, Tim and Kim Seiger, Cam and Jess Smith—it is such a blessing to have colleagues who are also friends—people who get it! Thanks to our care group friends—Rick Robinson, Ron and Linda Seiger, and Greg and Emerald Scaffe—for your encouragement and prayer. A special thanks to the Fire Friends—Brandon and Kristen Hershey and Andy and Kim Weikert—for doing life together, for laughing and crying around many fires, at restaurants, events, and in our text group. I'm deeply grateful to my parents, Harold and Beth Kime, my siblings, Jeff and Laura, and their families, my in-laws, Sandy and Diane, and Michelle's extended family for your support. But I am most thankful for my immediate family, for your support and encouragement. Thank you, Tyler, Mariah, Luke and Lily, and thank you, Connor and Katie; thank you, especially, for the multiple weekends I spent at your houses dog sitting, which gave me lots of time to write. Thank you, Michelle, Jared, and Meagan, for your patience as I read so many books and spent countless hours writing, many of which were away from home. I love you all. Thanks especially to my wife, Michelle, who has been a constant encourager and who also read numerous drafts and provided excellent feedback. I am grateful for this life together with you. I love you.

Introduction
Just Getting People Together Is Not the Point

Two groups of teenagers were staring at me, fear and loathing in their eyes. Without saying a word, they were begging me to stop what I was doing. I was their youth pastor, and I had just informed them that the two groups were going to mingle. From my vantage point standing in front of them, it was clear they did not want to mingle. Why was I making those teens do what they did not want to do?

I had been youth pastor at my church for about nine months when a sister church approached us with an idea. What if I would become youth pastor of their teenagers too, leading a combined group? Our church leaders and I thought it was a wonderful idea, so over the summer of 2003, I planned the merger. I was excited to embark on this new journey, but as a very inexperienced youth pastor, how would I help two distinct groups of teenagers come together as one?

I knew it would take time to build meaningful relationships, but I thought it might help to start with a symbolic act. As we will learn in chapter 13, rituals are symbolic acts that help us imagine and build new worlds. I wanted the two separate youth groups to imagine becoming one. For our kick-off event, our sister church rented the gymnasium of the school where they met for worship. Most of the new merged group meetings were going to take place at my church building, so we thought it appropriate for our group to make a selfless overture by holding the first event on the sister church's home turf. That evening, after some icebreaker games and sports, the groups ate pizza on the bleachers in the gym. I'm using "groups" intentionally in the plural because there were two very visible groups on those bleachers. The youth of each church had sorted themselves *apart* from one another.

My plan for the night was to have a devotional talk about unity, and it seemed the evening was starting with disunity. I was disappointed that none of the students from either church were sacrificially reaching out to one another. I can hardly blame them, because I have observed the same tendency with a variety of age groups. Most people stick with their friends, with those familiar to them, whether children or adults. That same dynamic was at work years later when I was senior pastor, and I asked the adults in a worship service to sit in new locations. Those adults sit in the same section of the same pews every week. After preaching for sixteen years, you could walk me blindfolded into the sanctuary on a Sunday, and I could point out with a high degree of precision who was sitting where. Whether adults or youth, we humans can struggle to open our communities to new people.

Back at that rented gym in 2003, I looked at the two youth groups on the bleachers, totally separate from one another. But I was ready. I had come prepared with my symbolic gesture. I queued up the Beatles' song "Come Together," and I gave the following instructions: as the song played, I wanted them to physically get up from their seats, move their bodies, and sit next to someone from the other church. I hit the play button, and as the Beatles crooned "Come Together," nothing happened on the bleachers.

It was at that moment when the teenagers' faces had filled with fear and loathing. After some further coaxing, the students begrudgingly rose from their places on the bleachers and came together. They were now physically together, but they were far from being together in any meaningful way. What kind of coming together was I seeking in the group? Certainly more than just sitting next to a new person for fifteen minutes one evening.

As the world learned during the COVID-19 pandemic, physical presence with others has great value, but that night on the bleachers, I wanted something much more than physical proximity for my students. The youth group merger lasted three years, and I believe a deeper, better unity eventually did form in *some* relationships. Yet, the goal of coming together did not occur in all their relationships, and even in the ones where relationship did form, the quality of togetherness was not always as deep or as meaningful as I had hoped.

During those three years, we had numerous youth group meetings, events, retreats, and mission trips. Then it was over. In 2006 the other church took occupancy of their newly constructed building, and they hired a part-time youth pastor, hoping to focus on their school district. We had a closing ceremony, and the groups separated. While I was glad for the opportunity to lead the combined group those three years, after that closing ceremony the groups barely interacted, and with rare exceptions, friendships did not continue.

Coming together is difficult. And yet, the word "together" is *everywhere*. It seems to me that it is one of the most popular words in America.

Politicians use the word together, claiming that our country is divided, and we should vote for them because they have figured out how to bring us together. Social media companies claim that their networks help people come together like never before. A home goods manufacturer suggests that if we use its time-saving cleaning products we'll have more time together with our loved ones. I could go on and on. Are you seeing the word "together" as much as I am? I doubt it, but keep reading and that may soon change. Why?

I see the word together so often because of the principle "familiarity breeds frequency." If you are thinking, "The phrase is supposed to be 'familiarity breeds contempt,'" you are right. We'll get to that phrase in a moment. I just searched online for "familiarity breeds frequency," and I couldn't find it, so maybe I've coined a new phrase. Actually, "familiarity breeds frequency" is just a new title for a common human experience. Let me explain. After purchasing a new car, if it is a model that is new to you, in the days and months after the purchase, you suddenly see that model of car all over the road. Before purchasing your new vehicle, that model rarely, if ever, stood out to you. It's not as though hundreds of people living in your community bought the same model vehicle around the same time. What happened? You grew a new familiarity with your model vehicle, and thus you are now aware of others like it, seeing them frequently. Familiarity breeds frequency. In the same way, when I became immersed in thinking and writing about togetherness, I started noticing the word together all the time. As you read this book, I suspect you'll begin to see the word together more often in our society also. In fact, I want you to see it. More importantly I ask you to evaluate how together is being used.

I am concerned that the frequent use of together and how it is being used might be a problem because of the truth of that other phrase, "familiarity breeds contempt." We humans can become so accustomed to something that we take it for granted, and when we take something for granted, it is liable to lose its meaning and impact. I have come to believe that the word together, and its related concept of "togetherness," are overly familiar in our society, leading many of us to wrongly assume we understand what these terms mean and how these terms can benefit society.

But don't take it from me. Test it out for yourself. Throughout the rest of your day, try to keep the word together in the forefront of your mind. Notice how often it is used in advertisements, in songs, in interviews, in print, online, and in many other conversations. As you listen for instances of the word together, evaluate how it is used. Do the people using the word together assume a meaning, or do they explain what coming together should look like and accomplish?

As I was writing an early draft of this introduction, I was listening to music in the background. At the very moment I was typing about the prevalence of the word together, the vocalist started singing the word together over and over. Not just three or four times, but dozens, almost as if to respond to what I am typing. It felt a bit eerie! The song is "Operation Spirit (The Tyranny of Tradition)" by the band Live.[1] As I have asked you to evaluate the occurrences of the word together you discover, I'm going to do so with Live's use of together in the song. What is the singer's intent in repeating the word together? Do the lyrics of the song help us understand "togetherness," or do the lyrics assume we already know what it means?

The lyrics talk about broken love, and the singer's hope that he and his former lover might get back together. But what kind of togetherness is he talking about? The writer uses the word together, and he does so while describing a quest for truth, but he assumes that all parties involved understand togetherness. Do all parties understand togetherness? My conclusion? I find the song's use of the word together to be vague and unhelpful.

As I ruminated about how the lyricist used the word together, I took a break to make a cup of coffee, and I checked my phone. I scrolled through one of my church's social media accounts, and I found another use of the word together. Along with posting a photo of a recording booth, an author I appreciate wrote this caption, "Only way we all keep going is together."[2] That message sounds similar to the lyrics in Live's song, but what does the post mean? What kind of togetherness is the author talking about?

The writer of the post, Sarah Bessey, had included a picture of the booth because she was participating in recording an audio version of a book by the late Rachel Held Evans being published posthumously. Evans passed away before completing the book, so several of her author friends worked together to complete the book and recently they published it. With that context, we can make an educated guess about the quality of togetherness that Bessey intended in her post.

It seems to me that she meant something like this, "By working together, we can grieve the loss of Evans and continue her legacy by bringing her words to the world." I propose that interpretation because I've previously read Bessey describing her close friendship with Evans and how she, Bessey, was in mourning over the tragedy of Evans's passing so young (she was only thirty-seven years old), and I have come to know something of

---

1. Live, "Operation Spirit."
2. Bessey, "Keep Going." The post was originally published Aug. 11, 2021 but was deleted at some later date.

the heart in Evans's previous works, which I've also read. Now compare my interpretation with Bessey's phrase. Here they are side-by-side:

Bessey's phrase: "Only way we all keep going is together."

My interpretation: "By working together, we can grieve Evans's loss and continue her legacy by bringing her words to the world."

Do you see how different they are? I find Bessey's phrase to be vague. If I didn't know the background of Bessey's relationship with Evans, and if I didn't know the heart of Evans's work, I would be left to inject Bessey's phrase with my own meaning of together. Bessey's Instagram post, "Only way we all keep going is together," gives the impression that togetherness is not only quite powerful, but togetherness is so vital that it is the "only way we all keep going," and yet she doesn't explain how or why.

Initially I want to cheer her use of together, given that I am writing a book arguing that a certain kind of togetherness, which I will call "flourishing-producing togetherness," is precisely what humanity needs. Having read both Bessey and Evans, I can confirm that their writing often promotes human flourishing, and thus Bessey's "together" likely has the same goal. That nuance of understanding Bessey's use of together, however, is only meaningful to people who read her own or Evans's books.

After reading my thoughts on the Live song and Bessey's post, I suspect some readers might be wondering, "Wait a minute. You're making way too much of your concern about togetherness. When people use the word 'together,' we know what they mean." I hear that concern, but let me push back. How many of us truly have a good sense of what coming together means and is supposed to accomplish?

Tracing its origins, "together" has Old English and German roots that you can see in the English words, "to" and "gether," roots that you might have already correctly guessed refer to the infinitive, "to gather."[3] To gather is to bring people into connection with one another. In its noun form, a gathering is that group of connected people. Gathering people, in and of itself, does not guarantee anything. A nation is a massive gathering of sorts, but it is a gathering that can be exceedingly unhealthy.

But you, reader, are likely not leading a nation or a state. Maybe you have experienced the difficulty of coming together in your business, team, church, family, or friendships. Getting people together can be confusing, complex, and frustrating. My wife will often say to me that though I am physically present with her as I sit next to her on the sofa in the evening, I am not always present with her in a way that she desires. The two of us have gathered, as we are in very close physical proximity, but my wife is

---

3. *Merriam-Webster Dictionary*, "Together."

dissatisfied with the quality of our togetherness. That might have something to do with the fact that I often fall asleep while sitting there. My snoring doesn't help. The same goes for when I am sitting next to her, but I am engrossed in playing a game on my phone. I am physically present, *together* with her, but as she would say, "I am not really present." In her mind, we are not together. Whether a nation or a husband and wife, what should "coming together" be?

I believe a sober evaluation of humanity reveals that we might not understand "together" or "togetherness" as much as we think. As Bessey suggests, we keep going, which is to say that humanity keeps surviving, and we nearly always do so together, but sadly, contrary to Bessey, we often get by with a quality of togetherness that is far from helpful. Survival together does not guarantee flourishing. I am writing this book to highlight the fact that not all togetherness leads to flourishing and provide an alternative approach, grounded in theology, that will help communities flourish together.

A quick survey through the history of humanity can give us examples of togetherness that led to the demise of many humans. War is hell, the phrase goes, because of its massive death toll on humanity. In the summer of 2013, my wife's cousin, Don, his wife Ang, their kids, and our family traveled fifty minutes west of our home in Lancaster, Pennsylvania, to visit the town of Gettysburg. We joined large crowds watching reenactors commemorating the 150th anniversary of the famously bloody battle during the United States' Civil War.

From the observation deck of the Pennsylvania State Memorial, we gazed across farmers' fields that a century and half earlier were littered with dead bodies. Down below, a group of sixty to seventy reenactors wearing Civil War military uniforms demonstrated how troops moved in their firing lines, row after row of soldiers loading their weapons, stepping forward, firing, then moving backward to reload while a different line stepped forward to shoot. As the firing cycle repeated, it was not lost on me that their muskets bellowed only smoke, blanks not bullets. Imagine the Battle of Gettysburg, where the numbers of soldiers and muskets were multiplied by thousands firing deadly projectiles at one another.

The original Battle of Gettysburg concluded when numerous lines of Confederate troops performed what became known as Pickett's Charge, together marching across a mile of open ground in a desperate, and likely arrogant, attempt to overrun Union high ground.[4] Northern muskets and cannons mercilessly mowed down the Southern soldiers, thousands losing

---

4. American Battlefield Trust, "Pickett's Charge," para. 2.

their lives in a matter of minutes. But Gettysburg was neither the bloodiest battle nor was Pickett's Charge the bloodiest day of the war.

Antietam holds that distinction, and I don't need to describe more gory details to make the point that war is a classic example of togetherness that leads to destruction. In the American Civil War, bonds of togetherness were exceedingly tight in both the Northern and Southern armies, but that kind of togetherness resulted in unimaginable death. The American Battlefield Trust estimates that 620,000 soldiers died during the Civil War.[5] If we wanted to, we could talk about other wars and genocides that have body counts in the millions. One person, working alone, cannot achieve such disastrous results. Look back through history, examine every war and genocide, and you will find people working together.

Perhaps war is too extreme an example of negative togetherness. Consider what my nephew shared with me about the swimming league he participated in when he was in elementary school. One team was disqualified from his league's final meet, which is like a championship, because some of the disqualified team's parents were falsifying their children's times, shortening them by seconds. Their team had not qualified for the league meet in many years, so those parents, desperate to give their kids a win, took matters into their own hands.

All they needed to do was shave off a few seconds from each event, and their kids could enjoy the thrill of making it to the final league meet. How did the parents attempt to fix the times? In my nephew's swim league, during dual meets, parents from each team volunteer as timers in each lane, one parent from each team per lane. The parents from the cheating team would time their kids, then subtract a second here and a second there, just enough to hopefully avoid notice by the other timers but still giving their kids the edge they needed to qualify for the league final.

How did they get caught? Because each lane is timed by one parent per team, the cheating was discovered when the altered times were checked against those recorded by the timer from the opposing team. Together, the entire cheating team was disqualified from the final league meet.

I suspect you could imagine numerous negative examples of togetherness that have occurred around you, maybe even some you participated in. When I was a teenager, for example, a handful of buddies and I called ourselves the Death and Destruction Club. While the name was way more aggressive than our reality, we did smash a few mailboxes, steal orange road construction cones to place on our friends' cars, and toilet papered our high school principal's house. I remember feeling a deep uneasiness about our

---

5. American Battlefield Trust, "Cost of War," para. 1.

club, especially when, in the act of launching toilet paper, our principal suddenly opened his front door, flicked on his porch light, and yelled at us. Certain the principal had identified us and was going to punish us, I experienced high anxiety for the next few days. Togetherness does not guarantee flourishing.

Obviously, there are also numerous examples of people working together for good. Consider a prosperous country wiping out the suffocating debts owed them by smaller struggling countries. Or how about a more local example? In my own community, the nonprofit Conestoga Valley SEEDS brings together representatives from a variety of community groups, such as churches, our school district, businesses, and social service agencies. They come together to help those in our community who have a variety of needs, such as for housing, mental health counseling, childcare, and more. SEEDS invites numerous community members to hold free English language development classes for community members who speak other home languages.[6] I suspect you can think of a variety of other positive examples of togetherness.

In addition to positive and negative examples, togetherness can be neutral, primarily when people gather in physical proximity. Vehicles driving through a busy intersection are people together but only circumstantially. Airports, shopping malls, and other common areas like parks include groups big and small, which are together but simply because they are using the geographic space. They are together in a neutral way.

These examples of togetherness, some neutral, negative, and positive, confirm that "togetherness" is the *quality* of being together. That's why this chapter is titled "Just Getting People Together Is Not the Point."[7] It is true that one definition of together is to be in physical proximity to others. But there are other ways to describe together, such as "being of the same mindset," or "in a relationship with another." When two people are dating, we say they are together. With so much variety of meaning, we would do well to examine "together" more deeply.

If togetherness is the quality of being together, defining togetherness can be complex precisely because quality can vary. The Live song and Bessey's social media post are examples of the frequent uses of the word together illustrating for us how much is assumed by the word. Most often, in my opinion, people use together as a positive sentiment, almost giving the impression that to be together is a cure-all for society's ailments. They

---

6. Seeds, "We Made a Video."
7. I am indebted to Doug Jacobsen, one of my dissertation readers, for this title.

are likely not thinking of simple geographic proximity; they are thinking of togetherness as something like unity around a set of beliefs or ideas.

It will not come as a surprise that in a sorely divided society, people can assume that the solution to the fracturing of society is simply for people to come together, to be unified. But unified toward what goal? While it is quite possible that the persons or groups who call for such a coming together might have flourishing as their goal, that goal is often assumed and rarely stated. Because people infrequently talk about the quality of the coming together they envision, instead simply issuing a call to come together, we who hear that call are left to create for ourselves and our communities the kind of togetherness we desire and what purposes the coming together is to achieve. This potential gap in meaning informs the heart of this book about togetherness.

When people use the word together it is not likely, in my opinion, that they have thought deeply about the neutral, negative, and positive aspects of togetherness. Instead, they often assume a generic positive goal of coming together. We might ask, What's wrong with assuming a generic positive goal of coming together? Is there any downside to that? If a group is being positive, is that not sufficient reason to come together? It is hard to argue otherwise, and yet I am going to try. I would suggest that if a group does not come together to produce flourishing, they are liable to come together in a way that falls short of that important goal.

I encourage you to ask yourself, When you think about the word together, what image forms in your mind? Better yet, is that image the correct image? Is there one correct version of togetherness? Could there be options? Certainly. Not only could we classify togetherness as positive, neutral, or negative, within each of these are many possibilities. There are many possible ways people could come together for positive goals. What I hope to demonstrate in this book is that biblical theology both suggests that and teaches how togetherness should produce human flourishing. In other words, what we will learn is that quality of togetherness God desires is a coming together for human flourishing.

My goal in this book is to examine togetherness so that communities of all shapes and sizes can understand and practice a quality of togetherness that will produce human flourishing. But what is human flourishing, and why should it be the goal of togetherness?

In part 1 of the book, through memoir and biblical study, I introduce the primary topic of the book, flourishing-producing togetherness and what I see as a significant cultural and theological barrier—individualism. In chapter 1 we define human flourishing, with its deep connection to justice. Next, chapter 2 will survey the potential sidetrack to flourishing, our American Christian individualist streak. In chapter 3, we'll look at how individualism has impacted our theology and Christian practice. Having identified that potential individualist sidetrack, in chapter 4 we seek a new goal, God's heart for human flourishing. But how will we arrive at that goal?

If you've ever hiked on a marked trail, you know that sometimes finding blazes on trees can be tricky. Theology helps us clearly identify the trail of togetherness that leads to flourishing. Thus, part 2 presents a theology of togetherness in which I survey the Hebrew and Christian Scriptures to describe God's heart for flourishing-producing togetherness. Part 2 will often feel quite different from part 1, in that we will be doing theology. As we'll learn, the work of theology involves a different kind of thinking. Therefore, part 2 will include less memoir, less story, and more biblical study and consultation with scholars. After chapter 5 helps us learn how to do theology, the remaining chapters in part 2 will examine the theological categories of God as Trinity (chapter 6), sin (chapter 7), salvation (chapter 8), covenant (chapter 9), kingdom (chapter 10), union with Christ (chapter 11), and solidarity with others (chapter 12). Put together, this section will create a biblical theology of togetherness.

With that theology in hand, part 3 will attempt to help Christian communities apply flourishing-producing togetherness to their many expressions of being together. Part 3 will likely seem to combine the storytelling of part 1 with the heady theological work of part 2. Chapter 13 will help us think about how to move from the heady work of theology to the heart, hands, and feet of practical action. The next five chapters will all focus on actively practicing flourishing-producing togetherness. First we will learn the world-shaping value of engaging in ritual together (chapter 14). Then we'll have two chapters about how flourishing-producing togetherness can bring healing to perhaps the two most divisive issues in our time—politics (chapter 15) and race/ethnicity (chapter 16). Finally, we conclude part 3 by learning about how communities can together practice repentance (chapter 17) and create new culture (chapter 18). I then conclude the book with a vision of human flourishing.

If I am right that contemporary uses of "together" suffer from the principles of "familiarity breeds frequency" and "familiarity breeds contempt," then togetherness needs to be injected with renewed meaning. That new meaning is what I am calling "flourishing-producing togetherness." In the next chapter, I examine that central claim by asking, What is human flourishing?

Part 1

Defining Human Flourishing and Togetherness

1

Flourishing

"What is human flourishing?" A fellow pastor stepped up to a microphone and posed that question to me in front of the 150-plus delegates to my denomination's annual national conference. All eyes were on me, and my attempt to answer his question did not go well.

I was on stage standing at the central podium in front of the delegates for what amounted to three hours, facilitating discussion and answering a variety of questions, such as, What is human flourishing?

For the previous two years I had served as the chair of the Amendments Committee of my denomination, the Evangelical Congregational Church (ECC). About every fifth year, the Amendments Committee's task is to receive, review, and propose amendments to the denomination's one-hundred-page book of order, which is titled *The Discipline*.[1] After working on amendments for about nine months, we bring our report of proposals to the meetings of the national conference, where delegates debate our proposals, propose further amendments, including amendments to the amendments, and ultimately vote on adopting them into the book of order.

This amendment process itself is an interesting example of coming together, as it occurs within the act of conferencing that happens when the denomination gathers each year. An important facet of conferencing is the debate and discussion, allowing any delegate to step forward to one of the

---

1. Harsh-sounding title, isn't it? The full title is actually, *The Creed, Ritual and Discipline of the Evangelical Congregational Church*. The word "discipline" is not meant in the punitive sense, though it includes a section about restorative church discipline. Amongst ourselves, because the title is so long, we ECers shorten it to *The Discipline*. Even after that explanation, I won't fault you if still find the title to be harsh. I do.

microphones stationed around the floor of the conference so they can ask questions and make comments.

At the May 2021 conference, as chair of the Amendments Committee, I was responsible to stand before the conference and give the committee's report. Our slate of proposed amendments was extensive, touching nearly every page of *The Discipline*. One amendment our committee proposed was a new statement regarding racial justice. Prior to this proposal, in its nearly one-hundred-year history, the denomination had included no official statement on racial justice in *The Discipline*.

Before the conference began, I reviewed all the amendments we were proposing, and I suspected most of them would pass quite easily. Open mics present a great unknown, however, and I thought I might get feedback, pushback, and questions, especially about the racial justice paragraph. I personally viewed the new racial justice paragraph as quite worthy of inclusion and long overdue, but because our nation and evangelicalism have a testy history with racial justice, which we will talk about further in chapter 16, I wondered if people would raise questions. *Did they ever.*

A first questioner motioned that we remove the paragraph entirely. Inwardly I bristled at this suggestion, and as his motion was seconded, I tried to remain composed in leading the ongoing discussion, knowing everyone was watching me standing before them. The questioner's motion was brought to a vote, and thankfully it failed. Then more questioners stepped to the mic, one by one, each motioning the removal of various sentences in the proposed racial justice paragraph. I wondered if, having lost the vote to delete the paragraph, they were part of a group now trying to dismantle it piece by piece.

In the end, only one phrase was removed, and another was enhanced. That enhanced phrase, prior to the enhancement, referred to "the Bible's . . . uniform call for human flourishing." That was the phrase that caused the delegate who is a retired pastor and friend of mine to come to the mic and ask, "What do you mean by 'human flourishing'? I don't know what it means," he said, "and if I don't know what it means, then there is likely little chance that the people in our churches will know what it means."

I will admit that his comment stopped me short, and my mind started racing. I wasn't ready to answer him. Human flourishing was not part of the paragraph that I thought would be questioned. Yet, I had to give the questioner credit. What does human flourishing mean? What did the Amendment Committee mean by the Bible's "uniform call for human flourishing"? If we are adding human flourishing to the denomination's book of order, then we are saying we believe in it, and we want the people of our local churches to pursue it. We need, therefore, to know what human flourishing means. The same is true for this book because I am making the claim that our practice of togetherness in Christian communities should have the goal of human flourishing.

Feeling those 150 sets of eyes bearing down on me, I floundered to articulate a cogent definition of human flourishing. I had studied the biblical vision of flourishing extensively, but in the intensity of the moment, my emotions got the better of me. A few seconds ticked by silently, and I began to mutter something like, "Human flourishing is God's desire for God's best for all humanity." Before I had finished that sentence, the retired pastor simultaneously talked over me into his mic. "If you can't explain what human flourishing is, then why do you include it in this paragraph?" I felt the flash of embarrassed heat course through my body.

Thankfully, two other delegates came to my rescue. One suggested that we look to Jesus' teaching in John 10:10 as a basis for understanding of human flourishing. Ultimately this Scripture became the enhancement to the phrase in the book of order. One of the two delegates motioned that we simply add that Scripture reference to the paragraph so that any future readers of the book of order could know that what Jesus talks about in John 10:10 explains the concept of human flourishing.

In John 10:10 Jesus remarks, "I have come that they might have life and life *abundantly*" (my translation). Jesus here indicates that one of his missional goals was that humanity would be able to experience abundant life. In teaching abundant life, Jesus is not only talking about life after death. He does specifically teach about life after death at other times, particularly when he uses the phrase "eternal life."[2]

Abundant life is the kind of life that Jesus desires people to experience both in the afterlife and in the here and now. The author of this passage, traditionally identified as the apostle John, uses the Greek word *perissos*, which is defined as "pertaining to a quantity so abundant as to be considerably more than what one would expect or anticipate—'that which is more than, more than enough, beyond the norm, abundantly, superfluous.'"[3] While this concept could be applied to physical abundance, the kind of life Jesus desires is not an outward abundance of material possessions, it is a deeper, more meaningful abundance that, as we will see, touches body, soul, spirit, relationships, and the entire created order.

In Matthew's Gospel, Jesus illustrates the flourishing life using the metaphor of a healthy fruit-bearing tree that naturally produces good

2. Though as we will see, when Jesus uses the term "eternal life" he is not exclusively referring to the afterlife. The terms "abundant life" and "eternal life" refer to the flourishing life in both the here and now as well as in the afterlife.

3. Louw and Nida, *Greek-English*, 598–99.

fruit, describing the person who is experiencing inner abundant life. Jesus teaches, "Make a tree good and its fruit will be good . . . out of the overflow of the heart a mouth speaks. . . . The good man brings good things out of the good stored up in him" (Matt 12:33–35). Jesus desires that humans will be changing inwardly so that what flows out of their lives is consistent with the abundant life that has taken residence inside them. If we want to see the evidence of whether a person is experiencing this abundant life, we can observe what is flowing from that person's life.

The early Christian writer Paul would further clarify abundant life in his teaching in Gal 5:22–23, referring to what he called "the fruit of the Spirit," which are the qualities of love, joy, peace, patience, kindness, goodness, faithfulness, gentleness, and self-control. The Spirit of God, residing in the life of the true disciple of Jesus,[4] works a change in the person from the inside out. As Paul describes in 2 Cor 5:17, "Therefore, if anyone is in Christ, he is a new creation; the old has gone, the new has come." In Paul's view, when a person is being transformed by the Spirit of Christ, the good fruit of the Spirit will be overflowing from a person's life. Human flourishing begins, then, through the inward experience of Christ's abundant life. But this inner flourishing sounds very individual, doesn't it?

Given that this is a book about what it means to come together, we need to talk about the abundant life from more than an inward individual perspective. The biblical writers describe human flourishing as the inward individual experience of abundant life that flows outwardly, enhancing humanity's ability to experience flourishing corporately. By using the word "corporate," I am not referring to the business world. In business, "corporate" often refers to a company's headquarters. Instead, I am referring to "corporate" as people sharing together, or working together, for flourishing.

As we will see, the biblical writers describe human flourishing as humanity's experience of abundance *together*. Throughout the book I will refer to this dynamic of people working together for human flourishing by the term "flourishing-producing togetherness." Flourishing-producing togetherness is the kind of togetherness that God desires, the kind of togetherness that leads to people striving for human flourishing, just like the tree that produces good fruit. Because we will study flourishing-producing

---

4. In future chapters will talk more about the Holy Spirit in the life of followers of Jesus. For now, consider the following two passages that describe the presence of the Spirit in the life of followers of Jesus. First, Paul writes in 1 Cor 6:19, "Your body is a temple of the Holy Spirit, who is in you, whom you have received from God." Paul's teaching reflects what Jesus had previously taught in John 14:16–17, "And I will ask the Father, and he will give you another Counselor to be with you forever—the Spirit of truth . . . he lives with you and will be in you."

togetherness in depth in future chapters, I will here only introduce the possibility for human flourishing, or abundant life, from a corporate perspective, drawing on the teaching of Jesus and the ancient Hebrew prophets. Let's begin with the Hebrew prophets.

Corporate human flourishing is described by the Hebrew prophets as the advancement of corporate justice and the rooting out of corporate injustice in such a way that all people can experience abundant life together, as well as individually. In the Hebrew Bible, the word that refers to abundant or flourishing life is *shalom*, most often translated by the English word "peace." But *shalom* is much more than the cessation of war or a process that brings two disputing parties into agreement. *Shalom* envisions wholeness in all relationships, first within the self, then to others, the natural world, and God.

Furthermore, societies and cultures who want to cultivate this *shalom* kind of flourishing life, the prophets teach, will move from injustice toward justice. Martin Luther King Jr. famously quoted the prophet Amos who writes, "Let justice roll on like a river, righteousness like a never-failing stream!" (Amos 5:24). Amos was prophesying not about the individual but instead about a vision of corporate justice that unceasingly runs through the people and structures of an entire nation, like a river that flows continually. Justice is not to be dammed up or dried up. God's desire is for human cultures to practice justice as the ever-present norm for all. Justice is necessary for flourishing.[5]

When you hear the word justice, what comes to mind? Courtrooms, judges, lawyers, juries, crimes, and punishments? I've been in courtrooms numerous times, including once when I was on trial. I've witnessed joyous adoption ceremonies, and I testified at a very difficult sentencing hearing for a man in my congregation. I visited that man in prison week after week, waiting for that hearing, and we discussed the question, What is justice? In the bible, God's heart beats for justice. The word used above in Amos 5 is the Hebrew *mishpat*, referring broadly to equality.[6] Justice, in God's eyes, is not simply about a punishment that fits the crime. God desires equality in economics, gender, ethnicity, class, culture, and society.

A wider study of the prophet Amos bears this out. Though from the southern Jewish kingdom of Judah, Amos's prophecy observes injustice taking place in the northern Jewish kingdom of Israel (Amos 1:1). Amos

---

5. But as my dissertation advisor theologian Douglas Jacobsen points out, flourishing and justice are not synonymous: "Justice is about what a person deserves; flourishing is about what and who people can become at their best." Jacobsen, pers. comm., Jan. 2021. This is a helpful distinction of the two related terms. As we will see, in God's kingdom, the pursuit of justice seeks to eradicate injustice so that all people can flourish.

6. Koehler et al., *Hebrew and Aramaic*, 651.

specifically pointed out how corporate injustice leads to corporate oppression, particularly for people struggling under the strain of poverty.

Amos illustrates that Israel's court system, the most obvious place where justice ought to rule, had become the purveyor of injustice toward the poor (Amos 5:12). Those in power marginalized groups with little or no power, committing injustices designed to maintain their power and enrich themselves. Here Amos identifies a societal expression of injustice embedded in the power structures of the Kingdom of Israel. Examples of this systemic oppression, Amos tells us, are not only poverty and injustice in the courts but also sexual exploitation (2:7). Amos concludes that the power brokers of Israel had turned justice into poison (6:12). Using farming imagery, that of producing fruit, Amos says that justice, which should have been the fruit of righteousness, had become bitterness.

Though it might seem that this systemic injustice provided flourishing for the powerful and oppression for the powerless, systemic injustice led to the opposite of flourishing for both the powerful and the powerless. On the surface, the systems of injustice they controlled grew the wealth of the wealthy and kept power in the hands of the powerful. What was below the surface, Amos reveals, is that the powerful, having dammed up the river of justice, became blind to their injustice. The powerful were deceived by their success. They believed that their position of power was a sign of blessing by God and thus an indication of his favor. Amos says they couldn't be more wrong.

God tells the powerful, through Amos's prophecy, that he will remove his favor from them because, in their wicked behavior toward the powerless, they broke the terms of his ancient covenant with them (Amos 2:6–16; 4:1–3; 8:1–6). At the risk of oversimplification, the covenant was an agreement between God and the ancient people of Israel. The terms of the covenant stated that if the people followed God's way, he would bless them, but if they did not follow his way, he would curse them (Deut 28). Because they perpetuated systems of injustice, the powerful oppressors in Amos's day were living proof and undeniable evidence that they had broken their covenant with God. As a result, God would allow them to face punishment and experience the opposite of flourishing if they did not repent of their ways and allow justice to flow like a river.

Much more obviously, the powerless were not experiencing flourishing because they were forced to live under the systemic oppression of the powerful. To restore the fruit of righteousness, to usher in corporate flourishing, Amos taught that the systems of injustice would need to be confronted and removed, thus allowing justice for all. The image of the fruit of righteousness—that is, justice—is an image of bountiful produce which flows from

God's heart to all the people of the land. It is, therefore, not simply an inner fruit of one's character or attitude, but it is also an outward fruit of systemic justice across the land that impacts every aspect of society.

Jesus would capture this idea for a new generation when he taught his disciples to pray, "Your kingdom come, your will be done, on earth as it is in heaven" (Matt 6:10). Jesus' inference is that God's will is always done in heaven, but God's will is not always done on earth. We see this in Amos's evaluation of his society, and we see it throughout history and still in our world today. The persistent presence of systemic injustice in our world is evidence that God's will is not always done on earth. When Jesus instructs us to pray that God's will would be done on earth now as it is in heaven, he envisions the eradication of systems of injustice in the world, replacing them with systems of justice.

Wherever justice flows like a river, God's kingdom is there, and we are to pray for and work toward that kind of present, real-world corporate justice in the places we live, work, and play. We are to pray for and work toward corporate justice in the here and now. I am suggesting that both the Hebrew prophets and Jesus call Christians to learn about and practice flourishing-producing togetherness that strives to eradicate systemic injustice. Unfortunately, too many Christians have not been given a biblical vision for that goal. I am one of those Christians. Let me tell you my story.

I completed both a bachelors degree at a Bible college and a master of divinity degree at a seminary, rarely hearing about God's heart for corporate justice through any of my classes. The important teaching of flourishing-producing togetherness was right there all along in places like the prophecy of Amos. But somehow, though my coursework assigned readings were in Amos and other prophets like Jesus, who often teach flourishing-producing togetherness, I viewed Scripture through a different lens. That lens was focused almost entirely on the individual trying to answer questions such as, What does the Bible teach about a person's individual relationship with God? Togetherness for human flourishing was not highlighted as it should have been in either my undergraduate or graduate studies. I will talk in depth about this absence of togetherness in favor of individualism in Christian theology in the next chapter.

I learned about God's heart for systemic justice not from my formal education but from a fellow pastor in my denomination. Bruce Ray grew up in and ministered in the city of Chicago, a culture and context far different from my own. My upbringing and church context is that of suburban Lancaster County, in southeastern Pennsylvania. Lancaster is famous for our Plain heritage, referring to our long history of Amish, Mennonite, and Brethren groups, which are still abundant in the county to this day. That heritage influences even the non-Plain people in our community, in the form of deeply held conservative and sometimes fundamentalist values.

When our denomination's national conference organizers matched Bruce and I to share a dorm room during the sessions of the conference one year, we represented a clash of cultures, the big city versus rural/suburban life. Thankfully our hearts and minds were aligned, and we struck up a friendship that continues to this day, more than a decade later. It was Bruce's investment in me that profoundly shaped my understanding of biblical justice.

What Bruce brought to that conference, and to our friendship, was something that God had been working in his life for many years. His Chicago church, Kimball Avenue, had previously started a group called Justice Watch, in which members would seek to learn God's heart for justice in Scripture, from passages such as those in Amos, and then apply the principles they learned to their own community. They already knew that injustice abounded in big cities like their hometown, Chicago, but as they made it their goal to seek God's heart to break down the dam of systemic injustice and allow the river of justice to flow, they got involved in numerous community activities. They advocated for fair housing, for just treatment of seniors in nursing homes, against violence, for creating community gardens in what was an inner-city food desert, and for fair lending practices by financial institutions to low-income earners.

To inspire their congregation to think about justice, each season of Lent they created what they called Lenten Compacts, a kind of formal agreement among the members of the church family. Kimball Avenue would agree together to practice fasting in line with Isa 58, where God, through the prophet Isaiah, tells the people that their fasting is a mockery to him if their actual lives promote systemic injustice, such as exploitation of workers (Isa 58:3–4). Often contemporary Lenten fasting is seen as a time to give up food to spend more time with God, which is a commendable spiritual practice, but one that tends to focus on the individual. The Justice Watch group of Kimball Avenue Church desired to practice fasting together in line with God's heart, as described in Isa 58:6, "Is not this the kind of fasting I have chosen: to loosen the chains of injustice and untie the cords of the yoke, to set the oppressed free and break every yoke?"

In this prophecy the Lord makes it clear that fasting should not simply be a religious ritual for personal spiritual renewal, but it should also break the dam of systemic injustice so justice can roll like a river. Through Isaiah, God gives practical illustrations of what he intends: sharing food with the hungry, providing the poor wanderer with shelter, clothing the naked, and caring for one's own family (Isa 58:7). When the people of God take a corporate view of injustice, they will submit their practice of religious rituals, like fasting, to the pursuit of justice, resulting in corporate flourishing—"Then your light will break forth like the dawn, and your healing will quickly appear; then your righteousness will go before you, and the glory of the Lord will be your rear guard" (Isa 58:8). Guided by this vision of corporate flourishing, Kimball Avenue created, year after year, Lenten compacts, which were corporate agreements to fast for justice together.

Bruce expanded his congregation's reach by inviting other churches to join them in the compacts, including mine, six hundred miles away in Pennsylvania. Given the friendship we struck up at the conference, I was eager to learn more. My church accepted his offer, and we adapted the compact for our context. During each of the three years we joined the compacts, we sought the Lord's help in performing a fast that would help us bring justice to our community. One year a compact focused on welcoming the stranger and foreigner, so we learned about refugee resettlement in our community. Another year, the compact addressed clean and sustainable energy, so we learned how to care for our planet through energy sources such as solar and wind. A third compact guided us in learning about food vulnerability. When the compact focused on affordable housing, we spent a night sleeping outside in a tent community to have a tiny taste of being unhoused. During that evening, we set up a video call with our brothers and sisters in Chicago, where they too had built a temporary tent community. We delighted in fasting for justice together across a six-hundred-mile divide. Soon we crossed that divide.

In the summer of 2010, a team of fifteen people from Faith Church traveled to Chicago to spend a week immersing ourselves in observing and learning from Kimball Avenue's Justice Watch group as they applied principles of flourishing to their context. We visited neighborhoods and met people whose lives were affected by systemic injustice in Chicago, all the while wrestling with biblical passages to learn God's heart for justice. In a major metropolis, it seemed easy to identify injustice on every corner, and we were grateful to learn how a group of people could apply flourishing-producing togetherness to their community. As a result, we returned to Lancaster passionate to start a Justice Watch group in our congregation.

We were surprised, though, when our passion dimmed because we couldn't easily see injustice in our community like we had seen it in Chicago. Driving through our lush farmlands and well-manicured suburban neighborhoods, our local community, Lancaster County, didn't appear to have injustice. There is no doubt that our community is beautiful, but as we kept looking, though it was slow going, we eventually discovered different kinds of injustice around us.

We learned from the school district social worker that each year more than one hundred children are classified as definitionally homeless in our community, often living in cars, motels, or with relatives. So many people live in local hotels that the school bus stops there to pick up kids. In the ensuing years, that number of definitionally homeless has increased to 150. In addition to the school social worker, we talked to police officers and other community leaders, listening as they described a serious human trafficking corridor just minutes away. We learned about the need for clothing, food, affordable housing, family mentoring, and financial counseling. We learned to ask if systemic injustice was anywhere present at the root of these concerns. This too we found was not an intuitive or easy process. It reminds me of my grandson.

As is true for every newborn, my grandson's eyes at birth had yet to develop the capability to see clearly. In those first weeks, we could tell that he was experiencing the normal cloudiness of vision for children his age. But as the weeks passed, his eyes started to follow me as I would sway back and forth in front of him. What a joy to experience him noticing me. Only months later, he would enjoy full visual awareness of his surroundings. Vision requires development and practice.

We were developing the eyes of justice, learning to evaluate the social systems of our community for possible injustice, thus helping to apply togetherness that can lead to corporate human flourishing. As of this writing, we have a long way to go in seeking flourishing-producing togetherness and much work yet to be done to bring the abundant life more and more in our community. Slowly our eyes are learning to focus more clearly, as we try to see life through the eyes of those in circumstances different from our own. Years later, one of the members of our church who was on that trip to Chicago participated in the community effort of togetherness to create Conestoga Valley SEEDS, which I mentioned in the introduction. SEEDS is like a Justice Watch for our community.

Because the goal of togetherness is human flourishing, and because many humans are not flourishing, we would do well to search for culprits that have impeded the achievement of flourishing-producing togetherness. I hinted at one such culprit above, when I talked about God's desire that individual disciples of Jesus experience the inner transformation of the Holy Spirit, so that the Spirit's fruit is growing inside them and flowing forth. I intended to describe a healthy individualistic approach to how the gospel leads to individuals experiencing flourishing as a precursor for how we can take a healthy corporate approach to flourishing. But we need to more deeply examine that individual approach. What we will find as we study individualism, sadly, is perhaps the greatest threat to God's vision for human flourishing—the unhealthy overemphasis on an individualistic gospel.

2

Individualism

IN RECENT SUMMERS, MY extended family has spent a week in one of Pennsylvania's gorgeous state parks. We've visited Black Moshannon, Ricketts Glen, Keystone, and Moraine. Some parks are in cellular dead zones, and they have no Wi-Fi. While the teens in the family sometimes go "hiking" (read, searching for a data connection), I find the dead zone to be glorious. For a whole week, I cannot be contacted. But just a short drive down the mountain, and our phones start buzzing and beeping as text messages, emails, and notifications light up our devices. On those vacations, we are off the grid but just barely.

Have you ever wondered if you could survive off the grid? I'm talking about something much more serious than a week in a state park. I'm asking, could you live off the land? Could you survive without modern conveniences such as indoor plumbing, electricity, and the plethora of grocery stores and service businesses we depend on for modern life? I would like to think I could, but I suspect living off the grid would be exceedingly difficult. The reality television show, *Alone*, awards one million dollars to a contestant who can exist in the wilderness for one hundred days. During one season the participants were dropped into the wilds of Alaska with limited gear and they had to build their own shelter, hunt or forage for their own food, and live off the land, all while filming their exploits on handheld cameras.[1] I find something about it compelling, a human individual surviving alone. It's why I am thankful for my wood stove.

---

1. Witt et al., *Alone*, sea. 1.

Years ago my cousin posted on social media that she was getting rid of a wood stove, and my wife and I scooped it up. We'd been paying exorbitant heating oil bills, and we both grew up with wood heat, not to mention that my father-in-law also has a small firewood business on the side. That meant free wood, and free wood meant free heat. Better yet, we would not be dependent on any grid, so it was a win-win. Since that time, in addition to splitting the many logs we've received from my father-in-law, I've lost count of how many trees I've felled. I split, stack, and cover the wood to let it air dry in advance of the next burning season. Then I cart loads of wood in my wheelbarrow, backing it up my deck steps and into our home, where I fill up the wood box. I've split, stacked, and carted wood in the humid summer and in the winter snow.

While wood heat is a lot of work and can be messy with all the bark, chips, and ash, I will admit it taps into something primordial deep inside me. I am heating my own home independently just like our ancestors did before the advent of electric, oil, or gas furnaces. When we humans resurrect that individualist spirit inside us, we often feel very good. Of course, in our contemporary connected culture, it is nearly impossible to be totally independent. My family's use of a wood stove, for example, is dependent on my father-in-law's firewood business. Still, consider how our use of a wood stove is individualistic. We do not rely on the electric power grid. When I told my Amish friends, whose culture is famously disconnected from the grid, that we use wood heat, a huge smile beamed on their faces as they exclaimed, "Good for you!" Why would they say that? What is so good about individualism?

Many, if not most, Americans throughout our 245-year history have prided ourselves in our individualism. Stephen Dubner says this tendency has been described as "rugged individualism" or even "wild individualism."[2] Scholars note that our American individualism finds its roots in the writings of seventeenth-century English philosopher John Locke, whose "ideal was an autonomous individual."[3] Our individualistic ingenuity goes back as far as the pioneering frontier entrepreneurial spirit, illustrated in the homesteaders who traveled west braving the wilderness, living off the land.[4]

When my youngest two children were in their elementary years, friends passed along some books about individual survival that their boys

---

2. Dubner, "Just Different," 6:40—7:10.

3. Bellah et al., *Good Society*, 265.

4. My thanks to my doctoral mentor Tony Blair who pointed out while reviewing a draft of this chapter that "the 'frontier thesis' was first formulated by historian Frederick Jackson Turner in the 1890s, precisely at the moment when the frontier was being considered 'closed,' as in filled in." Blair, pers. comm. with author, Jan. 2021.

had enjoyed at that age, thinking that maybe my son and daughter would as well. In *Hatchet*, Gary Paulson writes a fictional account of thirteen-year-old American Brian Robeson, who is the only passenger in a prop plane flying over the Canadian wilderness enroute to visit his father who was recently divorced from his mother. Mid-flight the pilot suffers a heart attack and dies, leaving Brian alone as the plane crashes into a small lake surrounded by endless acres of forest. Brian must survive with nothing but his clothing and the hatchet his mother gave him as a present before he left. Based on Paulson's time spent alone in the wilderness, the remainder of the story follows Brian's desperate attempt to survive.[5]

These "alone-against-the-wilderness" stories are compelling, inspirational attempts to bolster our spirits, filling our minds with the inner power of one. I remember reading *Hatchet* to my kids, thinking how amazing self-sufficiency must feel and that our world would be a far better place if we all learned to live alone in the woods. The survivalist Bear Grylls has popularized the power of one, inviting celebrities to join him in the wilderness where they brave the wilds and live off the land for a few days.[6] Yet, what researchers tell us is that Americans are somewhat unique in our individualism.

Dubner reports that "the American model is among the most successful—and envied—models in the history of the world. But it's also a tremendous outlier."[7] While there are likely examples of individualists in every country across the globe, it seems that America is one of the few nations, and possibly the only nation, in which individualism seems to have caught on in a widespread way. This is not simply anecdotal evidence.

The Asch Conformity Test studies how groups can influence individuals to conform to a crowd. The classic example of this is when a group of individuals walk into an elevator with a hidden camera. Normally, when riding an elevator, people turn to face the elevator doors. But in the test everyone in the group except one person is an actor with instructions to enter the elevator and stand facing away from the door. Very often the person who is not in on the secret instructions succumbs to a feeling of peer pressure and right away, or mid-ride, will turn to face the same direction as the rest of the riders, even if they are facing the elevator wall. The Asch

---

    5. Paulsen, *Hatchet*.

    6. If you haven't seen *Running Wild with Bear Grylls*, I highly recommend season 3, ep. 4, where Shaquille O'Neal joins the host in his wilderness expedition.

    7. Dubner, "Just Different," 7:25–7:35.

Conformity Test has been used globally in research, finding Americans least likely to conform.[8] Our individualist streak is scientifically verifiable.

Though I would sometimes love to be the consummate American individualist, despite my wood-chopping skills, reading *Hatchet* left me suspecting that if I had to survive alone in a wilderness, I would be incredibly inadequate to the task. Could I, like Tom Hanks's character in the film *Cast Away*, survive on and successfully escape, by myself, a deserted island?[9] Could I, like real-life survivor Louis Zamperini, brave the open sea for forty-seven days in a raft, after my bomber crashed in the Pacific, like Zamperini did during World War II, as told in the book and movie *Unbroken*?[10] Could I, like Aleksander Doba, kayak across an ocean, alone, not one or two but three times?[11] These accounts, both fictional and true, pull at my longings. Why? What is it about tales of individual survival that can be so compelling?

That inner pull toward individual achievement drives me to run long distances, a decidedly solo venture. While I have run numerous races of varying lengths, my three marathons were, by far, the most grueling, and in the end, the most satisfying. What many people don't realize is that, though running 26.1 miles is surely a feat of individual mental and physical strength, to shape my body into the condition where it can run for the approximately four hours it takes me to complete a marathon, I first completed five to six hundred miles over the course of eighteen training weeks. No doubt those final 26.1 miles are the most difficult. In each of the three marathons, when I crossed the twenty-mile threshold mid-race, I entered a whole new territory I had not covered in training.

On the training plan I used to prepare for that first marathon, the highest mileage week during the eighteen training weeks covers a total of forty miles across four days. The longest single training run is twenty miles. During each marathon, then, as I ran past the twenty-mile marker not only was I in new distance territory but, with six more miles to go to the finish line, my body already felt as though it wanted to stop miles earlier. Those last six miles are like a physical, mental, and emotional battlefield during which my mantra is "just keep running . . . just keep running . . . just keep running."

Step by painful step, I fight through leg cramps and the dark thoughts of why I ever considered this a good idea in the first place. Slowly the finish line appears, and I cross it welling up with emotion. At the finish line of

8. Dubner, "Just Different."
9. Zemeckis, *Cast Away*.
10. Hillenbrand, *Unbroken*; Jolie, *Unbroken*.
11. Vadukul, "Aleksander Doba."

two of those marathons, I broke down in tears. In all three marathons, I felt a deep elation and sense of accomplishment sweep over me. In all three marathons, during those last six miles, I was swearing angrily to myself that I would never do this again but then, beyond the finish line, a surprising feeling washes over me. I want more of that individual satisfaction. Maybe I'll sign up for another.

Have you felt it? The accomplishment of individualism is like a drug, filling us with peace, joy, hope, and worth. But just as drugs provide temporary, unsustainable highs that can lead to crushing emptiness, so too individualism has its shadow side. Some, in fact, say individualism is a harmful problem.[12] Like much else in life, there are pros and cons to individualism. On the positive side, individualism can inspire personal responsibility, self-accountability, and human achievement.[13] On the negative side, though, it can lead to arrogance, pride, and self-righteousness, which often result in anxiety and depression.[14] Individualists can be rife with selfishness and a general lack of self-awareness, both of which can create a callousness toward others. Individualism threatens togetherness.

Likewise, the English Rabbi Jonathan Sacks notes in his book *Morality* that Alexis de Tocqueville, a French sociologist who studied American culture, warned us centuries ago about a culture-wide erosion of togetherness. Labeling it "outsourcing," Sacks summarizes de Tocqueville's assessment of American culture as embodying an individualistic conscience from which people "cease to interest themselves in the welfare of others, and . . . leave that responsibility to the state."[15] But in decrying the loss of community, is de Tocqueville inadvertently providing an example of togetherness? What is dependence on the state if it is not an act of community, given that a government is a community, people working together?

One way we could answer this question is to look at de Tocqueville's central concern, the loss of responsibility for the welfare of others. If I can outsource to the state my human responsibility to care for others, I can be tempted to focus more on myself, thus growing within me an individualistic attitude. Increased dependence on the state, therefore, might be a mirage of togetherness. As a result, though they are depending on the state, more and more people across a society become individualistic in their mindset and action.

---

12. See, for example, Miller, "Radical Individualism."
13. Koch, "Individualism Good or Bad?"
14. Gross and De Dreu, "Individual solutions."
15. Sacks, *Morality*, 82.

Furthermore, as my dissertation mentor Tony Blair points out, there is a great irony in individualism turning over social responsibility to a government, as those governments tend toward authoritarianism, which often forcibly impose a uniformity that runs counter to individualism.[16] This counterintuitive movement from individualism to authoritarianism to uniformity is possible because individuals become so self-focused they lack the vision to see beyond themselves, and even if they do observe a rise in authoritarianism, they lack the heart to confront it.

Likewise, Sacks points to French social scientist Emile Durkheim, who wrote about the loss of *la conscience collective*, which Sacks understood as "the unifying body of ideas, beliefs, and attitudes that give shape and coherence to our shared social world."[17] What Durkheim suggests is that as individualism became increasingly accepted and applied within American society, togetherness declined. Or put another way, the rise of individualism led to a resultant rise in emotional and psychological struggle, authoritarianism, and the opposite of human flourishing.

The naysayer might respond that I'm blowing things out of proportion, that individualism is not nearly so disastrous as what de Tocqueville and Durkheim suggest. We would do well to investigate whether individualism has had far less an impact than I've claimed. Therefore, we need to examine individualism more closely, starting with the presupposition that it exists at all. In other words, is there such a thing as a truly individual endeavor? To the possible surprise of the naysayer, we will discover that there is no such thing as a purely individual endeavor. What we can learn by testing the claim that there is no purely individual endeavor will be instructive to our observations about togetherness, leading us to an important conclusion.

Consider long-distance running, which I suggested above is a distinctly individual act. Let's take a closer look. If there is no such thing as a purely individual act, then it is true for long distance running. When I run a marathon, for example, of course I do much on my own, but I am also heavily reliant on others. While in training for my first marathon, I ran the first few weeks using cheap sneakers I already owned. When the once-per-week longer training runs reached nine miles,[18] I knew I needed hydration and energy, especially given the hot humid eastern Pennsylvania summers.

16. Blair, pers. comm., Jan. 2021..

17. Sacks, *Morality*, 82.

18 That first training plan involved running four days per week, and those four runs were as follows: a short run, then a medium run, then a short run, and finally a longer run. For example, in week one, the four runs were three miles, three miles, three miles, and five miles. At the peak of training, the four runs were five miles, ten miles, five miles, and twenty miles. See Higdon, "Marathon Training."

I brought a handheld water bottle and mid-run tried to eat a dry, crumbly granola bar. Readers who are long-distance runners, laugh it up. It did not go well, and if you have done long-distance running, you know why. First of all, running long distances with a constantly sloshing water bottle is a nuisance. And, second, dry granola bars are very difficult to eat while running, and they do not provide the instant energy exhausted muscles crave.

After that nine-miler I felt sick to my stomach most of the day afterward. I battled discouragement and doubted I could run nine miles again, let alone 26.1 miles, which amounted to running nearly nine miles three times in a row, *on the same day*. After the nine-mile training run, I was not flourishing. A persistent stomachache had me concerned about the next Saturday with its long run slated to increase to eleven miles.

I had previously scheduled a gathering with a college friend later on the day of my rough nine-miler, and I told him about my nausea. He had experience running long distances, so he asked me about my mid-run food and water consumption. When he heard what I was doing, he made some very specific recommendations for improvement: eat a high-energy bar before the run, take instant-energy chews at least every three miles, and get a water backpack that can hold a lot more than a single water bottle, leaving your hands free for proper running movement. Then, he said, drink the water frequently during the run. The following week, I did as he said, and it worked! Never again, even after much longer runs, did I struggle with stomach pains. Instead, I flourished.

I have since completed three marathons, three half-marathons, and all the training runs. My flourishing in long distance running was not due to my individual determination alone. It was highly dependent on my friend and his investment in me. I had never experienced the unique nutritional and hydration needs of a body undergoing extreme exertion. My friend had that experience, however, and he produced flourishing in me by his willingness to share his knowledge and experience with me. Though my friend did not run the marathon with me, he embodied flourishing-producing togetherness. But as I think about my training to run that first marathon, though my nutrition and hydration problems were solved, as I continued training, I encountered a new barrier, one that introduced me to a much larger community supporting the idea of flourishing-producing togetherness in long-distance running.

The new barrier was a new sharp pain in my feet and knees. I played soccer throughout my middle school, high school, and college years, so I was accustomed to a lot of running. I had felt pain in my legs and feet before. But I had never run such long distances nor felt this kind of pain. I immediately feared injury, and with a couple months already invested in training, I worried I would not be able to complete the marathon. The level of pain was such that I could not continue training, and I contemplated seeing a doctor. At the same time, through more conversation with friends and reading articles about running marathons, it struck me that my shoes were old. Worse, those worn-out sneakers were bargain models, never designed for long-distance running in the first place. That prompted a visit to the local running store.

The experts at the store fitted me with specialty distance running shoes, and on my next run, the cushion of those new shoes was a revelation. I hadn't realized how much it would matter that the foam in my old shoes was not designed for long-distance running, and worse, after so many miles of pounding out those training runs, the foam had become compressed. I want to exaggerate and say that what I was running on had as much cushion as a block of wood. While my old shoes were not that bad, I can confirm that my knees and feet were not flourishing. In a matter of days of using the new shoes, however, my pain disappeared.

Much like my friend's nutrition and hydration advice, I would not have been able to complete the marathon without the flourishing-producing togetherness of the people at the local running store. My marathon community of flourishing-producing togetherness was expanding. Actually, when I think about those new shoes, the community supporting my marathon exploded in size exponentially. Think about it: who made my new cushion-y running shoes? Not the owner or employees of my local running store. So, take a journey with me, a journey of understanding the scope of flourishing-producing togetherness in a simple pair of running shoes.

The birth of a running shoe starts like any birth, with a conception. A slew of designers, researchers, and marketers working for the shoe company conceive of the idea, usually investing months, if not years, into running shoe technology, comfort, and appearance. Once plans and schematics are drawn, the company creates and tests sample shoes. A prototype is born. The list of people involved thus far is rather small. But once the initial team finalizes their design, the size of the team explodes.

Shoes require fabric, foam, rubber, and other components. Farmers, harvesters, and distributors across the globe grow and sell the raw materials that will be sewn into fabrics or molded into rubber foam and tread. Buyers purchase the materials, and shippers ship them to factories where they are sized, measured, cut, pressed, threaded, shaped, and glued by still more workers artfully using their own two hands or perhaps by operating machinery. Sadly, it is highly likely these workers are underpaid, working long hours in unsafe working conditions, and worse, some are underage. For me to flourish must they be kept from flourishing? We'll talk more about how flourishing-producing togetherness seeks to address the garment industry in a later chapter. Once fashioned at the factory of origin, finished shoes embark on a long journey to get to my feet.

From the factory, my running shoe team expands to include shipment prep workers, loading dock laborers, truck drivers, shipping container packers, sailors, and pilots. After my shoes arrive at an American port of entry, be it an airport or a shipping container dock, another group of loaders and shippers bring the shoes to the shoe company's distribution center. There my shoes remain in storage until my local running store visits the shoe company website to place a wholesale order. That website requires a staff of designers, customer service reps, and salespersons, all working together to process the running store order.

The running store's order is transmitted to the distribution center, where more staff or robots fill the order, including packing it for delivery to the running store. At some point on this journey, the shoes are stuffed with and wrapped in thin paper, then placed in typical cardboard shoe boxes, which are also made possible by a long list of people working for the company that makes cardboard containers.[19]

Finally, the delivery truck driver and store employees work together to transfer the shoes from the truck to the store inventory. Only then can store staff sell me the shoes that I put on my feet, walking around the store to see if they feel okay. In the end, likely hundreds of people had a part in my shoes. I wonder how many of them actually physically touched my shoes before I did? Flourishing-producing togetherness requires every one of them.[20]

This story of who made my running shoes could easily be expanded. Nearly all the people who worked on my shoes could only do so assisted by other people or equipment made by still other people. If we wanted to trace it, this chain of flourishing-producing togetherness likely circles the globe eventually including every human, except perhaps infants or some aboriginal tribal groups. My point is not to show that we are all connected or reliant on everyone else but instead to show that even in an event like a marathon that is very much a grand personal achievement, a runner is not achieving a feat of individualistic endurance—far from it.

Furthermore, I doubt I would have ever run a marathon without my friends Brandon and Matt. We have run each of the three marathons together, as well as the three half marathons. Others have joined us for a race

---

19. By the way, shoe boxes these days are works of art with literal artwork printed on them in attractive designs. Shoe boxes alone require artists, graphic designers, printers, presses, ink, paper, and cardboard.

20. For a detailed account of the shoe-making process, see Shoemakers Academy, "Online Footwear Courses."

here and there, which adds to the experience of togetherness. But without Matt first saying, "Guys, I think this year is going to be the year of the marathon," I can't imagine I would have thought it was something I ever wanted to do or could accomplish. Upon hearing Matt say that, though, I became excited about the possibility. Matt researched races, and we agreed to do the Baltimore Marathon. Once Matt and Brandon signed up, the pressure was on me. It wasn't long before I had followed suit.

With the money committed, and with Brandon and Matt also on board, I wasn't turning back. We found the beginner's training plan I mentioned above, since this was a first for all three of us, and we plotted out eighteen weeks of training to conclude right before the date of the marathon. The camaraderie of sharing training stories throughout the eighteen weeks was a weekly emotional boost to each of us. We would encourage one another, commiserate about running in the rain or humidity, and talk about how our bodies were handling the ever-lengthening runs each Saturday. As we acclimated to running ten, then fifteen, then eventually twenty miles, we told stories of aches and pains, and of the joy of being able to eat as much food as we wanted and still lose weight.

When the marathon finally arrived, our wives joined us, and we made a weekend of it. They were part of the team too. In fact, our wives started calling themselves the Marathon Widows, because the prep, run, and recovery time necessary for those long training runs could easily consume two to three hours every Saturday for eighteen weeks. Flourishing as runners required togetherness from an ever-expanding village of people.

As I said above, what initially seems to be a stunning solo achievement is the furthest thing from it. The same can be said for nearly every human endeavor. When my wife and I attended a graduation party for the son of some of our closest friends, I heard numerous people say to my friends' son something like this, "Congrats! You did it! Graduation from high school is a huge achievement." That is true, and yet there is more to the story. I know how much toil and agony my friends experienced to get their son to the point of graduation. I know the many moments when neither they nor he had confidence that he was going to graduate. I know the late nights arguing about homework, about studying, and the many tears shed by the son and by his parents on his behalf. When he graduated, my wife and I congratulated him for sure, but we tried to give his parents an even bigger congratulation because this was their graduation too.

Pure individualism, I propose, therefore, is a false concept. Pure individualism does not exist. We are a connected, supported people, and we always will be, whether we run a marathon or graduate from high school. I challenge the reader to find an example of pure individualism. Without question, there are acts of human achievement that are significantly individualistic. Running a marathon, for example, despite all the ways I described it as a together kind of endeavor, still requires one person to run all those training miles alone, and to run, in one fell swoop, 26.1 miles. The three marathons I have run are, far and away, the three most difficult individual physical experiences of my life.

I mentioned Aleksander Doba above, an endurance athlete who solo paddled across the Atlantic Ocean three times in a kayak. The account of his adventures is astounding, and I look to him as one, though thoroughly connected and supported in a variety of ways, who completed a supremely individual effort. Solo mountain climbers amaze me. Authors amaze me, as the task of completing a manuscript, often very much alone, is gargantuan, and worse than alone, it can be lonely. Perhaps you can think of many of your own solo performances or journeys. History is rife with examples. But none of them are purely individual. My conclusion is that even if an example of pure individualism could be found, it would be the exception that proves the rule.

If I am right that pure individualism does not exist, I find it curious that we Americans have had such an affection for individualism. Certainly, as I mentioned above, individualism can be viewed in a positive light, particularly from the perspective of personal responsibility, grounded in the Protestant work ethic. It is an American article of faith that working hard, so we do not have to depend on others, is a virtue, and thus we take pride and feel genuine emotional satisfaction when we complete a task on our own. By completing a task on our own we demonstrate a measure of responsibility.

I feel these emotions of satisfied responsibility deep within me, especially when something in my home breaks. A couple years ago my clothes dryer started making a grinding noise, which I didn't like but chose to ignore. I chose to ignore the noise because I had never fixed a dryer before, and in fact I have rarely fixed any appliances. I feared I would not be able to fix it. But I had an inner individualistic impression that I should be able to fix my dryer by myself. I am not physically incapable. I can learn things. Even better, if I fix it, it will almost certainly be cheaper than hiring someone. (Famous last words . . .) I felt torn, indecisive, and since the noise wasn't that bad, I did nothing. The dryer was, after all, still drying my family's clothes.

What started as a low grind, in a few weeks, went on to become a loud metal-on-metal screech, to the point where I could avoid it no longer. It was so loud, the rest of the family couldn't stand it, and I wondered if the rotation of the dryer drum was soon going to rub a hole through the dryer's exterior sheet metal. My anxiety spiked. I strongly wanted to avoid the cost of a professional repair person. I think to myself, "If I was independently wealthy, I would probably call someone."

At moments like these my wife will often say, "Call someone." What she means is, call a friend. We have numerous men in our church that are gifted in home repairs, and those guys have a wonderful spirit about them. They love to serve and help. They could be the perfect solution, demonstrating flourishing-producing togetherness. But I didn't want to call them.

Intellectually I agree with my wife that calling for help is a great idea. Emotionally, though, my individualism floods my thoughts. I do not want to admit that I need help, and I also don't want to be known as the guy who calls for help. When my wife suggests I call my church friends, I imagine them thinking, "He's always calling for help . . . He probably didn't even try to fix it himself. What a pain." The result is that the dryer is not flourishing, and because it is so loud, my family is not flourishing, and my individualistic pride has me in a bitter frame of mind, which also means I am decidedly not flourishing.

Individual pride won out. I did not call my church friends. Instead, I opened my laptop and visited the dryer manufacturer's website. There I found detailed videos explaining how to disassemble the dryer and look inside. Though I still felt the high anxiety of using a tool on my dryer, the videos emboldened me. Out came the tools, and part by part I opened the dryer and discovered the problem. A buffer made of thick felt keeps the spinning drum in place. Unfortunately, the felt had worn down over time, allowing the drum to eat through a plastic retention clip, which left the drum to spin against the metal frame and create that awful screech.

All I needed to repair the machine was new plastic clips and felt buffers, and the manufacturer was more than willing to sell me replacements. But they weren't cheap. Parts from the manufacturer are usually more expensive than third-party versions. I called a local parts distributor my dad once recommended, and they had the parts I needed at a fraction of the cost. After a quick trip to the distributor, with parts in hand, I once again followed installation videos online, and fixed the dryer. Like crossing the finish line of a long race, I felt a high. Individualism filled my emotional tank, and even as I type this years later, I have a twinge of joy. I didn't need help. I did it on my own. I was experiencing the elation of individualism.

There is a positive sense to this kind of individual achievement. As I mentioned above, the impulse to individualism can inspire us to try new things, to grow, to learn, and to have a healthy sense of venturing outside of our comfort zones. But my dryer repair success must be seen for what it was, a product of individualism combined with flourishing-producing togetherness. I could not have fixed the dryer without help from the manufacturer's videos, the parts store, the maker of the parts, and so on, all of which involve lots of people. While individualism has its benefits, individualism must be distinguished from pure individualism.

Therefore, because pure individualism is impossible or exceedingly rare, the next step is to examine what might be called basic individualism—what I have been calling an individualistic impulse or desire. What we will find is that while pure individualism is false, basic individualism is very real, but basic individualism carries an empty promise. In other words, the affection that we humans, and particularly we Americans, have for individualism, with its promise of self-satisfaction and personal responsibility, often turns out to be detrimental to human flourishing. The traditional view of American culture that prizes this basic individualism and does not give a proper nod to the reality of flourishing-producing togetherness has far too often led society astray. Yes, I fixed my dryer, and I even came away from the repair with an individualistic high of satisfaction. But in so doing I missed out on the opportunity for a potentially richer experience of spending time with a friend from church who has expertise in appliance repair.

We would do well, therefore, to evaluate our American individualistic streak in a balanced light, seeing not only the healthy, empowering side of basic individualism, but also its proclivity for isolationism, arrogance, and pride. In the Disney/Pixar film *The Incredibles*, about a family of superheroes, the father, Mr. Incredible, is known for his super strength and his catchphrase "I work alone." At the film's crisis moment, fearing danger to the rest of his family, Mr. Incredible boldly utters this phrase to his wife, Elastigirl, telling her to get their kids to safety, while he attempts to vanquish the enemy by himself. Throughout the film, and even at this moment, it has been abundantly clear, however, that Mr. Incredible cannot go it alone.[21]

To be victorious over evil, he must depend on the abilities of his wife, his children, and his friends. Together, not alone, they defeat the evil villain. Mr. Incredible's plight rings true because we share his fears and his pride. In a culture of individualism, we do not want to be viewed as incapable of handling life on our own. We too often want to be the superhero, the Mr. Incredible, of our own sphere of influence, such as home appliance repair.

I feel the lure of individualism as I write this book, which started as a dissertation. I want to do it alone, including the originating idea, the outline, the research, the writing, and even the editing. There is within me a strong desire to be self-sufficient in the entire project. Thus when my dissertation committee gave me feedback, while I appreciated it, I felt very conflicted. Should I take their advice? Shouldn't I do this alone?

---

21. Bird, *Incredibles*.

When I had submitted a draft of the outline for their review, one of the committee members responded with a suggested reordered and refocused outline. He was taking my ideas and main points and editing and rearranging them in a way that made more logical sense to him. I asked him to be on my committee for precisely this kind of deep thinking and feedback. When I read his suggested outline, I knew right away that it was better than mine. His order made a lot more sense than mine.

Just that fast, though, I felt an emotion creep up inside me. That emotion had a rebellious tone to it. While my intellect could not deny that my dissertation committee member's suggested outline was superior to mine, that emotion inside me balked hard. I want this to be my dissertation, start to finish, and thus, individualism tugged at my pride, telling me I should not rely on my committee member's input.

As a compromise with my individualism, I attempted to learn from the input and enhance my own outline but without rearranging it as he suggested. That way I was giving a nod to humility (so I told myself),but also satisfying my inner voice demanding individual responsibility. Then something strange happened. Or maybe it wasn't so strange. Rather than making forward progress by incorporating the clear-thinking logic of my committee member, my so-called compromise bogged me down in the emotion and guilt of my own individual shortcomings. My work ground to a halt as I became frustrated trying to follow my outline that had a confusing (il)logical flow. My pride, rooted in individualism, hurt my ability to flourish, and it voided my team's ability to help me flourish.

The danger of individualism is that it can erode the togetherness necessary for human flourishing. As I worked on writing my dissertation, I was not flourishing because I carried anxiety stemming from individualistic pride. I stuck to my convoluted approach in writing some chapters, but I did not have the benefit of a clear outline guiding my efforts. I could have had that clear outline if I would just throw off my inner longing for individual achievement and submit to my advisor's advice. When I finally swallowed my pride and did what my advisor suggested, I found the far better pathway of togetherness, and my writing picked up speed dramatically. I experienced flourishing.

For all the good individualism can do, we must see it for what it is. Individualism is limited. It is not pure or absolute. For individualism's positive aspects to be held in check and avoid pride, we need to know and embrace flourishing-producing togetherness. It is a lesson we may need to learn over and over throughout the course of our lives. What I propose is that theology can aid us in learning how to overcome individualism and experience flourishing-producing togetherness. Sadly, not only has individualism infected

American culture, but it has also infected the theology of some American church communities.

When I was sharing the topic of this writing project with a pastoral colleague from another denomination, he told me a story of how individualism impacted his US-based denomination. His denomination is organized as four independent entities that are designed to support one another by working together. One of the four is a central governing body that provides oversight to the other three bodies—a pension organization, a foreign mission agency, and a domestic mission agency.

A few years ago, the foreign mission agency came up with an idea to create awareness and raise funds for its endeavors by hosting gatherings in each of the denomination's geographical regions across the country. To entice people to attend, the mission agency brought in an engaging guest speaker. This standard fundraising event sounds well and good until you learn that the mission agency did not communicate its plans to or collaborate with any of the other three national entities. To make matters worse, the guest speaker's topic was networking and collaboration. This tone-deaf display of individualism at the corporate level led to deeply negative feelings throughout the denomination.

As we will see in the next chapter, individualism has affected the church and some American Christian approaches to theology and the gospel, becoming yet another deterrent to flourishing-producing togetherness.

3

Christian Faith as Individual and Together

"WE STAND ALONE TOGETHER." What do you think about the two ideas in that short phrase? Alone, and together. Does it make rational sense to pair "alone" with "together"? Is it self-contradictory? That phrase is a real phrase used by a Christian community to describe their mission.[1] Why would a Christian community think that phrase a good fit for their mission? Further, would it surprise you that it was the slogan of an American church's men's ministry? In the previous chapter, we looked at both the positive and negative sides of individualism. I mentioned my opinion that individualism's negative side has influenced the church. Now let's investigate that further. I'm going to attempt to demonstrate that individualism has not only negatively influenced the church but that this influence comes from individualism infecting our American Christian theology, which, if I am correct, could present a significant hurdle to flourishing-producing togetherness. That brings me back to the slogan above, "We stand alone together." I learned about it from a pastor friend.

Four pastors in my denomination and I have an ongoing text message group that is our attempt to harness technology to experience togetherness as we travail the sometimes bumpy road of pastoral ministry. A few years ago one friend in the group texted us that he had to confront his associate pastor who my friend felt had improperly interpreted a text of Scripture during a sermon. My friend asked us for feedback on the approach he was

---

1. I have amended the phrase for anonymity.

going to use in talking with his associate, and we tried to encourage and affirm him that it seemed like he had indeed developed a wise, healthy response to his associate. It would mean, however, that my friend would have to confront his associate.

Those kinds of confrontational discussions can be exceedingly difficult for certain personalities, and for any personality, doing a good job of holding someone accountable is complex. Sensing that emotion and tension within himself, my friend said to us, "I could never do this alone," and he thanked us for our willingness to collaborate with him by giving him feedback and encouragement. Another one of the friends texted back, "No one should be doing this alone, no one." A third friend texted that at a previous church where he served, the slogan for the church's men's ministry is "We stand alone together." The slogan leapt off the phone screen at me, as I have been thinking and writing about individualism and togetherness. What is the slogan trying to say?

On its face, because it includes both concepts of "alone" and "together," the slogan "We stand alone together" might be an example of an oxymoron. Do "alone" and "together" cancel one another out, leaving us with a phrase devoid of meaningful content? Or is it possible that the slogan describes something important about reality? Could it be that there is a sense in which we are alone and yet simultaneously together and that combination of ideas accurately represents humanity and our relationships?

Perhaps the slogan "We stand alone together" represents that balanced understanding of individualism and togetherness we seek. Is there a healthy way to balance individualism and togetherness? Or to put it in terms of a question this chapter seeks to answer, Can Christian faith be both individual and together?

Simply put, yes. To begin answering the question of how Christian faith can be both individual and together, though we are cautious about individualism, it is important to note that individualism is not all bad. In the previous chapter, we examined that, while there is no pure individualism, individualism has been identified as a compelling force in some human cultures, including that of my own context, American culture.

We also observed in the previous chapter that people have varying opinions about the influence of individualism. On the one hand, individualism is sometimes viewed positively in our culture, inspiring the human spirit, achievement, creativity, and responsibility, all of which can lead to flourishing in society. On the other hand, individualism can be viewed negatively leading to selfishness, narcissism, and a lack of concern for the other, all of which can lead to the crippling of flourishing in society.

As we think about Christian faith as being individual, it is my position that individualism's negative aspects often outweigh its positives. Furthermore, as we think about Christian faith as being together, it is flourishing-producing togetherness, properly applied, that will keep the negative aspects of individualism in check. To be fair, unhealthy extremes are possible in both directions. I have already highlighted the unhealth of individualism, an individualism I hope to counter with the concept of flourishing-producing togetherness. But togetherness can also have its unhealthy extremes.

We humans have attempted numerous approaches to togetherness throughout the ages. One of those approaches to togetherness is communitarianism, which is the practice of smaller groups working together.[2] Think of communes. Some communes can be healthy, while some become cults forcibly mandating near-total togetherness, often led by a charismatic authoritarian leader or team and frequently ending in disaster.[3] In my county, the Ephrata Cloisters were such a communitarian experiment in the 1700s, dominated by a powerful leader, Conrad Beissel, who mandated celibacy for all members. The members slept on fifteen-inch wide wooden benches, with woodblocks for pillows. The members genuinely attempted to be hardworking kind neighbors. When I toured the cloister, now a Pennsylvania historical site, the tour guide presented Beissel as an overbearing strict leader. After Beissel passed in 1768, the cloister slowly faded.[4]

Communism is another approach, striving for an extreme togetherness at a national level, which has often led to horrible consequences. Communist nations, however, have committed horrible atrocities, including the slaughter of millions of their citizens.[5] Socialism is yet another approach to togetherness, with both ardent supporters and detractors. By observing these sometimes aberrant projects of togetherness, achieving healthy togetherness in Christian communities will need checks and balances to avoid extremes. We will learn how flourishing-producing togetherness provides that kind of needed accountability.

What I am suggesting in this chapter is that American society, while dabbling from time to time with those negative experiments in togetherness, has largely been individualistic to its detriment and that individualism

---

2. See Persons, *Socialism and American Life*, 125–52. An example, the Catholic Worker Movement, started by Dorothy Day in the Great Depression of the 1930s, grew into a series of farms where workers live communally. The Catholic Worker Movement reports that there are over one hundred such communities still in existence today. Cornell, "Brief Introduction," para. 9.

3. For example, Budziszewski, "Problem with Communitarianism."

4. Ephrata Cloister, "History."

5. Haven, "Stalin Killed Millions."

has negatively impacted how American Christians understand their faith. Let's consider how individualism can infect Christian communities negatively, even to the point of warping a Christian understanding of theology.

We're going to spend time in chapter 6 becoming more acquainted with theology so that we can harness its analytical prowess. For now, as we think about the possibility of individualism harmfully infecting American Christian communities, let us simply consider how a beautiful feature of theology is that it can provide a lens through which to view and evaluate all other aspects of life. Therefore, if individualism has warped our understanding of theology, it is possible that Christian communities have lost an important measure of accountability that theology's lens can provide. This task of evaluation will require, then, some healthy self-awareness to be able to ascertain if we in fact have allowed our theological lenses to be scratched and fogged by unhealthy individualism. Are we seeing clearly?

In the early twentieth century, theologian Walter Rauschenbusch claimed that American Christians were not seeing theology clearly. In his book *A Theology for the Social Gospel*, Rauschenbusch argued that the individualistic gospel had become a detriment to societal transformation.[6] What is the individualistic gospel? Rauschenbusch suggests that the individualist gospel is a theological view of the story of Jesus, focusing on getting people to accept Jesus as their personal Savior so they can believe they are saved from punishment in the afterlife in hell. In fact, he claims that individualism so warped theology that the biblical gospel's social concern, in some Christian circles, had become nearly unrecognizable.[7] In the one hundred years since Rauschenbusch wrote, both conservative and progressive Christians have embraced social causes. Has American Christianity corrected itself?

Consider the pro-life movement, which some Christians hold to be a social justice effort protecting the life of the vulnerable unborn. Many Catholics and conservative Protestants strongly oppose abortion. The pro-life cause is historically pro-conception and pro-birth. Some Christians express a more holistic understanding of life by fighting the alcohol industry, stemming from a concern about the destructiveness addiction can have on many lives. Likewise, other Christians have advocated for life through the abolition of the death penalty. Though these concerns, temperance and oppposition to the death penalty, are not typically labeled "pro-life," they align with a Christian social theology under the umbrella of what could be called God's heart for life. Given this multifaceted pro-life advocacy, can we say that the conservative American Christians Rauschenbusch critiqued

---

6. Rauschenbusch, *Social Gospel*.
7. Rauschenbusch, *Social Gospel*, 26–27, 100–101.

one hundred years ago have transformed to become aligned with the social gospel? Would Rauschenbusch, if he were alive and could evaluate the past century of American Christianity, say, "Well done! You've read my book and you changed!"?

Despite many contemporary Christians emphasizing a variety of pro-life social concerns, and many others related to ethnicity, economics, and classism, I believe Rauschenbusch's concern about an overly individualistic gospel remains valid a century later. Let me explain why, and it has everything to do with theology.

I am an American evangelical. One of the central tenets of evangelical theology is that the gospel of Jesus is the good news for the salvation of individuals. This individual salvation has as its goal the hope of a flourishing eternal afterlife. Individualist theology argues that the temporal world is just that, temporary, and as a result our focus should be eternal. Temporal social concerns, the individualist gospel argues, pale in comparison to real flourishing, which is in the afterlife and almost *only* in the afterlife. It is this individualistic approach to theology and the gospel that seeks to assure a person of their place in that afterlife.

In the evangelical subculture in which I was raised in the 1970s through the 1990s,[8] one of the phrases commonly expressing this individualistic theology was the need for everyone to "accept Jesus as their personal Savior." This acceptance was often explained by using the acronym, ABC, which stands for admit, believe, and confess. What this phrase envisioned was a person making a mental choice to admit that they are an individual sinner in need of a personal Savior, so they must individually believe that Jesus is their personal Savior, finally leading them to individually confess their personal sins, thus starting the new life that Jesus wants them to live.

If a person prayed what was often referred to as the Prayer of Salvation, they as an individual had accepted Jesus as their personal Savior. This is the individualist understanding of the gospel, the good news, that individual sinners[9] can be forgiven of their sins and have the hope of eternal life.

Clearly evidenced by the repetition of the words "personal" and "individual," this version of the gospel story focuses on individual salvation, promising the individual a future of eternal bliss. This version of the gospel is a beautiful story of God's love for people. It depicts a God who created

---

8. Noll writes that because America was so diverse, even in its founding era, Christian theology in America followed suit, and yet the result was a "tremendous explosion of individualized, creative, ever-restless, earnest, word-infatuated religious talking and writing." Noll, *America's God*, 228.

9. Here the biblical teaching should be clarified—all humans are sinners. See Rom 3 for the apostle Paul's description of human sin.

humanity out of a deep desire to be in relationship with them. But humanity, in their selfish individualism, chose to deny God's love, rebel against him, and break away from that relationship. God as lover, however, is exceedingly passionate about restoring a relationship with individual humans, to the point that he would give his life, through Jesus' crucifixion and resurrection, to rectify the brokenness,[10] giving each human the individual opportunity to choose to be back in relationship with him. This message truly is good news. That which is wrong can be righted.

If this individualistic gospel is such good news, why does Rauschenbusch critique it? He does so because its individualistic focus does not represent the totality of the biblical view of the gospel. What he goes on to teach in *A Theology for the Social Gospel* is a filling in of the gaps, a needed corrective to a truncated gospel. Rauschenbusch walks through the New Testament teachings, both by Jesus and the other writers, explaining a gospel that not only provides the hope of eternal life but also the possibility for what I am calling flourishing-producing togetherness, what the Hebrew Bible calls *shalom*, and what Jesus himself called "abundant life" (John 10:10, my translation).[11]

Supporters of the individualistic gospel might respond, however, that their view was not devoid of a corporate or collective emphasis. The way that flourishing-producing togetherness flowed from an individualistic approach to theology, they claim, is that as the number of individuals who become followers of Christ increase not only will individuals experience transformation but the collective result will be the transformation of society.

To illustrate this, they needed only to point to the revivals of years past, when numerous individuals in one community would decide to receive Christ as their personal Savior, and those new followers of Jesus would renounce sins such as consumption of alcohol, gambling, and carousing. Church worship service attendance would rise. Crime would decrease. Jails would empty out. Society would flourish. In their view, God's plan for human flourishing in society was first to change the individual heart and mind.

To be fair, many of the revivalist preachers truly advocated social change. America's Second Great Awakening spread like spiritual fire across the young nation during the span of 1795 through 1810. Historian Mark Noll says the title "Second Great Awakening" has been "used in so many different ways, and for so many different periods, that it is almost meaningless."[12] But he goes on to suggest that "from 1795 to about 1810 a broad and general

---

10. For more on "rectification," see Rutledge, *Crucifixion*, 147n3, 296, 327.
11. See Rauschenbusch, *Social Gospel*, 104–5, 108.
12. Noll, *History*, 151.

rekindling of interest in evangelical Protestantism spread throughout the country."[13] The impact of the revival was not only spiritual. Prominent evangelist Charles Finney's "contribution to the abolitionist movement was substantial,"[14] write sociologists Michael Emerson and Christian Smith. They describe Finney as declaring from his revival pulpit that slaveholders could not take Communion, declaring them not Christian. Finney's passion for abolition, though, paled in comparison to his passion for evangelism, and he eventually broke with the abolitionist movement. Emerson and Smith write that "although some of the more outspoken abolitionists were evangelicals, most evangelicals were not outspoken abolitionists."[15] By and large, evangelicals focused on promoting the individualist gospel during the Second Great Awakening.

Given the societal transformation some communities experienced through people believing in the individualist gospel, perhaps Rauschenbusch, writing in 1918, was wrong to react so strongly against the individualist gospel? Rauschenbusch's context was quite different from that of the Second Great Awakening. After the revival fires cooled, a new movement was afoot in Protestant Christianity in the second half of the 1800s. The new movement was a byproduct of the growing theologically liberal wing of the church, with its critique of the Bible, and the new scientific theory, particularly evolutionary biology from the likes of Charles Darwin, who published his revolutionary *On the Origin of Species* in 1859.

In response to evolutionary biology and liberal modernist theology, theologically conservative Christians in the late 1800s began to mount a defense of a highly literal interpretation of the Bible. Often referred to as Christian fundamentalists, they sought to preserve what they believed was primary—the individual salvation approach to the gospel. Theological controversy only heightened between modernists and fundamentalists into the early decades of the 1900s. As Rauschenbush observed the claims of the fundamentalists about individual salvation, he published *A Theology of the Social Gospel* in 1918, attempting to recover what he believed was lost. His claim was that the gospel had always included a social concern, and thus those teaching an individualist approach were not teaching a fully biblical gospel. The social gospel, Rauschenbusch said, included not only a theological concern for individual salvation but also a concern that the

---

13. Noll, *History*, 152.

14. Emerson, and Smith, *Divided*, 32. For more on this era, see Bebbington, *Evangelicalism*, 108, 120-22, 132-37; Marsden, *Fundamentalism*, 80-85; and Sweeney, *Evangelical Story*, 162-64.

15. Emerson and Smith, *Divided*, 33-34.

gospel would impact society and structures.[16] Rauschenbusch's claim was that God's heart for human flourishing included both individual salvation and social transformation. He pointed out, though, that the fundamentalists were abandoning the social side of the gospel.

We will interact further with his claims in future chapters. For now, I think it is important to ask the question, Who is right? Are those who hold to an individualistic gospel correct? Does individual transformation lead to the transformation of society? Or does Rauschenbusch's view of the social gospel provide the superior interpretation of biblical theology?

Might we find balance between the two views? Do we "stand alone together"? Does a theology of flourishing-producing togetherness miss out on the necessary individual perspective of the gospel? Is it one or the other, individual or together? Or is there a way to understand the gospel as relating to both the individual and the collective? To attempt to answer these questions, we examine the concerns of those who hold to an individualist view of the gospel. I know that individualistic view, as it was deeply embedded in my undergraduate studies.

I attended a conservative evangelical Bible college, which was founded about one decade after Rauschenbusch wrote *A Theology for the Social Gospel*, when the modernist-fundamentalist controversy was raging in the 1920s and 1930s.[17] Sixty years later, in the mid-1990s when I was a student, the college continued to have a strong dose of those early influences. Theology professors taught us that Rauschenbusch and those that held to a theology of the social gospel were using incorrect hermeneutics, a word that refers to the art and science of interpretation. Instead, my professors taught, the individualistic gospel was the correct way to interpret Scripture. Also, the professors feared, the social gospel led to a denial of Scripture and God's heart for salvation of individuals. They taught us to focus on one question of utmost importance: Where would people spend eternity? Helping people answer that question with the word "heaven" was to be our passion, and "heaven" was to be the theological lens through which we would interpret Scripture and understand the world.

As a result, I held a rather negative view of any churches or Christians that emphasized the social gospel, as if they were polluting the truth in their quest to make life better for people here on earth. My classmates and I believed there was something commendable about addressing injustice, and we certainly read how Jesus himself cared for the poor, sick, and abused. But our focus was on the question of heaven and hell. What would it matter,

---

16. Rauschenbusch, *Social Gospel*, 118–130.
17. See especially Marsden, *Fundamentalism*, 194.

we reasoned, if we fed the hungry but did not care for individuals' eternal souls? We saw the purveyors of the social gospel as all too willing to ignore individual eternal destiny, which was, in our eyes, far more important than some temporary societal ill such as hunger or poverty.

My wife and I graduated from college in 1996 and were married soon after. We earned degrees in biblical studies and cross-cultural ministry, and we believed God wanted us to become missionaries so we could devote our lives to telling people about the individual gospel. In three year's time, we were accepted to serve as church planting missionaries with a mission agency focused on the Caribbean, and God provided the funds for us to be fully supported. We moved our family, which now included our two young sons, to Kingston, Jamaica, to help a team of American missionaries start new churches in partnership with a Jamaican denomination.

Though we regularly walked through extreme poverty in Kingston's ghettos, where many of our Jamaican friends lived their whole lives, our missionary team focused on communicating the content of the individual gospel. If we could only get people to assent to the propositions of that gospel message, they would not only have hope of eternal life in heaven, which was better by far than any comfort in this world, but perhaps they would also change the temporal state of their lives. What we thought was going to be our life's work ended quickly as a one-year stint, because we had some emotional and relational healing and growing up to do, and we moved back home.

A year after we moved back to our hometown of Lancaster, Pennsylvania, I was hired at Faith Church, and we started making relationships within our denomination, the Evangelical Congregational Church. Through denominational connections, Michelle met a woman, Aiyana, who along with a few other friends desired to make a difference in the world. They had some connections in Cambodia, and they invited Michelle to join them on their next exploratory trip.

In Cambodia Michelle saw crushing poverty that was far worse than the truly awful poverty we encountered in Kingston. Michelle, Aiyana, and their friends traveled through Cambodia, desiring to learn how they could help, even if in some small way. They talked about the famous quote, "Not all of us can do great things, but we can do small things with great love."[18] The small thing they decided to do was start a nonprofit, Who Cares?, which was dedicated to supporting a Cambodian ministry to alleviate poverty and grow opportunities in the Poipet area of Cambodia.

---

18. These words are often attributed to Saint Mother Teresa, but they do not appear in any of her works.

Through the newly founded nonprofit they raised funds among family and friends in the United States, seeking to sponsor clean water wells, an AIDS treatment center, toilets, and schools "on a mat." Village parents who could not afford to send their children to school would allow the kids to attend "school on a mat." An itinerant teacher would spread out a tarp for the children to sit on, and the teacher would instruct using an easel supporting a chalkboard. For many kids, "school on a mat" could be their only educational opportunity.

In those first few years of her travels back and forth to Cambodia, when Michelle would talk with people in our church about her trips and the goals of clean water and education, some people would ask, "But when did you share the gospel? Did anyone pray the prayer of salvation?" The people questioning Michelle were thinking with the same individualistic mindset that we had been taught in college, that a school on a mat was nice, but what was far more important was the children's eternal destiny. Their view of gospel results only included metrics based on the individualistic gospel.

Through Michelle's journeys to Cambodia and the work of the nonprofit Who Cares?, from which Michelle and Aiyana would go on to birth a business called Imagine Goods, we learned that the individual gospel is true but truncated, not sufficient to account for the wealth of biblical teaching on flourishing. A biblically holistic gospel includes sharing the content, the words of the story of salvation made available by Jesus, but usually not before expressing the deeds of the gospel.

Does one really come before the other? Is there a priority in gospel proclamation of word and deed? Take Poipet, Cambodia, as a test case for answering this question. The reality of life in Poipet was systemic poverty that fueled human trafficking. Poverty forced some parents to choose which of their children they could afford to send to school and therefore which children would not receive an education. The harsh reality of a school-age child remaining uneducated was that the child was far more vulnerable to be trafficked for labor or for the sex trade. The lack of financial margins in the parents' world left little opportunity for parents or for their children.

To people in that desperate situation, it would have been biblically inconsistent to say, "Let me tell you about Jesus who wants to offer you eternal life in heaven so that you don't have to go to hell when you die,"[19] without caring for the physical needs of their families. When communicating with

---

19. In writing these words, I am not suggesting that these words equate to the content of the good news story. I am simply suggesting that those from an individualistic gospel background often use words like "heaven" and "hell" when they give a message of salvation. I believe the gospel story is best communicated with a great deal more grace and nuance, which I believe is more in line with the heart of God.

people like those Cambodian families, we would do well in most situations to live the deeds of the gospel first, and only after a solid loving, caring foundation has been established will we share the content of the good news story of Jesus.

This is a perspective based not simply on wisdom, seeking to honor the dignity of the other, but it is also modeled by Jesus himself who demonstrates this order quite often in his ministry. Of course, sometimes he preached first and he helped meet needs afterwards. Sometimes he preached and didn't meet needs. Each situation is unique, but as we study the accounts of Jesus' life, he often cares for people's physical needs before sharing the content of good news. Because of Jesus' example, I affirm a critique of individualist gospel proclaimers who focus on preaching the content of the salvation story without considering the life situation of their hearers. For that kind of preacher, it seems to be all "pie in the sky," which is not in line with the ministry of Jesus.

There is absolutely a time and place to share the content of the story of Jesus' love with families like those in Poipet, but first and foremost, those families needed help in a variety of ways to provide stability and safety for their children. Clean water wells close to home not only meant healthy water for their bodies but also meant they would no longer have to send their vulnerable young children on long walks to the nearest well.

School on a mat in their own village meant that families had opportunity to educate all their children rather than choosing which children can attend school. Schooling is so vital because education opens opportunities for work and advancement, which can assist the family in overcoming poverty and the plethora of difficult social issues brought on by poverty and lack of margins. Many systems of injustice work together to create the perfect storm for trafficking and slave labor to thrive, and thus a proper response must include a gospel of deeds to bring justice, because justice can lead to human flourishing.

So often, when those of us from Western or developed countries travel to developing countries, we have a goal of bringing flourishing to the people of that country. This good motivation can hide a shadow side, as we can also believe that we are the solution to their problems. Perhaps we believe that those in developing countries need the solution of the individualistic gospel. Perhaps we believe that our finances can help them. While it is not wrong to have a heart that desires to help, a heart of service, we must examine our desires to see if they are truly motivated by flourishing-producing togetherness. Michelle and Aiyana learned that flourishing-producing togetherness surprisingly moves in two directions.

As Michelle and Aiyana spent time in Cambodia, though they wanted to help the Cambodians they met, they learned that so often it was the Cambodians who helped them. Togetherness with Cambodian friends produced flourishing both ways. This two-way flourishing was only possible if all involved desired it. As Americans Michelle and Aiyana brought opportunity and resources the Khmer people could benefit from, but something was missing. During their time in Cambodia, as they listened and learned, the Khmer people taught Michelle and Aiyana a deeper perspective. They learned God's love for all people, the impact of joy, the power of prayer, and the beauty of culture. Together both cultures and groups of people began to have moments of flourishing, learning, and growing from each other.

While Michelle became more involved in Cambodia, and I went on the trip working with our sister church in Chicago, as I mentioned in a previous chapter, Michelle and I also studied God's word, learning anew about his heart for justice. We became convinced that the proclamation of the gospel must balance word and deed. Nearly fifteen years into this process of learning, I read Rauschenbusch for the first time.

Page after page I was shocked by what I was reading. His words and his approach to understanding the gospel were not heretical like we had been taught. Instead, he balanced the gospel of word and deed. He critiques the individualist gospel that emphasizes the word, the content of the story, but he only does so to point out the wealth of biblical theology that teaches the deeds of the gospel and the corporate, collective need for Christians to overturn injustice wherever they see it. As I finished reading his book, I was left wondering how my evangelical fundamentalist forebears could have any problem with such quality analysis of the biblical text. But I know how. There are many reasons.

First, my evangelical fundamentalist forbears emphasized the individualistic gospel because it is attractive. The promise of personal salvation and bliss in heaven taps into human craving for comfort, entertainment, and pleasure. The thought that we can be free of pain, experiencing nothing but joy and perfection all the time in heaven, is a deliciously tempting idea. The individualistic gospel promises that bliss precisely because it locates flourishing in another world yet to come. Its rhetorical pull is not unlike the health and wealth message of the prosperity gospel.

The prosperity gospel suggests that if an individual has genuine faith in Jesus, God will bless them with bodily health and financial wealth in the current life. Likewise, the individualist gospel suggests a kind of health and wealth, what some might believe to be the ultimate health and wealth, though attainable only in the life to come, in heaven. While the prosperity gospel has, in my opinion, only a sketchy basis in the biblical text, the individualist gospel of giving people hope for heaven is theologically sound. But it falls short when it fails to incorporate the social gospel and its call for human flourishing now.

Second, my evangelical fundamentalist forbears emphasized the individualistic gospel because it is not nearly as messy as the social gospel. The individual gospel requires less of us. It is primarily a matter of an individual assent to the content of the story of Jesus, believing that story in one's own heart and mind. The social gospel, however, almost always involves engaging in long-term relationships and in fighting the battle of injustice, which can be complex and painful. Systemic structures of injustice are in place for a reason, usually because people who have power and wealth want to retain their power and wealth. Here the story of Jesus is instructive. His social message ran counter to the power brokers of his society, and it got him killed. Talk about messy.

Finally, my evangelical fundamentalist forbears emphasized the individualistic gospel because the individualist gospel is countable. When we were students in Bible college, every year the college would report how many people made individual "decisions for Christ" through student outreach ministries. It sounded impressive to hear that a couple hundred people were now followers of Jesus. In the chapel service when the president reported that statistic, people would applaud. The college promoted the number of conversions in its fundraising mailings. Even if not all, perhaps many of those individual decisions were sincere, resulting in people becoming genuine followers of Jesus who experienced the transformation of the Holy Spirit, not only having the hope of eternal bliss but also flourishing now.

Knowing the amazing way God works, I believe it possible that some of those people are experiencing that hope and flourishing to this day, and maybe they can even point back to a day years ago when Bible college students told them the content of the gospel. But when the college counted those statistics, they never included the deeds of the gospel, the social gospel. Why? The social gospel is far more difficult to count. It is not impossible to quantify, however. In recent years, Christians have suggested that our metrics need to change, including metrics that record the deeds of the gospel. But how do we count people lifted out of poverty? How do we count injustice overturned? It is possible, but it is also difficult.

Thankfully, the biblical text tells us that no matter how costly, difficult, or complex the social gospel remains, balanced with the individual gospel, the social gospel is of utmost importance. While humans are individuals who can have personal relationships with God, especially as the Holy Spirit lives in us (1 Cor 6:19), we can also embrace a gospel of flourishing-producing togetherness.

By itself, though, individualism, even though it has some benefits, is insufficient at best and utterly damaging at worst. Individualism does not naturally lead to flourishing of humanity, precisely because its greatest good is the flourishing of the solitary human in the afterlife. As we will see in part 2 of the book, theologians Miroslav Volf and Matthew Croasmun provide a corrective—theology, rightly interpreted, expresses much more than individual salvation, a far superior flourishing-producing togetherness.[20] But what makes flourishing-producing togetherness superior?

Embracing a gospel of flourishing-producing togetherness will not only retain the wonderful news of hope of eternal life for individuals, but it will also provide the impetus for the kind of abundant life on earth envisioned by the kingdom of God. In the chapters to come, we will expand that answer. For now, perhaps one example can whet the reader's appetite for more to come.

That example is Facebook, the social media conglomerate that rebranded itself as Meta in 2021. Over the last ten years, perhaps no company has embodied the idea of togetherness as has Meta. Its social media properties, including the behemoths Facebook, WhatsApp, and Instagram, boast billions of users globally, seemingly connecting people together like never before.[21]

When I graduated from high school in 1992, the internet was in its infancy. I first learned about a social network called CompuServe that fall in my first semester of college.[22] Very few people had heard of the internet, and even fewer used it. The summer after high school graduation, I said goodbye to numerous high school friends, never to see them again. Thirty years later as my own children have been graduating high school, they have every expectation of maintaining connections with as many of their high school friends as they want to, through the kind of togetherness social media provides.

But Meta has been under scrutiny in recent years as whistleblowers claim that the company, though long aware of its severe downsides, did little to mitigate the situation.[23] Those downsides include social media addiction, election misinformation, and child endangerment. Social media has given birth to what are called troll farms, many of which are run by malintents who spread lies, most famously attempting to affect the outcome of national

---

20. Volf and Croasmun, *For the World*.
21. "Introducing Meta," para. 6.
22. "About CompuServe," para. 2.
23. Andersson, "Social Media Apps," para. 9.

elections. These troll farms create fake articles meant to deceive and create mistrust.[24]

To be fair, Facebook responded, deleting "1.3 billion fake accounts between October and December of 2020, and [employing] over 35,000 people working on tackling misinformation on its platform. The company also removed more than twelve million pieces of content about COVID-19 and vaccines that global health experts flagged as misinformation."[25] But the damage was done.

Writer M. G. Seigler suggests that "the problem is that Facebook created the greatest tool ever to connect . . . human beings." How is connecting people a problem? Seigler goes on to suggest that "connecting people is good! Right? But, as it turns out, it's not. It *sounds* good. We all *want* it to be good. But it's a . . . disaster. Because humanity is a disaster."[26] While he admits that he may sound harsh in those last few sentences, his point is well taken. Connecting people, and therefore, togetherness, is not an absolute good because people are not absolutely good. In the case of social media, people are connected like never before, but they continue to experience the devastation of humanity's tendency to "disaster."

Worse still, the algorithms used by Facebook and other social media platforms have also come under fire for being addictive, bringing a rush of endorphins much like slot machines in casinos. People, and especially teens and children, have a very difficult time disengaging from the use of social media, as the artificial intelligence running the show is designed to keep their focus. Yet Meta and the other social media companies have long been aware of the addictive nature of their products.[27] Since its advent in recent decades, social media addiction has been classified as a genuine disorder, and communities have created detox programs to help free people from its grasp. When viewed this way, social media engages the worst impulses in humanity, making it exceedingly difficult to break away.

What would the proponents of the individualist gospel say about the crisis of social media addiction? Can the individualistic gospel impact such a ubiquitous problem? To answer these questions, I invite you to entertain a thought project with me. Imagine that a widespread acceptance of an individualistic approach to the gospel story resulted in massive numbers of people becoming followers of Jesus who now had a hope of eternal life in heaven. Also imagine that the individualist gospel motivated them to

24. Hao, "Troll Farms."
25. "Facebook Fake Accounts," para. 1.
26. Seigler, "Facebook Is Too Big to Fail," paras. 9, 10 (italics original).
27. Andersson, "Social Media Apps."

change their individual lives. While that would be excellent, giving people hope for the future and strength to live a better life, addictive social media platforms remain.

No matter how many people become Christians, social media platforms still captivate our baser instincts and do so with addictive qualities baked into their programming. Seigler is on to an important theological discussion, which we will talk about further in a future chapter, that of human depravity and how that depravity gets in the way of the kind of togetherness that produces human flourishing. But what Seigler does not mention is the significant addictive qualities of social media. The individualistic gospel does not address that systemic structure.

Those Christians who emphasize the individualist gospel could respond that if enough people became Christians, then Christians in leadership roles at Facebook or other social media companies could eventually lead those companies to eradicate the addictive quality of their products. That view, however, is a grand "what if" statement that is potentially unrealistic. One could also argue the opposite. What if that many people do not become Christians? Or consider the possibility that a dramatic increase of people converting to Christianity within one society might not make that society increase its level of human flourishing.

China is a case in point. In the last century, Christianity has grown significantly in China. In response to that we must ask, Has the presence of millions of Chinese Christians changed that nation, eradicating its injustices? Anecdotal evidence of that is sparse. What is more prevalent is the ongoing perpetration of injustice by the Chinese government. Whether in China or in response to social media or any other systemic ill, what is needed is a holistic gospel for both individual and society. We need not wait for the "what if" of individualistically fueled cultural change.

Rather, flowing from the teaching and example of Jesus himself, the gospel calls us to preach good news in word and deed so that individuals can have hope of eternal life and abundant life. Christian theology leads us to think about how to address injustice now. If we can understand flourishing-producing togetherness, we will have practical principles to apply to the injustices committed by social media, thus protecting children and adults who are susceptible to misinformation and addiction.

We return to the slogan with which we started the chapter, "We stand alone together." Is each human foundationally alone, though when we gather in supportive groups, like a men's ministry, we offset the negative sides of individualism? No. Humans are individuals who are integrally together. I visited the website of the church with the men's ministry slogan, as my friend has not pastored there for a few years, wondering if they still used the slogan. I discovered the slogan had changed to "Standing together." It is a promising change away from individualism.

Likewise, we must view biblical theology through a lens of togetherness in addition to and more intently than through a lens of individualism. When we view biblical theology through the lens of togetherness, we will be able to understand how biblical theology informs and inspires flourishing-producing togetherness. It is a theology of togetherness that will help us define and employ flourishing producing togetherness. As we have seen, togetherness is a neutral concept that refers to the qualities or characteristics of how people are together. Not all togetherness produces flourishing.

For a doctoral course, I studied my denomination's response to the American civil rights movement in the 1950s and 1960s through the reporting of its magazine at the time, the *United Evangelical* (UE). The civil rights movement had at its heart a concern for the many people in the United States who were not flourishing because of racial injustice, segregation, and racism. Pastors and laypeople of my denomination, the Evangelical Congregational Church (ECC), wrote numerous articles and letters to the editor, commenting on Supreme Court civil rights decisions and the civilian reaction to those decisions, reactions that often included protests, marches, and other demonstrations. The ECC's official response was to form committees to study the issues and produce papers, which were eventually published in the magazine.

In these papers my predominantly white northern denomination concluded that the best approach to the civil rights movement was what could be called spiritual individualism, which is the individualistic approach to theology that so concerned Rauschenbusch, as I will discuss further in chapter 4. As I wrote in that chapter, the rationale of individualist theology is that once individuals are saved, they will live out the fruit of the Spirit (Gal 5:22–23), treating people with loving kindness. Therefore, what our country needed during this difficult time, the ECC claimed, was more and more individuals to believe in and become disciples of Jesus.[28] First change people, then society will change.

Additionally, many civil rights protests and uprisings, the committees and magazine authors declared, were almost always illegal, which is

---

28. Emerson and Smith report that many white American evangelicals in the civil rights era believed that "equality is spiritually and individually based, not temporally and socially based." Emerson and Smith, *Divided*, 58. See also their chapter "Color Blind," 69–91. In this chapter, they reveal how free will theology has led white evangelicals toward an individualistic view of racism, thus being opposed to viewing racism systemically. "White Americans favor individualistic explanations over structural ones." Emerson and Smith, *Divided*, 109.

unbecoming of Christians and therefore ill-advised. Christians should practice evangelism, not social justice. Evangelical historian Mark Noll remarked that in that era the same tendency filled the pages of the most prominent American evangelical magazine, *Christianity Today*. Flourishing, they believed, would come through individual salvation.[29]

What is fascinating is that the ECC in those same years held a nearly opposite view and approach to another social issue: temperance, the prohibition of alcohol. While applying an individualist theology to the injustices of the civil rights era, when it came to prohibition of alcohol, the church strongly advocated for not just an individual spiritualist approach but also a systemic approach, which included legislative options and aggressive social action. Every issue of the *United Evangelical* included one page devoted to attacking the systemic injustice of intemperance and alcohol abuse. The UE also included numerous articles and editorials addressing temperance and alcohol. Many Christians in our day approach the social issues of abortion and sexual ethics with similar inconsistency.[30]

To address this inconsistency, Christians must see that the spiritual individualist view is not the only view of the gospel, and this relates to Rauschenbusch's central claim. There is a social aspect to the gospel, and this social aspect was always intended by Jesus and the New Testament writers to be integral to any explanation or demonstration of the gospel. When Christians proclaim the gospel, in other words, we do so in word (proclamation of content) and deed (social justice). Therefore, to follow God's heart for flourishing for all, Christian communities will implement flourishing-producing togetherness, which will include working toward the eradication of unjust societal structures.

In the pages of the *United Evangelical*, authors expressed admiration for Martin Luther King Jr. and his passion to remove unjust structures in society, but they also disagreed with his focus on the deeds he promoted such as marches or boycotts. King, however, knew that the unjust racist structures were often being upheld by people who claimed to have experienced

---

29. Noll, email message to author, Aug. 20, 2019. I am indebted to my uncle James Ohlson, who put me in touch with Noll. For more analysis of *Christianity Today*'s coverage of the civil rights era, see Emerson and Smith, *Divided*, 46, 56.

30. Consider the massive decades-long systemic movement to overturn Roe v. Wade. That movement included marches and protests, some of which were illegal, including, sadly, the bombing of abortion clinics. Pro-life supporters far more often peacefully advocated through the political and legal means, seeking to elect pro-life politicians. Pro-life anti-Roe efforts culminated in President Donald Trump's selection of conservative Supreme Court justices who gave the court the numbers to overturn Roe on June 24, 2022, in the Dobbs decision. See Frame, "Violence Escalates"; Hurley, "Overturn Roe v. Wade."

individual salvation. Public schools were segregated in states where most of the people fighting to keep school segregation also claimed to be Christians. Injustice was not being eradicated simply because people were self-identifying as Christ followers. The roots of injustice go deep, supported by a divisive theological construct that prioritizes individual salvation to the detriment of social justice. I have been guilty of that imbalance in my own life.

My wife and I attended her cousin's wedding in the late 1990s; it was held at a United Methodist Church. In the lobby, I perused pamphlets describing that congregation's concern for social justice. Having been raised in an evangelical subculture that promoted individual salvation, I immediately had a feeling of discomfort upon realizing that we were in a social gospel church. If, as Rauschenbusch claims, Jesus and the other New Testament writers taught a social element to the gospel, why was I taught to be concerned about an understanding of the gospel focused on social justice?

The reason for this fear is an imbalance, in which some churches or denominations abandoned the individual aspect of the gospel in favor of the social. The fear was that the biblical individual aspect of the gospel was being lost, and thus people were not truly being saved, not truly disciples of Jesus. This fear was not ill-founded. Some churches were over-reacting and becoming social gospel churches, neglecting and sometimes abandoning individual emphases in their evangelism. As such, there was an equal and opposite reaction to emphasize individualist theology, and some churches, mostly in the evangelical and fundamentalist streams of Christianity, began to promote an exclusively individualist gospel, which is clearly seen in my denomination's approach to the terrible injustices of the civil rights era. Rauschenbusch, therefore, was writing to recapture the balance.

Sadly, in individualistic evangelical circles, Rauschenbusch's work, especially with the word "social" in its title, was considered suspect at best, heresy at worst. As I mentioned previously, reading his writing with new eyes, I found it to be quite biblical and balanced. *A Theology for the Social Gospel* recovers the lost emphasis on how the gospel has a social aspect and application. If the ECC would have embraced that balance in the 1950s and 1960s, they could have welcomed the work of Martin Luther King Jr. rather than finding him suspect. There were social injustices that needed a social response, especially when those who called themselves Christians were promoting the injustices.

Furthermore, the gospel does have something to say about social justice. While an individual's salvation is an important topic and goal, the gospel also calls for injustice and evil to be defeated. What we will see in part 2 is that a theology of togetherness is indebted to the social gospel for helping us balance the individual and social, the word and deed, for the goal of human flourishing.

A theology of togetherness, while similar to the social gospel and sharing some of its viewpoints, is unique in that it can speak to all kinds of communities, impacting the wide variety of collaborative groups. A theology of togetherness specifically seeks to help Christians think theologically about the quality of the togetherness in the communities in which they, the Christians, and all others, participate, so that working together as Christian communities, they can produce human flourishing.

When considering togetherness in Christian communities we should not assume that everyone is on the same page in their understanding of what it means to be together. Instead, we need a source outside of ourselves, a guide to help us discover the kind of togetherness that produces flourishing.

My claim is that theology can help us evaluate togetherness to arrive at flourishing-producing togetherness. As we will begin to see in the next chapter, doing theology, studying the Scriptures, will help us to learn the qualities of togetherness that can help Christian communities achieve human flourishing.

Part 2

Theology and Togetherness for Flourishing

4

What Is a Theology of Togetherness?

A FORMER COWORKER OF mine described herself and her husband as theology nerds. What she means is that the two of them very much enjoy reading, thinking about, and discussing God. They love theology, and yet theology is a word that can cause people discomfort. I concluded the previous chapter by suggesting that in this next section of the book, we will do theology, studying the Scriptures to understand and apply flourishing-producing togetherness in our communities. What I mean is that theology will help us see the world. When we put on those theological lenses, we will be doing theology. It might feel intimidating to think about doing theology. You might wonder, How does one *do* theology? Can I do theology without training? Perhaps you are a professor or pastor reading this, and if so, this chapter might seem rudimentary. I would recommend you skim over it, as in the next chapter we'll begin the actual theological work. If you have not had theological training, I would encourage you to read this chapter, as I believe you'll find that after learning some basic terms and concepts, you'll be able to join in the discovery.

Doing theology, then, is engagement with ideas, and in particular, ideas about God. When we do theology, we purposefully think about God and how those ideas about God relate to our world. I have preached, for example, on a theology of space exploration, a theology of artificial intelligence, and a theology of lawn care. In those sermons, I attempted to help my congregation think theologically about life and culture, whether in outer space, cyberspace, or the space just through their front door. In this book, I invite you to think theologically with me about togetherness. I don't know if this will turn us into theology nerds, but I hope it will help us consider how to understand flourishing-producing togetherness more deeply and implement it in our communities.

DEFINING THEOLOGY: THE STUDY OF GOD

Let's begin by defining the word "theology." The English word "theology" is a combination of two Greek words, *theos* and *logos*. *Theos* refers to divinity, to the things of God. In their lexicon, Greek scholars Louw and Nida note that this term can be understood as referring to a being with "(1) benevolent disposition and behavior, (2) creative and sustaining activity in the world, and (3) supreme power."[1] On the one hand, Louw and Nida's definition of God is contextual, coming from Christian biblical scholars steeped in a Western worldview. On the other hand, Louw and Nida's guiding purpose for their lexicon is to explore a word's semantic range of meaning, thus aiding translators working in a variety of cultural contexts, resulting in definitions that strive to remove cultural biases. I point this out at the beginning of theologizing because it is vital to admit that our understanding of God can be significantly impacted by our culture, experiences, and language.

Theologians and philosophers from a variety of contexts around the globe, including those adhering to other religions, have varying perspectives on the definition of God. I recognize that I am a Christian biblical scholar raised in the Western worldview, and thus my view is uniquely attuned to my contextual way of looking at divinity. Given that perspective, it is my hope to communicate a picture of God that is faithful to Christian theology, which understands God as a deity whose power is controlled by his love. I believe this view of God is not only faithful to the Scriptures, but it is applicable to other contexts. It is important to keep that context in mind as we combine *theos* with *logos*.

Logos is a word the Greeks used for a variety of concepts. It could mean "word," but it could also refer to conceptualizing something, to putting an idea into words, like our English concept of a logo. A logo is an artistic symbol that refers to a company, a sports team, a church or any number of groups. When you see the Golden Arches, you think of the fast-food chain McDonalds. The symbol carries meaning.

Often, the Greek *logos* is used in English as "the study of." We see it in the names of the sciences. Biology (*bios* and *logos*) the study of life. Put together, *theos* and *logos* refer to the study of the divine, the study of God, or

---

1. Louw and Nida, *Greek-English*, 136.

specifically a study of how the loving power of God is expressed or applied in the world. Theology is thinking deeply about God and seeking to apply our understanding of God to any topic or idea.

When we "do theology," we use philosophical (the art and science of thinking about life) and hermeneutical tools (hermeneutics is the art and science of interpretation) to evaluate religious texts, scouring them to learn about God and apply what we learn to any topic or idea. For the purposes of this book, I focus on Christian theology and thus focus my investigation in the Christian Scriptures.[2] These are my own faith commitments, but I attempt to write in such a way that those from other faith commitments could benefit.

I seek to apply the tools of philosophical reflection and hermeneutical inquiry to the Christian Scriptures to study what God has to say about how Christian communities can pursue flourishing together. In other words, I want to answer the question that is at the heart of this book: What quality of human togetherness does God desire? When people are working together, what kind of working together is aligned with God's vision for humanity? We will be doing theology to help us answer those questions.

THE PURPOSE OF THEOLOGY: HUMAN FLOURISHING

As I've previously noted, in their book *For The Sake of the World*, theologians Miroslav Volf and Matthew Croasmun suggest that the purpose of theology is human flourishing.[3] Since this is a book about how a certain kind of togetherness should produce human flourishing, and since we are about to start doing theology to help us discover that flourishing-producing togetherness, Volf and Croasmun are giving us a very affirming definition of theology. But are Volf and Croasmun correct? Is human flourishing the purpose of theology? Other theologians argue that the goal of theology is the glory of God, thus finding Volf and Croasmun's definition, that the goal of theology is human flourishing, too human centered.[4] Shouldn't the task of theology be God centered? Shouldn't we seek to do theology to give God glory? This is a valid concern, rooted in Paul's teaching in 1 Cor 10:31, "whatever you

---

2. Many Christians also include the books of the Old Testament apocrypha, and though I have great appreciation for those books, I will not be referencing them in this study.

3. Volf and Croasmun, *For the World*, 11. See also McKnight, *Fellowship*, 191–236.

4. Bingham and Nichols, "What Is the Goal?"; Carson and Reeves, "Studying Theology"; Ferguson, "Goal of Doing Theology."

do, do it all for the glory of God," and the Westminster Shorter Catechism, which says, "The chief end of man is to glorify God and enjoy him forever" (WSC 1). Clearly, when we do theology, it is biblically correct for the glory of God to be the goal of theology. Before we've even started doing theology, have we encountered a roadblock? If we are headed in a human-centered direction, when we ought to be headed in a God-centered direction, our entire project could be undermined. So what about Volf and Croasmun? Can they also be correct that the goal of theology is human flourishing, thus affirming our theologizing that specifically leads to human flourishing?

To attempt to resolve this apparent tension, that of competing goals of theology, let's practice doing theology. Let's think about what the Bible says about God and his goal for humanity. First, God's loving relational nature led him to create humanity in the first place. We read in Gen 1 that God's creation was good and he wanted humanity to flourish. Second, the Christian doctrine of the incarnation refers to God taking on human flesh in the person of Jesus. In so doing, there is a sense in which God changed for the purpose of connecting with humanity. God who previously did not have flesh became human. God embraced change so we who were separated from God could be reconciled with him. Why?

God changed to connect with humanity because God is a relational being. A proper view of God, therefore, is not one in which God is impervious to the whims of humanity. Instead, we are affected by God, and God is also affected by us. In fact, as we will see in our study of Scripture, God's heart aches when his creation is not flourishing.

Therefore, with Volf and Croasmun, it is right and good to view the human activity of theological reflection as an act in which the created glorifies the Creator, enjoying him, for the purpose of human flourishing. Theology is a task that connects humans with the divine to bring the flourishing that God's heart so desires for us. It is not only proper to envision human flourishing as a good goal of theology but theology helps us have togetherness with God.

Theology is a kind of lens by which we can evaluate all human endeavor, seeking to ascertain whether any human endeavor is promoting flourishing.[5] When viewing life through that theological lens, we assume that God cares about all communities, the work those people working together do, and the people who comprise them. If we can understand God's goal for humanity, then we will likely be heading in the right direction to answer what quality of Christian community is in line with theology. As I have already suggested, doing theology is engagement with ideas, and in particular, ideas

---

5. See Heschel, *God in Search*, 4.

about God. Therefore, when we do theology, we purposefully think about God and how those ideas about God impact the quality of communities in our world. My hope is that our study of theology will give us a wonderfully detailed picture of what God desires flourishing-producing togetherness to look like. In other words, theology will show us how people can work together in all kinds of Christian communities, the places where they live, work, and play, in such a way that those communities will be marked by flourishing-producing togetherness.

Two more analogies might help us understand in practical terms how theology helps us understand and live flourishing-producing togetherness. I already suggested that theology is like a lens through which we view the Scriptures. Additionally, the process of doing theology will be like a trainer, helping Christian communities to grow and strengthen the kind of togetherness that produces flourishing. Finally, the process of doing theology will be like a guide, showing us the way to think and learn about the kind of togetherness that produces flourishing. What we will specifically do to follow theology as our trainer and guide is scour the Scriptures for places where the Scriptures teach principles or qualities of togetherness.

Given the massive quantity of material in the Scriptures, this will not be a comprehensive investigation. We will contain the present investigation to an examination of common theological categories from a perspective of togetherness, which we begin in the next chapter. I am writing to Christians who share certain foundational commitments, and I want to spend my energies not explaining or defending these commitments but building on them, seeking to help us understand the kind of togetherness God desires.

As we venture into the sometimes thick jungle of theology, it can be quite helpful to follow those who have gone before. Thankfully there are many who know the lay of the theological jungle. I have introduced you to some previously, Walter Rauschenbusch and Jonathan Sacks. Rauschenbusch was a Protestant Christian pastor; Sacks was a Jewish rabbi. They each bring a helpful theological perspective on togetherness. We will converse with them, and a few others, along the way, as they show us how a theology of togetherness helps us reimagine some of the standard categories of theology.

My hope is that each Christian community can benefit by applying a theology of togetherness to their unique situation. Theology, therefore, is not ethereal or irrelevant. Similarly, I once heard a saying about philosophy that was something to the effect of, "A conversation in a Paris coffee shop can be the cause, even decades later, of war." Journalist Agnes Poirier and historian Jessica Pearce Rotundi write that the philosophical discussions in coffeehouses in Paris and America were all influential in those nations' revolutionary wars.[6] In other words, ideas matter. It might take a long time, but they can have exponential impact. This is abundantly true for theology, and it is why the task of theological reflection is so important. It is also why I invite Christian communities of all kinds to join with me in doing a theology of togetherness, so that your community might apply flourishing-producing togetherness to your context.

We now begin reflecting on some major theological categories through the lens of a theology of togetherness to help us understand what flourishing-producing togetherness can look like in the real world. What we will see is that the Trinitarian view of God (major theological category number one) provides a foundation for a theology of togetherness and gives us a vision for human flourishing.

Humanity, however, does not always flourish. Why? Humanity's struggle with sin (major theological category number two) has put us in need of salvation (major theological category number three). That salvation is found in covenant (major theological category number four) with God, a covenant which finds its fruition in God's kingdom (major theological category number five). Finally we will learn that we can apply the principles of union with Christ (major theological category number six) and solidarity to help usher in the kingdom, which is another way of saying that we will be learning how to have flourishing-producing togetherness.

---

6. Rotundi, "How Coffee," para. 1; Poirier, "Coffee and Revolution," para. 7. Rotundi notes that "King Charles II's father, Charles I, had been decapitated during the English Civil War, so he was understandably paranoid about his subjects gathering to talk politics. On June 12, 1672, Charles II issued a proclamation to 'Restrain the Spreading of False News, and Licentious Talking of Matters of State and Government,' which read in part: 'men have assumed to themselves a liberty, not only in Coffee-houses, but in other Places and Meetings, both public and private, to censure and defame the proceedings of State by speaking evil of things they understand not.' To combat this 'evil,' Secretary of State Sir Joseph Williamson embedded a network of spies in London coffee houses and in December of 1675, Charles II went as far as ordering the closure of all coffee houses in London. The ban lasted just 11 days. The people had spoken: Coffee was here to stay." Rotundi, "How Coffee," paras. 6–7.

5

God as Trinitarian Community

CHRISTIAN PASTOR AND SPIRITUAL writer, A. W. Tozer wrote in his book, *The Knowledge of the Holy*, "What comes into our minds when we think about God is the most important thing about us."[1] Do you agree? Disagree? Why? Why not? I think Tozer is right. If we have incorrect thoughts about God, then it is very likely that we will think incorrectly about everything else in life. What Tozer is getting at is that our thinking about God is foundational to our view of life. How we think about God will affect our choices, our behavior, our relationships, and our communities. It is essential, therefore, that we begin our theology of togetherness by considering God.

Christians hold to the view that God is a Trinity.[2] When Christians refer to God as a Trinity, they are suggesting that their view of God is that God is three yet one. There are three persons who, together, are unified as

---

1. Tozer, *Knowledge*, 7.

2. Some Christians and Jews disagree with the notion of a Trinitarian God. For Jews, a central biblical passage is Deut 6:4, which says, "Hear O Israel: the LORD our God, the LORD is *one*" (emphasis mine). Also, as seen in their name, *Unitarian* Christians disagree with the concept of God as triune. The Christian belief in a Trinitarian God is admittedly complex, and it has a mysterious quality to it. The close reader will find neither the word "Trinity" nor the description "three in one" in the Scriptures. Because others have done excellent work in providing a biblical and theological rationale for a Trinitarian view of God, and because it is outside the purview of this book, I will defer to other scholars and suffice it to say that the New Testament is replete with evidence for the doctrine of the Trinity. See for example, Volf, *After Our Likeness*. For another perspective from the viewpoint of Roman Catholic liberation theology, see Boff's *Holy Trinity*. Boff writes, "If God means three divine persons in eternal communion, then we must conclude that we also, sons and daughters, are called to communion." Boff, *Holy Trinity*, 2. For a fictionalization of this social view of the Trinity, see Young, *Shack*.

one God. A Trinitarian view of God is careful to explain that it is not suggesting there are three gods. Instead, there is one God but that one God is a kind of divine community, with three expressions working together. Some Christians theologians have described the three expressions of God as persons,[3] and in so doing they are not wrong.

For the purposes of our discussion, we need to clarify that the Trinitarian God, as a community, is not the same as human communities. In human communities, the people of that community are together, but they are also distinct individuals. God as Trinity is mysteriously three yet one. God is also spirit, not to be equated with physical human persons with bodies. If we describe God as a person, then, it is only in the sense of a divine "person."

God as Trinity is fundamentally a community, a community of divine persons working together. Philosophers Moreland and Craig have termed this view "Social Trinitarianism," such that "in God there are three distinct centers of self-consciousness, each with its proper intellect and will," but this social view does not go so far as to separate the three persons of the Trinity into three distinct gods, a nonorthodox view called "tritheism."[4] Moreland and Craig conclude that Social Trinitarianism is best understood as "Trinity monotheism," such that God is one soul with three complete sets of rational cognitive faculties, each sufficient for personhood.[5]

What, then, do we observe about the Trinitarian nature of God? We see collaboration, equality, communication, and oneness. When we think about these Trinitarian qualities, we conclude that God, in and of himself, is a togetherness. In fact, Moreland and Craig write, because "God is by definition the greatest conceivable being . . . God's love is necessarily directed [internally] to himself."[6] This self-giving love of the Trinitarian Creator God, then, flows outward to all creation. Father, Son, and Holy Spirit work together as coequals for the cause of human flourishing. We will now examine a group of biblical passages that support this view of Trinitarian theology and inform flourishing-producing togetherness.

In the Gospels we read that God the Son is Creator who eventually takes on human flesh, as John writes, "In the beginning was the Word, and the Word was with God, and the Word was God" (John 1:1). The Word,

---

3. Some Trinitarians describe God as "tripersonal." See Moreland and Craig, *Philosophical Foundations*, 575.

4. Moreland and Craig, *Philosophical Foundations*, 583. See also Moreland and Craig's discussion of the three views of Social Trinitarianism in *Philosophical Foundations*, 586–95.

5. Moreland and Craig, *Philosophical Foundations*, 594.

6. Moreland and Craig, *Philosophical Foundations*, 594–95 (brackets original).

John tells us, was involved in the creation of all things,[7] and eventually "the Word became flesh and made his dwelling among us" (1:14). Who is the Word that John is talking about?

John reveals that the Word came from the Father (v. 14) and that the Word is Jesus Christ (v. 17). Together the Father and Son initiate and fulfill their plan to convey grace and truth to humanity, and as a result John states, "From the fullness of his grace, we have all received one blessing after another" (v. 16). In this verse we observe God's collaborative work between Father and Son, which leads to human flourishing. But what about the third person of the Trinity, the Spirit?

Jesus, later in John's Gospel, teaches his disciples that, though he was going to leave them and return to his Father, he would send his Spirit as their counselor and guide, to comfort and empower them (John 13–17). We will return to this theme more fully in chapter 11 when we talk about union with Christ, as it is the Spirit of Christ that enables us to have ongoing union with Jesus.

For now, notice how the apostle Paul connects the ongoing work of the Holy Spirit with flourishing in Gal 5:16–26. In this passage, we see the collaborative work of the Trinitarian God. As promised, Jesus sends the Spirit to the disciples (the events of which we read about in Acts 1–2), and the Spirit provides empowerment for ongoing human flourishing in what Paul calls the fruit of the Spirit (Gal 5:22–23). Love, joy, peace, patience, gentleness, kindness, goodness, faithfulness, and self-control are the fruit of a life lived in step with the Spirit, a picture of flourishing.

In Acts 4, we read another instance of the filling of the Spirit that demonstrates how the togetherness of God, via all three persons of the Trinity, leads to flourishing in the Christian community. The context of Acts 4 begins with the events of Acts 3 where Peter and John perform a miraculous healing at the temple, preach to the crowd, and are arrested by the religious authorities. The next day at their hearing, they preach to the authorities who cannot decide what to do, and so they release Peter and John.

The disciples return to the gathering of their Christian community, and we read that the community "raised their voices together in prayer"(Acts 4:24). In the prayer, they mention God as speaking through the Holy Spirit, and they describe Jesus as "holy servant" (Acts 4:27, 30). All three persons of the Trinity are included in the prayer as one deity in three persons, working together. At the conclusion of the prayer, the Spirit of God manifests in the room, filling and empowering the community to minister boldly. This leads, in the conclusion of the chapter, Acts 4:32–37, to a description of

---

7. See also Paul's affirmation of Jesus as Creator in Col 1:16.

flourishing, whereby the Christian community is unified, practicing sacrificial generosity so that "there were no needy persons among them," and they experienced the power and grace of God. The togetherness of the Trinity is not only a model but also a means of flourishing-producing togetherness in the Christian community.

While it is not my goal to attempt a comprehensive biblical examination of the collaborative work of the Trinitarian God, there is one other passage that bears mentioning. Paul prays in Eph 3:14–19 that the Ephesian Christians would experience the collaborative work of the Trinitarian God in their lives. All three persons of the Trinity are mentioned coequally as strengthening each Christian's inner being, so that they might know the expansive love of God and be filled with the fullness of God. Let's look more closely at this prayer, examining how Paul envisions the togetherness of the Trinity leading to human flourishing.

First, Paul writes that he kneels before God the Father, praying that he, the Father, would strengthen the people with power. Second, he prays that this strengthening would occur through God the Spirit in their inner being. Third, he prays that God the Son, Christ, would dwell in their hearts through faith. All three members of the Trinity are involved in this profound inner formation. Furthermore, when Paul writes "strengthen you" he is writing in the plural or as we would say in English, "you all." In other words, while God is desirous of deeply filling separate individual hearts so that individuals might experience the love of God, he is also desirous the Christian community experience his filling together.

It is hard to overstate how meaningful this prayer could be for the flourishing of humanity. Imagine the love the persons of the Trinity have for one another. That same love God desires his people to grasp so that they can be rooted and established in that expansive love. In fact, he wants the community to so completely identify with his love that those in the community will encounter it in a way that surpasses knowledge. God wants his people to experience his love together. Clearly, the Trinitarian God collaborates as a community for the purpose of human flourishing.

If God is a community, then it follows that we, his people, would do well to emulate him. This communal, collaborative emphasis in Trinitarian theology provides a solid foundation for examining all other doctrines from a perspective of togetherness. We have already spent time describing how humanity is communal, how there is no absolute individualism. This makes sense when considering that God is also communal. It is wholly appropriate therefore to view the gospel from a perspective of togetherness. We turn now to examine a core tenet of the gospel, human sinfulness, that which separates God and humanity. The Trinitarian God is sinless, while humanity is sinful. But how does a theology of togetherness view sin?

6

Sin as Selfishness

BEFORE WE CAN VIEW sin through the lens of a theology of togetherness, we need to have a grasp of what we are talking about when we talk about sin. What is sin?

Sin, as the biblical authors use the term, can be defined variously, such as "to miss the mark or target, to do wrong,"[1] and "to act contrary to the will and law of God, wrongdoing."[2] Put these concepts together and the definition of sin could be "to do that which is not aligned with the heart of God." A traditional understanding of sin is that of humans choosing to engage in a willful act in which we do one of two things: either sins of commission, in which we *commit* a sin, actively doing what does not align with God's heart, or sins of omission, in which we *omit* doing the right thing, avoiding doing what does align with God's heart.

When considering what human actions or inactions of thought, word, and deed are in line with God's heart, we should not view God as selecting random activities that he forbids and others he commands adherence to. God is not random. Instead, God's will and way flow from who he is, from his heart, which is best understood as perfect love (1 John 4:8, 16). Sin is when we choose, therefore, to do something that is out of line with God's perfect love or when we choose to omit something that is in line with God's perfect love. When we sin, we miss the target, which is God's heart of love.

---

1. Koehler et al., *Hebrew and Aramaic*, 305. This is the definition of a common Old Testament Hebrew word for sin, *hata*.

2. Louw and Nida, *Greek-English*, 772. This is the definition of the most common New Testament Greek word for sin, *hamartia*.

This common understanding of sin, which is often applied to individuals, also applies corporately. A theology of togetherness moves beyond the individual, viewing sin corporately, whereby collectives of people engage in sinful acts of commission and omission together. In fact, when they sin, those groups of people willfully collaborate in the sinful act. It is of particular importance for us to notice that Christian communities of all kinds can sin collaboratively, together.

A theology of togetherness brings a unique perspective on sin because it does not simply view sin as individual action/inaction with individual consequences or even as individual action/inaction with potentially corporate consequences. While sin can move, in its consequences, from the individual to the community, sin can also occur corporately via the collective.[3]

Consider the prophets of the Hebrew Bible as they confronted sin in the nation of Israel. From time to time the prophets set their sights on individuals, such as Ahab and Jezebel (1 Kgs 16:29—22:40), and likely they also delivered confrontational prophetic words to other individuals not listed in Scripture. Despite that, the overwhelming testimony of Scripture is that of prophetic utterances to corporate bodies, such as the religious elite, the wealthy class, or most of all, the nations.[4]

The prophets declared a corporate word of woe because of the cyclical wickedness committed by the nation of Israel and by the people groups dwelling in surrounding nations. A biblical historian could list a plethora of examples of Israel's corporate or national evil, such as their idolatrous rebellion during the Exodus travail, extending what should have been a journey of perhaps a couple months or years, to one that lasted forty years in the wilderness.

Another prominent example is found in nearly the entire account of the Hebrew Bible's book of Judges, which details the repeated pattern of the people rebelling against God by worshiping the gods of the nations around them, in response to which God would allow nations to invade them. The cycle continued as the people would cry out to God for help, and God graciously acquiesced by raising up a judge to rescue them. When the judge

---

3. Rauschenbusch pointed to this communal reality of sin when he wrote that "society is so integral that when one man sins, other men suffer, and when one social class sins, the other classes are involved in the suffering which follows on that sin." Rauschenbush, *Social Gospel*, 182. We'll discuss this further below using the Korean concept of *han*.

4. Again, Rauschenbusch explains how prophets focused on the community: The prophet's "woe did not come through fear of personal damnation, but through his sense of solidarity with his people and through social feeling; his hope and comfort was not for himself alone but for his nation." Rauschenbusch, *Social Gospel*, 20.

passed on, the pattern would repeat as the people sinned together over and over.

Further the reader can examine the many stories of national injustice and sin throughout the centuries when Israel was ruled by its kings, many of whom "did evil in the eyes of the Lord,"[5] leading the nation to worship foreign gods and practice injustice. There are certainly instances of God interacting with individuals, but the wider context of the history of Israel is one of God's attention directed to Israel and other nations as corporate entities. The promises and pledges in God's covenant were binding with a collective people and thus his prophetic judgment falls on the whole nation as well.

Examples of national sin are not only abundant in the history of Israel but also across the globe and throughout history. Whether by war or genocide, nation has committed atrocity against nation and community of people against community. Contemporarily we need look no further than Rwanda in the 1990s, Cambodia in the 1970s, or Communist nations committing atrocities against their own peoples in places like Russia and China.

Moving backward in history, Japan and Germany in World War II slaughtered millions, most despicably in the Jewish holocaust perpetrated by the Nazi regime. In Muslim nations, we could point to centuries of brutal treatment of women and to acts of terror against and persecution of peoples who are not adherents of Islam. Fundamentalist factions such as the Islamic State have desecrated or destroyed ancient artifacts, and they have beheaded people to draw attention to their cause.[6]

Lest we think that we Americans are free from accusation, let the USA remember its original sins of racism, enslaving captured Africans, and of genocide, nearly wiping out indigenous populations who lived in North America long before Europeans visited its shores. The scars and pain of our ancestors' brutality remain, fueling the fires of racial injustice we see broadcast on the daily news.

While injustices individuals commit against other individuals or groups is sadly prevalent in our world, causing deep pain, it is groups of people that have amplified the problem exponentially, creating structures of systemic injustice, often put in place by communities, by people working together. Therefore, we need to view the lack of flourishing in our world as a community ill. To help humanity understand our corporate sin,

---

5. For a few examples, see 1 Kgs 11:6; 14:22; 15:26, 34; 16:19, 25, 30. In 1 & 2 Kings there are twenty-nine total instances of this phrase.

6. See Abdelaziz, "ISIS Smashes Artifacts"; Larson, "ISIS Beheadings."

theology must move beyond the individual to communities, just as the Hebrew prophets well knew. What, then, is at the root of communal sin?

SIN AS EVIL POWER

First, one possible root of communal sin is described theologically as evil power. Sin is not only the collaboration of people but also the presence of evil in the spiritual and physical realm. Sin is evil power. It is not the purpose of this book to describe a theology of the spiritual realm. Others have done so quite capably.[7] Suffice it to say that the writers of the biblical texts communicate to us the existence of a spiritual realm that includes evil power. Those powers of evil can work within individuals as well as within groups corporately.

In Col 1:16, for example, Paul lists numerous created beings and groups, including thrones, powers, rulers, and authorities. On the surface, Paul seems to be referring to a variety of government leaders. Upon closer examination, however, it is possible that Paul intends us to interpret his list as including both spiritual and physical leaders. McKnight comments that "it seems 'thrones' and 'powers' are heavenly, invisible potentates, while 'rulers' and 'authorities' are more likely their earthly, visible servants."[8] By including this phrase, Paul wants his readers to see that Jesus is the Creator Son above all, and that Jesus' supremacy in creation is cosmic, including being supreme above evil power. What we surmise from this is that, in addition to human sin, there is also evil power at work in the world. Sometimes that evil power manifests itself through humanity individually and corporately, and sometimes through systemic structures.

---

7. Wright points out that "we humans have thus, by abrogating our own vocation, handed our power and authority to nondivine and nonhuman forces, which have then run rampant, spoiling human lives, ravaging the beautiful creation, and doing their best to turn God's world into a hell (and hence into a place from which people might want to escape). . . . Some of these 'forces' are familiar (money, sex, power). Some are less familiar in the popular mind, not least the sense of a dark, accusing 'power' standing behind all the rest." Wright, *Revolution Began*, 76–77. In another place Wright notes that "alongside this Israel-and-God story there runs the deeper story of the good creation and the dark power that from the start has tried to destroy God's good handiwork. I do not claim to understand that dark power. . . . I don't think we're meant to." Wright, *God and the Pandemic*, 14. Volf suggests that "to commit sin is not simply to make a wrong choice, but to succumb to an evil power." Volf, *Exclusion*, 96.

8. McKnight, *Colossians*, 152.

SIN AS SYSTEMIC COLLABORATION OF THE COLLECTIVE

Second, a theology of togetherness helps us understand how the roots of evil power and sin manifest in systemic structures. In his attempt to explain sin from a social gospel perspective, Rauschenbusch describes this category of communal sin well. He illustrates it by drawing attention to social ills in his day when he says that "attention is concentrated on questions of public morality, on wrongs done by whole classes or professions of men, on sins which enervate and submerge entire mill towns or agricultural states. These sins have been side-stepped by the old theology."[9]

In other words, what he calls the old theology, the theology which focuses on individual sin, missed an entire, and perhaps larger, emphasis on corporate sin. In his day a conglomerate owning mills could commit sin in a collaborative way by refusing to pay a living wage, by providing substandard housing, or by forcing workers to risk their lives in unsafe workspaces. In so doing, a collaborative sin has been perpetrated systemically, with far-reaching consequences that stunt human flourishing.

SIN AS GENERATIONAL

A third way that a theology of togetherness views sin collaboratively is through the concept of generational sin. Generational sin understands the corporate nature of sin by viewing sin's tentacles reaching across the boundaries of time. In the book of Genesis, we see an example of generational sin in the life of Abraham. He practiced deception (Gen 12), hiding his marital status. Years later Abraham's son Isaac did the same (Gen 26), lying about his wife. Then Isaac's son Jacob lied about his identity (Gen 27). Many generations later, Israel's great King David committed sins of adultery and murder that his descendants would go on to repeat, with devastating consequences. There can be in some instances a generational quality about sin.

Furthermore, studies have shown the disastrous mental health impact of slavery, a systemic corporate sin, on succeeding generations of African Americans, even after they are no longer enslaved.[10] Dashort et al. found the same tendency in survivors of the Nazi Holocaust.[11] Freeman explains this generational component of sin when he says that

---

9. Rauschenbusch, *Social Gospel*, 36.

10. Halloran, "African American Health." See also DeGruy, *Post Traumatic Slave Syndrome*.

11. Dashort et al., "Intergenerational Consequences."

sin is not a *legal* problem. It is not about what is fair or unfair. It is about a mystical burden that we experience as debt, hindrance, oppositional weight, weakness, brokenness and corruption, or just the starting place of our lives. Virtually everything in our lives is gifted to us, and there are many 'gifts' that we would prefer never to have received. It is part of our incarnational existence. We are the offspring of others. To have an embodied existence in space and time is to have a body burdened with the DNA of eons and a family and culture that is both the product and carrier of history. Our own existence is a consequence of everything that has come before us. We cannot rightly suggest that such a contingent existence comes free.[12]

The social dynamic of humanity is so rooted in our collective existence that we can barely conceive of any sin that would be exclusively individual.[13] In fact, togetherness is part and parcel of sin. For example, Park notes that one way to view sin is collaboration.[14] This is not to say that all collaboration is sinful but that sin has a collaborative aspect, such that when we sin, we always sin against someone else. First and foremost, we sin against God. Our sin affects our togetherness with God because our sin is an affront to his heart of love. Second, when we sin, we often sin against other people. Park suggests that Christian theology would do well to borrow from the Asian concept of *han* to help us understand this connectional aspect of sin.

Han, is "the ineffable experience of deep bitterness and helplessness" that victims of sin feel as pain.[15] Park notes that too often the Christian view of sin is individualistic; *han* provides a helpful corrective, as our sin has profound effects on God and others. Furthermore, *han* can be understood in the collective.[16] When oppressed people revolt, for example, they often reach the point of such deep collective grief over the sin that has been perpetrated on them, they revolt against their oppressors. One thinks of uprisings of enslaved persons in the nineteenth-century American south, fueled by centuries of beatings, overwork, indignity, and rape, among other atrocities they endured.

---

12. Freeman, "Sins of a Nation," para. 6.

13. Rauschenbusch adds that there might be something inherently social to sin when he writes that "a theology for the social gospel would have to say that original sin is partly social. It runs down the generations not only by biological propagation but also by social assimilation." Rauschenbusch, *Social Gospel*, 61.

14. Park, *Wounded Heart*, 177.

15. Park, *Wounded Heart*, 10.

16. Park, *Wounded Heart*, 36–40.

Park goes on to point out that sin and *han* can cause a chain reaction of more sin and *han*. Take the example of a revolt by enslaved persons that I mentioned just above. The owners and abusers of enslaved persons have committed manifold sinful atrocities against the enslaved. As a result the enslaved together experience the depths of *han*. The enslaved get to a point where the *han* is so great that they rise up and revolt, committing injustice against their oppressors, often through killing and maiming them. *Han* helps us understand how deeply relational sin's effects can be.[17]

SIN AS SELFISHNESS

Fourth, and perhaps most foundationally, a theology of togetherness helps us see that sin is rooted in selfishness. At its most basic level, sin is doing what I, the individual, want to do when I do not want what God wants me to do. Sin is focused on the will of the self and acting on that will when it is misaligned with God's heart. Sin looks inward rather than outward. Conversely, a theology of togetherness promotes an outward focus.

When humans apply togetherness rightly, they will not only consider their own desires but also God's heart and how their choices will impact others. Notice how Sacks describes the ramification of this selfishness to Christian communities of all kinds: "When the 'I' takes precedence over the 'We,' the result is weakened relationships, marriages, families, communities, neighborhoods, congregations, charities, regions and entire societies."[18]

If we connect these observations about sin to what we previously noted about absolute individualism, an important principle emerges. In chapter 2 we discovered that absolute individualism is a false idea. We humans are always connected, and thus the choices of our lives have communal ramifications. Sin, likewise, must be seen as connectional, as corporate.

There are ramifications to not seeing sin as corporate in nature. Christian communities can be guilty of avoiding accountability for perpetrating collective sin by promoting the idea that sin is exclusively individual. If it is true that sin is only individual, then the community can claim that it is not culpable for sin or sin's consequences. If sin is only individual, then the community can suggest that it is only the individuals who need to change, not the community or the structures it promotes.

In chapter 4, we noted that during the civil rights era, some Christian denominations claimed that the solution to racial prejudice and segregation was not social justice but individual salvation. A theology of togetherness

---

17. Park, *Wounded Heart*, 69–70.
18. Sacks, *Morality*, 17.

counters this by suggesting that sin is both public and private, both communal and individual. Likewise, a theology of togetherness sees an exclusively individual approach to sin as selfish or as a potentially dangerous self-focus. This self-focused conception of sin is itself selfish, giving Christian communities license to commit sin in a wider way. When viewed through the lens of a theology of togetherness, sin is selfishness.

Because of its societal, consequential, and generational impact, our understanding of sin must include a corporate dimension. Therefore, the traditional notion that sin only applies to the individual is insufficient. A theology of togetherness teaches us that sin can be corporate. To sum it up, sin is both the individual and communal use of human free will to choose what is out of alignment with God's perfect love, and sin is also the forces of evil, the enemies of God, which can inhabit and empower communal sin.

Through the lens of a theology of togetherness, then, we see how sin is not just individual but together. For an illustration of this togetherness view of sin in American Evangelical Christian subculture, consider Liberty University. While its genesis seemingly flowed from a desire to advance God's kingdom, Liberty has in recent years been mired in numerous illicit scandals.[19] What does a Christian community do when they are found to have committed institutional sin? They need to be saved.

Rauschenbusch opened the door to a communal understanding of sin when he suggested that "the social gospel seeks to bring men under repentance for their collective sins and to create a more sensitive and modern conscience."[20] The practice of corporate repentance, which we will examine in-depth in chapter 17, is only possible if we first understand the communal nature of salvation from sin. How then, does a theology of togetherness understand salvation from sin?

---

19. French and Chang, "Liberty University."
20. Rauschenbusch, *Social Gospel*, 5.

7

Salvation as Selfless Emancipation

IN THE SUMMER OF 2005, my wife and I took members of our church's youth group to Kingston, Jamaica, on a short-term mission trip. On a sightseeing day, we drove the team to the island's north shore to climb the famed Dunn's River Falls. My older two sons joined us, and midway up the falls, we came to a tricky spot, as it required a bit higher climb than other sections of the falls. I was between them, with my oldest going first and my second son following us. All over the falls, the rocks are quite slippery, and as my son shifted his weight to reach up to attempt that higher climb, his foot slipped, and he fell toward the rocks maybe six feet below. In one of those dad moments, from just above him, I shot my wet hand downward and grabbed his wet arm, desperately hoping that my grip would hold. Relief swept over me as my grip held and my son was saved from what could easily have been a serious injury.

Likewise, in Christian terms, salvation is the state of being saved. When we are saved, we are saved from something or, as we will see, saved for something. In the book of Acts, a regular refrain in the preaching of the apostles is "believe in the Lord Jesus Christ, and you will be saved."[1] Jesus' life, death, and resurrection open the door for humanity to be forgiven of their sins and thus experience salvation from that sin. This salvation includes the forgiveness of individual sins, restoring relationship with God but also making it possible to experience restoration with others and all of creation.

---

1. See for example Acts 2:21, 4:12, 11:14, and 16:31.

Salvation, then, viewed through the lens of togetherness is not limited simply to individual salvation from sin, or even to the communal spiritual sense of the church as the group of those who are saved. Instead, salvation, from the perspective of a theology of togetherness, because of the corporate nature of sin, can be viewed as applicable broadly to Christian communities. What we will see, though, is that salvation is such a rich concept that it has application to any community, any instance of people working together, creating the situation whereby all people can experience human flourishing.

Rauschenbusch explains that "conversion has usually been conceived as a break with our own sinful past. But in many cases, it is also a break with the sinful past of a social group."[2] Just as we have surveyed the sinful past of many nations and cultures, it is only by salvation that we remove the barricades of the non-flourishing past and work toward a flourishing future. Whether it is wars or slavery, genocide or environmental pollution, the sins of the nations are endemic, regularly causing the opposite of flourishing. To remedy this, communities of all sizes need conversion, or salvation, because of the connected power they wield.

Because Christians can be so accustomed to thinking of salvation in individual terms, an illustration might help us begin to think about salvation through the lens of togetherness. Consider the recent phenomenon of the Me Too movement. Me Too observed many societal structures that harmed women. The movement called for sweeping changes, a kind of conversion of our society. Me Too is a collaborative community that sought the salvation of the entertainment industry and of government and spawned sister movements such as Church Too, which had the goal of uncovering and eradicating abuse in the church.[3] Me Too and its offshoots aimed at saving communities, as we will see, in line with a theology of togetherness.[4]

To begin our exploration of salvation through the lens of a theology of togetherness, we connect the dots with what we just learned about sin. Sin is selfishness, both in its motive and its focus. Salvation is freedom from sin, or put another way, to be free not to sin. Putting sin and salvation together from the perspective of a theology of togetherness, humans demonstrate corporate salvation, a saved life of togetherness, when they embrace their freedom to move from selfish viewpoints to other-centered viewpoints. We can know when people have embraced a theology of togetherness, therefore, when they demonstrate selflessness, which will be evident in their choice

---

2. Rauschenbusch, *Social Gospel*, 99.
3. See "You Are Not Alone."
4. Griswold, "Silence Is Not Spiritual."

to live lifestyles that promote flourishing-producing togetherness. If sin is selfishness, then salvation is selflessness.

What has been called the New Perspective on Paul[5] is another way to view salvation through a lens of togetherness. Coming out of the Protestant Reformation's reaction against what it saw as legalism in the Roman Catholic Church, the new Protestant theologians taught an individualistic view of salvation that was by faith alone (*sola fide*) and grace alone (*sola gratia*). They found what they believed to be source material for their disagreement with Catholicism in two New Testament places: (1) Jesus' strong opposition to the hypocritical legalism of the religious leaders of his day, and (2) the writings of Paul, particularly in his epistles of Romans and Galatians, where he discusses Christian theology's interaction with the Mosaic law.

Though not in either Romans or Galatians, perhaps the concise and well-known writing of Paul that best summarizes this teaching is Eph 2:8–9, "For it is by grace you have been saved, through faith—and this not from yourselves, it is the gift of God—not by works, so that no one can boast." Following what Paul fleshes out more fully in Galatians and Romans, Protestant theologians taught that individuals, by placing one's faith in the grace of God, would be justified before God, and saved. Conversely, a person could not earn their salvation through good works, or as Paul says, by keeping the law. This non-legalistic, and very individualistic, approach became the standard evangelical way to understand the theology of salvation.

Scholars who hold to the New Perspective on Paul, however, bring a potential corrective. E. P. Sanders, for example, suggested that the traditional Protestant view, that Paul was reacting against legalism, misunderstood Paul's Jewish covenantal approach to salvation. The covenant was God's agreement with the nation of Israel, and the law stipulated the terms of that covenant relationship. Jews did not obey the law, Sanders wrote, to gain entrance into the covenant. They were already in. Instead, Jews obey the law to *stay* in the covenant. Salvation, in other words, from a Jewish perspective was understood corporately within that covenantal framework. Why, then, does Paul take such a strong stance against the law, if by keeping it, people remained together in the covenant?

Let's look at a specific passage again. Given their disagreement with Roman Catholic theology, Reformation-era Protestant theologians read a passage like Rom 3:20, "No one will be declared righteous in God's sight by the works of the law," and they understood Paul as combating a theology of individualistic works righteousness, which is the idea that a person can

---

5. For more on the New Perspective see Wright, *What Saint Paul Really Said*; Sanders, *Paul and Palestinian Judaism*; Dunn, *Theology of Paul the Apostle*.

save themselves by doing good works. James Dunn, agreeing with Sanders, wrote that Paul, however, was reacting against Jewish ethnic privilege. Paul was essentially arguing that Jews are wrong to assume that, because of their historic covenant with God, they have cornered the market on salvation. Instead, Carson and Moo, summarizing Dunn, write that "it is ethnic exclusivism, not personal legalism, that Paul finds wrong with Judaism."[6]

The New Perspective on Paul opens a door to evaluating the individualistic approach given to us by the Protestant Reformers, thus seeing salvation from the viewpoint of togetherness. This does not mean that the New Perspective must be accepted entirely, such that any view of Paul as teaching individual salvation must be discarded. On the contrary, numerous scholars have critiqued the New Perspective.[7]

Therefore it seems best to seek balance. Salvation is not only individualistic, and it is not only corporate. Salvation is broad enough to encompass both views. My point is that adherents of the New Perspective help us think beyond the individualistic-only approach to salvation. A theology of togetherness follows that lead, viewing salvation not just of the self but of the collective. It is not just the New Perspective theologians, but Jesus himself demonstrates this.

Paul so eloquently presents the other-centered view of salvation when he writes in Phil 2:3–8,

> Do nothing out of selfish ambition or vain conceit. Rather, in humility value others above yourselves, not looking to your own interests but each of you to the interests of others. In your relationships with one another, have the same mindset as Christ Jesus: Who, being in very nature God, did not consider equality with God something to be used to his own advantage; rather, he made himself nothing by taking the very nature of a servant, being made in human likeness. And being found in appearance as a man, he humbled himself by becoming obedient to death—even death on a cross!

Jesus' individual action of selflessness clearly illustrates the kind of self-denial necessary for salvation from individualism, thus benefiting the

---

6. Dunn, *Paul the Apostle*, 334–89, referenced in Carson and Moo, *Introduction*, 376–77.

7. See Carson and Moo, *Introduction*, 379–85, and Blomberg et al., *From Pentecost*, 142–45. Blomberg et al., referring to the scholarly response to the New Perspective, write, "Some accept it uncritically; others uniformly censure it. Both of these extremes usually reflect over-simplification and lack of sufficient nuance. Most, though, recognize both strengths and weaknesses of the movement." Blomberg et al., *From Pentecost*, 143.

common good. To pursue flourishing, a theology of togetherness also calls us to develop Christian communities that practice self-denial.

Christian theology emphasizes the need for salvation from sin so that we can pursue selflessness or self-denial. Consider, for example, Jesus' teaching about discipleship, that disciples must follow him by dying to themselves (Luke 9:23; Matt 16:24; Mark 8:34). In so doing, Jesus' disciples revoke the notion that they can accomplish human flourishing on their own. Certainly, this decision is an individual choice that motivates individuals, but it motivates the individual to corporate action.

Death to self, therefore, is not saying that individuals, or even individual action, should be somehow eliminated. Instead, death to self is an ongoing decision to orient one's life toward a togetherness viewpoint and activity. Death to self admits the limitations of the self, pointing out that the individual, devoid of corporate connection, cannot on their own accomplish the mission of human flourishing.

Together with the example of Jesus above, his repeated invitation—"Follow me" (John 1:43, 21:19, 22; Matt 4:19, 8:22; Mark 1:17, 10:21)—and his teaching—"Remain in me . . . [for] apart from me you can do nothing" (John 15:5)—are foundational for the Christian who desires to accomplish the mission of God. While the individual Christian has individual dignity, made in the image of God, loved by God beyond all measure, that individual Christian is not equipped to sustain the mission of God in a solitary fashion. The individual Christian will always have individual choices for taking personal action, as that is the starting point for all human activity. But as that individual Christian follows Jesus, abiding in him, the Christian will consistently take individual action toward the salvation of their community, which includes the goal that all in the community will experience flourishing.

The Christian dies to any self-sufficiency and individualism in favor of the kind of action that will most significantly create human flourishing. In other words, the action that will best lead to human flourishing will be corporate action, starting with the action of abiding in Christ, which is the basic unit of togetherness, otherwise known as union with Christ. We'll talk about a theology of union with Christ in depth in chapter 11 For now, suffice it to say, embedded in this tenet of Christian theology is a principle easily transferable to any pursuit of human flourishing. People must die to the notion of isolationist, solitary, or individualistic action. This death to self is the beginning of salvation, as viewed through the lens of a theology of togetherness.

To illustrate, in the midst of what was perhaps humanity's most horrific example of communal sin, the Nazi death camps that slaughtered millions,

Sacks notes that psychologist Victor Frankl, working with survivors, developed "an entirely new method of psychotherapy that he called Logotherapy: psychological healing based on man's search for meaning," such that "the essence of this mission had to be a call from outside the self."[8] What Frankl suggested is that healing occurs when humans embrace an outward-focused view of and pattern of life. In my own ministry, I've often counseled those struggling with loss or lethargy to consider volunteering in roles that help others. When they have given rides to students attending ESL class or when they have assisted people at the food bank, they have not only helped others flourish but they themselves experienced flourishing anew.

We can see Frankl's affinity with Paul's theology in Phil 2 above, when Paul taught the earliest Christians to look beyond the self, to consider others as better than oneself. In so doing we follow in the footsteps of Jesus, raising our eyes to the other, serving the other, as a collective. Sacks suggests this is essential to counter our inherent human sinfulness, which is selfishness. "Being human is always directed, and pointing, to something or someone other than oneself: to a meaning to fulfill or another human being to encounter, a cause to serve or a person to love."[9]

A theology of togetherness, then, sees salvation as rooted in Jesus' call to discipleship, that his disciples would die to themselves and follow him. By "die to yourselves," Jesus was referring to a change, such that disciples would dedicate their lives no longer to their own cause. Salvation, in Jesus' view, called the disciples toward the flourishing-producing togetherness that would be found via collaboration in his kingdom. In his kingdom, Jesus said, salvation is also emancipation.

SALVATION AS EMANCIPATION, WHICH LEADS TO FLOURISHING

In addition to the concept of "death to self," a theology of togetherness describes salvation as emancipation. Organizational theorist Bruno Dyck and theologian Elden Wiebe write that salvation, conceived communally, "in our contemporary culture is more likely to be called by its secular expression *emancipation*."[10] In their telling, emancipation becomes a synonym for flourishing. Too often, though, this emancipation is individual. The individualist gospel suggests that salvation is emancipation from the guilt and consequence of sin, so that an individual can have hope of eternal life when

---

8. Sacks, *Morality*, 42.
9. Sacks, *Morality*, 42.
10. Dyck and Wiebe, "Salvation Across the Centuries," 300 (italics original).

they die. A theology of togetherness, however, views emancipation collaboratively, for the freedom of humans held in bondage by systemic structures.

In Luke 4, we read an episode in the life of Jesus that illustrates salvation as emancipation. After returning to his hometown, Nazareth, on the Sabbath day, Jesus enters the synagogue. Jesus reads from the scroll of Isaiah, chapter 61, verses that state, "The Spirit of the Lord is on me, because he has anointed me to preach good news to the poor. He has sent me to proclaim freedom for the prisoners and recovery of sight for the blind, to set the oppressed free, to proclaim the year of the Lord's favor." He rolled up the scroll, and he said to those in attendance, "Today this scripture is fulfilled in your hearing" (Luke 4:18–19, 21).

By applying this passage to himself, Jesus suggests that flourishing in his kingdom involves multiple emancipations. When he talks about preaching good news, Jesus has in view emancipation from sin, which Paul affirms when he writes in Rom 6:6–7, "we know that our old self was crucified with [Jesus] so that the body of sin might be done away with, that we should no longer be slaves to sin." It is important that we retain a theology of individual emancipation from sin, but Jesus reminds us that we must also envision an emancipation from corporate sin.

As Jesus' taught in his reading of Isaiah, the mission of the prophecy that was fulfilled in him is an emancipation from the structures of society that keep people from flourishing. The passage from Isaiah illustrates a number of these structures. Take note of the collaborative nature of "freedom for prisoners," "release of the oppressed," and a proclamation of "the year of the Lord's favor." All three include a corporate element.

That last idea, "the year of the Lord's favor," is a description of the Jubilee, in which God sought to bring justice across the land in a corporate way, as debts were forgiven and ancestral lands were returned to original family ownership. In Lev 25:10, God establishes the Jubilee year when he says, "Consecrate the fiftieth year and proclaim liberty throughout the land to all its inhabitants." The Jubilee is truly for all, both the haves and the have-nots. When debts are forgiven and land returned, it could be tempting to see the have-nots as the primary benefactors of Jubilee emancipation.

But the Jubilee is also for those who have abundance, as it taught them that all their possessions were truly God's, and it emancipated the wealthy from the false view that they could trust in themselves. God's heart in the Jubilee, a heart which Jesus captures in his teaching and ministry, was for human flourishing through salvation by emancipation. Flourishing grows exponentially through a communal or collaborative practice of emancipation.

SALVATION FROM MAMMON

Thus far a theology of togetherness has taught us that salvation includes both death to self and emancipation. Next, a theology of togetherness teaches us salvation from mammon. "Mammon" is a word Jesus used when he taught his disciples that "no servant can serve two masters. Either he will hate the one and love the other, or he will be devoted to one and despise the others. You cannot serve both God and *money*" (Matt 6:24, emphasis mine).

In Matt 6:24, the word "money" is a translation of the Aramaic word *mammon*, which is almost a personification of worldly wealth "with a strongly negative connotation."[11] A professor of mine once described, for example, his view that shopping malls are "temples to mammon." Mammon is akin to a god that is worshiped, and thus it could be said that some Christian communities worship at the feet of the god Mammon. When a Christian community becomes enthralled by mammon, they put profit over people.

Churches can do the same, even as they claim to worship at the feet of Jesus. In their book, *A Church Called Tov*, responding to recent moral failures in some churches, biblical scholars and father and daughter Scot McKnight and Laura Barringer helpfully point out how churches can be saved from worshiping mammon.[12] Instead of pursuing larger buildings, increasing budgets and bodies in the pews, which might be evidence of mammon-worship, churches can be saved by the Hebrew concept of *tov*, which is translated "goodness." God's heart is a heart of goodness that desires all people to flourish.

Sadly, when communities of all kinds pursue mammon, the flourishing of humanity can suffer. A theology of togetherness, as Jesus taught his disciples, views salvation as turning away from mammon and pursuing God's goodness. The goal of the community should not be the flourishing of the community but the flourishing of humanity. The goal of the community is not to promote the community but to consider how it can serve the common good.

SALVATION LEADS TO HUMAN FLOURISHING

Once we see salvation, through the lens of a theology of togetherness, as death to self, freedom from any kind of enslavement, and a turn from mammon toward God's goodness, the way forward for actual flourishing

---

11. Louw and Nida, *Greek-English*, 561.
12. McKnight and Barringer, *Church Called Tov.*

becomes clear. Individualistic views of salvation are revealed to be anemic precisely because they lack the vision and impetus for human flourishing. A communal approach to salvation is not only rooted in a biblical and theological understanding of God's choice of the people of Israel as well as his church as together "in Christ" (Eph 1) but also brings the transformational force of collaborative action.

The basic unit of such a communal approach is the family, and it is from family that flourishing first emanates. This is not an argument for a specific definition of family, so much as it is an observation that children flourish in the community of a caring family. In receiving care from family, children experience not individual salvation but the salvation of community as emancipation from neglect. Families then make connections with other families or individuals to form covenant communities of salvation, which continue to care for one another. This is not individual salvation that promises hope for eternal life. Instead it is a togetherness view of salvation, which leads to human flourishing now.

In addition to families and extended families, we can also see how other communities pursue human flourishing in line with a theology of togetherness for salvation. In the business world, B Corps are an example of how people work together for flourishing. A company or corporation can attain B Corp status, a private certification of for-profit companies that achieve specific social and environmental goals and abide by accountability measures. B Corp is not the same as the legal status "benefit corporation." B Labs, the nonprofit community that issues B Corp certification, reports that there are currently 4,720 certified B Corporations in more than seventy-eight countries and over 155 industries.[13] Ben & Jerry's ice cream and Patagonia clothing are examples of B Corps.[14] While B Corp certification is not inherently Christian, it is an example of how communities can pursue human flourishing in line with a theology of togetherness's understanding of salvation. All businesses would do well to pursue B Corp status.

Stroopies is a B Corp located ten minutes from me in nearby Lancaster City.[15] While their stroopwafels, coffee, and ice cream are delicious, it is their business model that is especially rich. Stroopies is the embodiment of flourishing-producing togetherness. They hire refugee women from all over the world who are being resettled in our area, paying them a fair wage, and giving them thirty minutes of English class while they are still on the clock. Each day when they take lunch, the women bring food to share, food from

---

13. B Lab, "Make Businesses a Force for Good."
14. Ben & Jerry's, "Ben & Jerry's Joins," paras. 1–4; Patagonia, "B Lab," para. 1.
15. Stroopies, "More than Making Cookies."

their home countries, and they form bonds across ethnic and language barriers. Stroopies employs a staff member to organize cultural trips to help the women learn about life in Lancaster and the USA. They even visited Washington, DC, to help the women prepare for citizenship tests. For each of the cultural trips Stroopies pays all costs, and Stroopies also pays the women their regular hourly rate for their time. Stroopies owners, managers, and English teachers have become deeply involved in the women's lives, helping them flourish in a new land.

In summary, to embody and apply flourishing-producing togetherness, a theology of togetherness teaches Christian communities, both inside and outside the church, that salvation is death to self, emancipation, and a turning away from mammon. To help achieve this goal, we now look at the concept of covenant.

8

Covenant for Community Flourishing

My wife Michelle and I sat in the living room of a young couple, listening to them talk frankly about struggles in their relationship. Only one year had passed since we had done their premarital counseling and wedding ceremony. Now one of them said to the other, "I don't feel love for you anymore." The other spouse burst into tears. How does a heart change and so fast? We clearly remembered the overwhelming joy of their dating years, their engagement, and finally their wedding day. We could feel the burning hot glow of love they had for one another when they covenanted to each other, before God and their family and friends, that they were going to love one another for the rest of their lives. Marriage vows are rightly seen as a covenant. Now, the covenant that bound their small community of two together seemed fractured, if not broken beyond repair.

A theology of togetherness' understanding of covenant can help guide the Christian community, especially when the community faces seemingly irreconcilable differences. Sacks suggests that "in a covenant, two or more individuals, each respecting the dignity and integrity of the other, come together in a bond of love and trust, to share their interests, sometimes even to share their lives, by pledging their faithfulness to one another, to do together what neither can achieve alone."[1] Given our definition of communities as people working together, Sacks's definition of covenant applies not only to marriages but to any size community. Covenant is possible, however, only

---

1. Sacks, *Morality*, 62.

when individuals working together have previously at least begun to embrace and practice death to self, which we explored in the previous chapter about salvation.

Additionally, it is important to distinguish between a covenantal approach to communities and a contractual approach, especially when considering how humanity swims in the water of a contractual society. A contractual approach to community is one in which relationships are predominantly understood economically. One person or group provides goods and services for which another person or group compensates the provider. While this arrangement is standard in business, a contractual approach can also be the common way people in the broader society view one another. In a contractual society most relationships can also be unconsciously conceived of in terms of payers and providers, even when no money is exchanged, and even when no contract is written.

A contractual view of relationships can be so ingrained in the conscience, so habitual an assumption, that the payer and provider are wholly unaware of the contract. It exists in their psyche. A person reveals that they believe in the contractual view when they erupt with negative emotion when they do not believe they are receiving what is due them. This contractual assumption (and eruption!) can be found in marriage, in friendship, in volunteer communities, and certainly in employment situations. In fact, contract is arguably the dominant form of relational understanding that undergirds communities in many contemporary cultures. The problem, Sacks notes, is that "contract is a transaction. A covenant is a relationship."[2] In order to counter a contractual view of society and culture, the theology of covenant is a rich concept that Christian communities can practice, thus, finding salvation from collective sin in order to pursue flourishing together.

Theologically, covenant is central to the Hebrew Bible. While God makes covenants with some individuals such as Noah and Abraham, he also covenants with groups, most famously the nation of Israel. God's covenant with people and groups demonstrates a radical departure from a contractual arrangement. The covenants are based in God's love, in which God himself sacrificially provides for his people, fashioning them into a new covenantal community for the purpose of flourishing.

In the midst of harsh cultures that practiced human sacrifice and other atrocities, God entered into a covenant relationship with Israel so that together they, and the world around them, would flourish. It was the Mosaic covenant that established this new vision, rooted in the Abrahamic covenant, through which God said Abraham's descendants would be a blessing

---

2. Sacks, *Morality*, 62.

to the whole world (Gen 12:1–3). We will examine this further in chapter 18 when we talk about creating culture, a practice of flourishing-producing togetherness that flows from the theology of covenant.

The harsh reality of covenant is that it can be broken. After agreeing to the covenant through the leadership of Moses, the nation of Israel would centuries later sever their covenant with God. Whenever they chose to live outside the covenant agreement, they would experience the opposite of flourishing, including surrounding nations invading, defeating, and oppressing Israel. The culmination of this oppression took place when the nations of Assyria and Babylon forced the people of Israel and Judah into exile.

Though the people had broken the covenant, one of the beautiful aspects of God's heart for covenant with his people is that he promised a new covenant, by which his peoples' hearts would be transformed. This new covenant, as described in the prophecy of Ezekiel (Ezek 34, 37), is also communal in nature, coming to fruition centuries later in God's covenant with the church (Heb 8–9). What both the Hebrew and Christian view of covenant teaches us is that God desires Christian communities to experience heart transformation. Heart is normally conceived of as the domain of the individual. Covenant, however, helps us understand that Christian communities also have collective hearts that can be transformed as they practice covenant with one another and God. When a covenant is broken, though, how is it renewed?

I started this chapter mentioning a young couple whose marriage covenant seemed to have shattered. How did this happen? One spouse had removed themselves from the covenant of marriage, and that spouse's heart grew cold. Sadly, this story is all too familiar. A heart on fire can grow cold. That goes for an individual heart, such as one spouse in a marriage, and also the heart of a community that breaks covenant with one another and God.

In the previous chapter we noted how B Corps, to maintain their certification, must have internal accountability to abide by practices of social and ethical responsibility. B Corps enter a kind of covenant with one another and with B Labs. Communities can lose their B Corp certification if they break the terms of the covenant. Any Christian community can break covenant with the people connected to their community and with God, if they chose to worship mammon rather than follow God's heart for human flourishing.

When a covenant is broken, thankfully there is hope. God describes the process whereby the nation of Israel could enter a new covenant with him. In Ezek 36:24–32, God mentions multiple steps of covenant renewal, and they are flooded with a two-word phrase that is repeated over and over: "I will . . . I will . . . I will." God will do it. This is a promise from God's mouth about what he will do. What will he do? He will do the work of empowering rebellious, disobedient people to be transformed into the people of God, and he will enter into a new covenant with them.

This new covenant comes to fruition in the life, death, and resurrection of Jesus, followed by the gift of the Spirit who enters the hearts of all disciples of Jesus, transforming them into a new covenant community, from which flows the fruit of the Spirit—love, joy, peace, patience, kindness, goodness, faithfulness, gentleness, and self-control (Gal 5:22–23). When I taught my grandson how to play the computer game *Fruit Ninja*, his little fingers would fly across the screen as he sliced and diced watermelons, apples, and oranges. Suddenly, a "fruit frenzy" would break out as loads of fruit flew across the screen.[3] Imagine the community flourishing of groups of Christians who produce a frenzy of the fruit of the Spirit toward one another.

Whether a church or nonprofit or business, as any community embraces and lives out that fruit-filled covenant, individually and collectively, the community welcomes any and all, expanding the flourishing to as many as want to enter the covenant. It is no wonder that Sacks writes that "my firm belief is that the concept of covenant has the power to transform the world."[4] Covenant transforms the world because it leads to flourishing.

Remember the couple in which one spouse said, after about one year of marriage, "I don't feel love for you anymore"? They're still married. They did the work of honest self-evaluation of their hearts and minds, work that led to still more work to nurture actions that showed hearts can change.

Likewise, in Ezek 37:26, God says, "I will make a covenant of peace with them; it will be an everlasting covenant. I will establish them and increase their numbers, and I will put my sanctuary among them forever." What a vision of hope is found in this new covenant! In fact, in Ezekiel chapters 40–48, the Lord gives Ezekiel a new vision of the sanctuary, the temple; from the temple flows a river that brings flourishing (Ezek 47:1–12). Finally God tells Ezekiel that the new name of the city is "THE LORD IS THERE" (Ezek 48:35). This is the place where the longings of our hearts are satisfied because their covenant with God is restored, and God is there. When God is there, we are living together in his kingdom. Kingdom is the next theological principle we will examine.

---

3. Halfbrick, *Fruit Ninja Classic*.
4. Sacks, *Morality*, 322.

9

A Kingdom of Loving Togetherness

WHEN YOU THINK OF the kingdom of God, what comes to mind? Heaven? God sitting on a throne? Streets of gold? Let me suggest another description of the kingdom of God. The doctrine of the kingdom is an approach to human flourishing, rooted in the perfect love of God for all, by which all kingdom people partake in and share God's love with one another. In the Gospels we see Jesus teach and live this new vision of the kingdom, and then in the book of Acts we watch as his first followers, the earliest Christians, begin to implement a new community of flourishing based on the principles of life in the kingdom. The casual observer of the account of the life of the Christians in the book of Acts will see a people working together for flourishing in their community in Jerusalem and then extending that flourishing to the far-flung reaches of the Roman Empire.

Two millennia later, Christianity encompasses the globe. As a result, human flourishing should be obviously present in almost every corner of the planet because Christians, if they are following the way of Jesus, carry with them the mission of human flourishing. From the vantage point of contemporary Christianity, however, the pattern of flourishing established by Jesus and demonstrated by the early church now often seems quite foreign. How so?

Christians lost or diluted the theology of the kingdom, replacing it with a different, individualistic theology, resulting in a view of God's purposes that God never intended. Into our overly individualistic culture, there is hope. As Rauschenbusch claimed, "The social gospel has already restored the doctrine of the kingdom of God, which held first place with Jesus but which individualistic theology carefully wrapped in several napkins and forgot."[1]

In other words, we need a return to the theology of togetherness as demonstrated in the kingdom of God, because flourishing finds its ultimate expression in the kingdom of God. In the kingdom of God, humanity flourishes when we follow the heart and way of the King. In a kingdom it is the monarch that reigns and rules. In God's kingdom, as his rule and reign expands, human flourishing expands.

One of the ways the biblical writers talk about human flourishing in God's kingdom is the concept of happiness. The ancient Greek philosopher Aristotle wrote about *eudaemonia*, "happiness," in his *Nicomachean Ethics*. Eudaemonia has a connection with flourishing. Reflecting on Aristotelian eudaemonia, Sacks writes, "*Eudaemonia* is a matter of living nobly, courageously, temperately and wisely. It is not about having wealth or popularity or power. It is about what kind of human being you become."[2] But how does Scripture describe happiness in the kingdom of God?

In Gen 25:8, for example, we read that Abraham's life, before he passed away, is described by the Hebrew concept of *sabe*, which refers to being "satisfied" or "having eaten or drunk to the fill."[3] In other words, Abraham was one that lived a full life, one who experienced flourishing. Likewise, Ps 1 refers to individual flourishing when the psalmist uses the Hebrew word *asre*. Often translated "blessed" or "happy," *asre* refers not to emotion but to one who is fortunate.[4] The psalmist adds a distinctly theological element to his understanding of *asre* when he describes how a person attains that fortunate position of flourishing. To do so a person delights in God's law, meditating on it day and night, thus becoming "like a tree planted by streams of water, which yields its fruit in its season and whose leaf does not wither—whatever they do prospers" (Ps 1:3).

The Hebrew *asre* is quite similar to Jesus' conception of beatitude in Matt 5. Matthew uses the Greek *makarios*, which means "happy, fortunate or blessed."[5] When one practices the principles in the statements of beatitude, they experience *makarios*, happiness, as the rule and reign of the King washes over their lives. In fact, Jesus goes so far as to say that they can experience this happiness even when they are being persecuted (Matt 5:10–12).

---

1. Rauschenbusch, *Social Gospel*, 21.
2. Sacks, *Morality*, 100–101.
3. Koehler et al., *Hebrew and Aramaic*, 1304.
4. Koehler et al., *Hebrew and Aramaic*, 100.
5. Louw and Nida, *Greek-English*, 301.

No doubt, the vision of flourishing in Ps 1 and Matt 5 can be understood individualistically. This does not mean, though, that these passages are applicable only in an individual sense. As I mentioned previously, the effects of individual action are rarely contained to the individual but nearly always overflow to their communities. In Deut 24:5, the writer gives us an illustration of shared happiness in that smallest of covenantal communities, marriage: "If a man has recently married, he must not be sent to war or have any other duty laid on him. For one year he is to be free to stay at home and bring happiness to the wife he has married."

When my wife and I were engaged, we were students in Bible college, so we asked a trusted professor to do our premarital counseling. We learned much from his experience and wisdom, including some practical advice based on Deut 24:5. He suggested that just like a newly married soldier should not go to battle for a year, any newly engaged couple would be wise to devote their first year of marriage to each other, purposefully avoiding opportunities that would keep them apart. A new bride and groom headed to ministry, for example, could commit the first year of their marriage to relationship building before they pursue ministry. Together we experienced *asre*, happiness, under the rule and reign of the King as we applied his words to our new marriage. This flourishing was so beneficial to us, we now encourage premarital couples we counsel to do the same, even if they are not headed toward professional ministry careers.

Another example of *asre*, happiness, demonstrates how the doctrine of the kingdom produces flourishing. In Deut 16:11, we see shared happiness in a family or a community during a festival. "And rejoice before the Lord your God at the place he will choose as a dwelling for his Name—you, your sons and daughters, your male and female servants, the Levites in your towns, and the foreigners, the fatherless and the widows living among you." This passage takes us beyond shared happiness, bringing flourishing to those who are not presently experiencing flourishing, the marginalized, the vulnerable. God's heart was that they, too, could gain entrance into the covenant community, as the rule and reign of his kingdom expanded to them.

Finally, Deut 26:10–11 describes worship that is communal in the context of a celebration to the Lord for his blessing of the harvest. As with the shared happiness of the festival celebration, the harvest worship extends covenantal flourishing to those in need, the Levite and the alien. The theological source material is rife with a vision of flourishing that not only impacts those who have directly experienced blessing but extends the blessing to those in need, inviting all to experience flourishing in the kingdom. The heart of the King is for the expansion of his kingdom, not for his own gain but for the flourishing of all people.

This vision of flourishing in the kingdom is rooted in the doctrine of the *imago dei*, that all humans are created in the image of God (Gen 1:26–27); thus the King desires all to be a part of his kingdom. The image of God has both individual and communal nuances.

Viewed individually, each human is a singular being of inestimable value, and viewed communally, the image of God places all humans on an equal plane. In other words, all humans are together in their standing before God, equally loved. The imago dei turns our gaze outward, because we are all made in the image of God, and we desire others to experience the benevolent rule and reign of the King in their lives. This realization of equality leads us to act in love and generosity, the building blocks of flourishing, toward every man, woman, and child, inviting them to enter the kingdom. As a result, the vision of flourishing a theology of togetherness presents to us is the necessity of salvation into the covenantal kingdom of God.

Our understanding of the kingdom of God, then, must avoid at least two misconceptions of salvation into the kingdom. The first misconception, as we learned previously, is that of salvation only or primarily applicable to the individual. In that individualistic view, salvation is concerned with salvation from personal sin through a personal Savior so that after they die a person can have a personal mansion in heaven. Therefore, the individualistic view often describes the kingdom of God as only attainable after death. A theology of togetherness, however, sees the kingdom of God as the covenant community of people together, saved for the flourishing of humanity now.

The second misconception about salvation into the kingdom is regarding the church. The church can become focused on itself, seeking to advance the church, erroneously believing that whenever the church is advancing, so also is the kingdom of God. When the church becomes self-focused, it can convey the idea that people need to be saved so that they can enter the church. The two, the church and the kingdom, however, are not one and the same. The mission of the church is to invite people to salvation so they can experience the flourishing of the rule and reign of the kingdom. Certainly, the corporate fellowship and nurture of the local church, and its relational connection through denominations, is vital for many reasons. But the church would do well to see itself as a servant of the kingdom.

These twin temptations of individualistic theology and self-focused churches are significant barriers to the advancement of flourishing. When these individualistic temptations manifest in the life of Christians and church, they reveal that those Christians and churches have lost focus on the kingdom of God. The church, when focused on itself with an intent to maintain its practices, emphasizes public worship services and buildings to the detriment of human flourishing. The practices of gathered worship and building spaces to hold that worship are not inherently antithetical to flourishing. Those practices, though they seek to support the corporate gathering of the church community, which is a form of togetherness, often promote an inner self-oriented focus.

When a Christian community gives itself to focus on the rule and reign of the kingdom of God, Rauschenbusch says that the community has rightly given its allegiance to "the Kingdom Ideal."[6] The kingdom ideal is the heart of God for the church and society. The kingdom ideal is rooted in the theology of togetherness' view of salvation we studied earlier. When Christian communities are saved into the kingdom, they will practice death to self, emancipation, and worship of God rather than mammon. In a word, the heart of God is love, which defines and guides all cooperation in the kingdom. The result is that the kingdom ideal leads to human flourishing because it is embraced and practiced by Christian communities that seek to embody God's heart of love.

Any community, church or otherwise, can forget the kingdom ideal. How often we hear about people working together to launch nonprofits that promote human flourishing, but as time passes, they begin to focus inwardly on maintaining and promoting their nonprofit. Their budget expands to cover overhead and salaries rather than programs to help people flourish. The kingdom ideal is a theological principle that holds Christian communities accountable to focus on the mission of Jesus for human flourishing in both abundant life now ("your kingdom come . . . on earth as it is in heaven," Matt 6:10) and eternal life in the future.

Finally, a theology of togetherness of the kingdom of God describes it as a covenantal community of love. Jesus said, "By this everyone will know that you are my disciples, if you love one another" (John 13:35). The New Testament writings are filled with "one another" phrases,[7] all of which are anchored by this teaching of Jesus: "A new command I give you . . . love one another" (John 13:34). The covenant community of the kingdom of God is ruled by love, and it operates by love. Love for one another is a transferable principle for any community.

With an understanding of the loving covenant community of the kingdom of God, we now turn to exploring how that covenant community is guided by the concept of union with Christ.

---

6. Rauschenbusch, *Social Gospel*, 135.

7. The New Testament writers used the Greek word *allelon*, which is most often translated "one another." By my count, *allelon* appears about one hundred times in the New Testament, of which approximately fifty-one are commands teaching disciples of Jesus how to treat one another. For an helpful infographic that finds forty-seven such uses of allelon, see Kranz, "All the 'One Anothers.'"

10

Union with Christ Together

As I MENTIONED IN the previous chapter, when my wife, Michelle, and I were engaged to be married, we asked one of our Bible college professors to lead us in premarital counseling. He agreed, using the workbook *Before You Say, "I Do"* by H. Norman Wright and Wes Roberts. We found it helpful and have used it, along with other resources, in pastoral ministry when we have provided premarital counseling for engaged couples. One reason we appreciate the book is that at the end of nearly every chapter, the authors repeat the same question, tailored to the content of that chapter.

In their book's chapter one, "What is Marriage?," Wright and Roberts introduce the question with a theological observation: "You may be thinking that when you marry there will be two individuals involved in that marriage. That is true, but there is a third party who can give an even greater meaning to your individual and married life. That person is Jesus Christ. In what way will the presence of Jesus Christ make a difference in your marriage?"[1] How is Jesus present in a group, even if the group numbers as few as two people? How does that group connect with the presence of Jesus together, and what difference can he make? Can you see how these questions relate to the idea of flourishing-producing togetherness?

When Wright and Roberts mention the "presence of Jesus in your life," they are referring to the theological concept known as union with Christ. Furthermore, Wright and Roberts believe that people who have this union can somehow connect with Jesus' presence to receive help from him. This relational connection with the presence of Jesus residing within

1. Wright and Roberts, *Before You Say, "I Do,"* 8.

a true disciple can occur many ways, one of which is through the spiritual practice of contemplation. Wright and Roberts are on solid theological and practical ground, then, in their assumption that Jesus can be present in our lives through union with Christ, and that by connecting with his presence through contemplation, Jesus can have a measurable impact on our lives toward human flourishing.

Additionally, Wright and Roberts correctly apply contemplation and union with Christ to marriage, thus moving beyond a purely individual application to that of a community, a married couple. In other words, the concept of union with Christ suggests that it is not just that the two spouses have individual relationships with Jesus but also that they can have a relationship with Jesus together through the practice of corporate contemplation.

But Wright and Roberts's insinuation goes one step further to say that Jesus' relationship together with a married couple is vital for producing a marriage that flourishes. But why stop there, with marriage? Is it possible that the concept of contemplation of union with Christ is broad enough that we could expand the range of application even further, beyond the individual, beyond marriage, to Christian communities?

Jesus himself taught, "Where two *or three* gather in my name, there am I with them" (Matt 18:20, emphasis mine). Jesus opens a door for us to consider how the concept of contemplative connection with his presence might apply to larger groups, and thus how his presence grows flourishing-producing togetherness through communities. When examining the scriptural foundations for the theology of union with Christ, it is first rightly understood in an individual sense. In other words, an individual Christian is indwelt with the Spirit of Christ.

But how does union with Christ occur in a corporate sense? Does union with Christ impact a Christian community simply by virtue of the individuals in the community bringing with them the presence of Christ in their personal lives? Or is there a real sense in which Christ makes union with whole groups of people together, at the same time? This chapter will seek to examine how the doctrine of union with Christ and the practice of contemplation on that union with Christ is essential for flourishing-producing togetherness. To start, we need to understand what the terms "union with Christ" and "contemplation" refer to.

Union with Christ.[2] A subset within Christology, which is the theological exploration of Jesus Christ, union with Christ falls under the category of incarnation. Incarnation describes how Christ took on flesh (from the Greek *en carne* which means "in flesh"), becoming a human (John 1:14;

---

2. See Oden, *Life in the Spirit*, 205–57.

Phil 2:5–11). Likewise, we will discover that the practice of union with Christ incarnates Christ in his followers, as he lives in not only the individual Christian but also in Christian communities, by his Spirit.

Contemplation. In their recent book *Embracing Contemplation*, numerous biblical and theological scholars help us define contemplation in connection with the theology of union with Christ. First, theologian Tom Schwanda defines "contemplation [as] a loving attentiveness or grateful gazing on God."[3] But how do humans look at God when he is invisible? Hans Boersma suggests, "Whenever we look to God through faith in Christ, we engage in contemplation of him."[4] So the act of contemplation is when we, in faith, think about Jesus and who he is, flowing from a heart of love and thankfulness for him.

Some have claimed that this kind of contemplation is nothing more than Eastern or New Age meditation and should be avoided. Countering that claim, Schwanda remarks that the apostle Paul's "frequent reminders of the life we are called to live in union with Christ (e.g., Gal 2:20; Eph 3:17; Col 2:6–7) have been recognized as an affirmation of contemplation."[5] Further, Ryan Brandt says that "contemplation follows from the reality of union with Christ."[6] The contributors to *Embracing Contemplation* show us that there is within biblical theology a connection between contemplation and union with Christ for flourishing.

With this preliminary understanding of union with Christ and contemplation, we must now examine what underlying assumptions might be affecting our ability to understand the concepts of union with Christ, contemplation, communities, and human flourishing.

EXAMINING ASSUMPTIONS

First, evangelical Christians, especially those from a word-centered stream, might not be accustomed to thinking of the incarnation of Jesus in terms of union with Christ. The word-centered stream of Christianity, particularly evident within evangelicalism, is the stream that believes the word of God, as present in the Bible, is the primary way to experience God. There is within the word-centered stream a somewhat rationalistic understanding of the indwelling of the Spirit of Christ, believing the indwelling to occur at the moment a person first places their faith in and gives their life to follow Jesus.

3. Schwanda, "To Gaze on the Beauty," 100.
4. Boersma, "Beatific Vision," 206.
5. Schwanda, "To Gaze on the Beauty," 104.
6. Brandt, "Gospel-Centered Contemplation?," 188.

What indwelling am I referring to? Word-centered evangelicals believe that when an individual makes a genuine decision to trust in and give their lives to Jesus (Rom 10:9–10), the Spirit of Christ enters our lives, and our bodies become the temple of God (1 Cor 3:16, 6:19). This indwelling is not necessarily something that needs to be perceptible to the senses, some evangelicals suggest, but the indwelling is instead a doctrine to believe.

When marrying the doctrine of union with Christ to a contemplative theology of togetherness, those from a word-centered stream will need to guard against skepticism about the present work of the Spirit and about mysticism. Such skepticism could prevent them from taking seriously that union with Christ might impact their communities for the purpose of human flourishing.

But there are many Christians from other streams. Those within a *Spirit*-centered stream are, for example, accustomed to the filling of the Holy Spirit as a palpable reality in their lives and thus will need to guard against placing inordinate emphasis on the felt experience of the filling of the Spirit. If Christians from a Spirit-centered stream overemphasize the manifestation of the Spirit, they potentially diminish grounding theology in Scripture, as well as marginalizing a practice of contemplation.

We also cannot assume that Christians have heard of, let alone understand, the concept of union with Christ or that Christians have gained the ability to practice contemplating the presence of Jesus to such an extent that the practice will lead to flourishing in their lives and in their communities. It is possible that some Christians are deficient on both understanding and practicing contemplation. We can lack an understanding of union with Christ in our lives, except perhaps a knowledge that the Bible tells us we are in relationship with him. Additionally, we can have a weak ability to feel the reality of Jesus' presence in the circumstances of life. With these cautions in mind, we turn to grounding our theology in Scripture, in hopeful discovery of the beautiful gift of union with Christ.

A SCRIPTURAL BASIS FOR CONTEMPLATION TOGETHER ON UNION WITH CHRIST FOR HUMAN FLOURISHING

Jesus himself prepared his disciples for the soon-coming day when he would no longer be bodily present with them but when, through his Spirit, he would empower them inwardly. In Matt 18:15–20, Matthew strings together numerous teachings by Jesus referring to the numbers "two or three."[7] Given our understanding of communities as "people working together," Jesus is here perhaps doing a bit of theology of togetherness, moving beyond the individual. He illustrates the "two or three" principle first with the handling of relational brokenness (Matt 18:15–18), second with corporate prayer (Matt 18:19), and third with the statement, "Where two are three gather together in my name, there am I with them" (Matt 18:20). It is this final claim that relates to union with Christ.

In Matt 18:20, Jesus describes a Christian community as two or three coming together in his name, and when they come together in his name, he promises that he is there with them. A community is Christian when it comes together in the name of Jesus, which is to say, for his honor and the purpose of his kingdom. When this occurs, Jesus says, he is present, incarnated, *with* them. The New International Version 1984 translation of "with" is perhaps too vague, as Matthew uses the Greek word *mesos*, which carries the idea of "a position in the middle of an area (either an object in the midst of other objects or an area in the middle of a larger area)."[8]

In a Christian community, then, Christ is central not because the community wills him to be but because he promises to be central, in their midst. The only two stipulations to the fulfillment of his centrality in a community, Jesus says, are (1) that "two or three" gather and (2) that they do so in his name. Thus Jesus teaches that union with Christ is possible in a corporate sense. He gives no indication that his presence among them is individualistic. Instead he is there with them corporately, precisely because they have gathered together and invited him to be part of their community.

Jesus teaches more about the concept of union with Christ in John's Gospel in his Upper Room Discourse, John 13–17. Having just celebrated Passover, Jesus and his disciples are together in the room when he gives them a treatise filled with instructions and doctrine, resources they can draw on after he departs. In John 14 when he brings up the topic of his departure, promising to return for them (14:1–4), his disciple Thomas asks a question that the rest of the disciples were probably thinking, "Lord, we don't know where you are going, so how can we know the way?" (John 14:5).

Jesus responds by promising that, though he himself is leaving them, the Father will give them an "advocate to help you and be with you forever—the Spirit of truth" (vv. 16–17) if they love him and show their love by keeping his commands. Even better, they will know the Spirit because

---

7. Jesus is referring to Deut 19:15, which discusses the "testimony of two or three witnesses."

8. Louw and Nida, *Greek-English*, 713.

"he lives with you and will be in you" (v. 17). Jesus remarks that there will soon come a day when, though the world will not see him, his disciples will see him because he is in the Father, they are in him, and he is in them. He concludes by repeating his teaching that his disciples will show their love for him by obeying his commands, and as a result they will experience love from the Father and Son, who will show himself to them (14:15–21). Consider how, in John 14, Jesus has expanded his teaching from Matt 18:20, when he said, "Where two or three gather in my name, there am I with them." Jesus mentioned union with Christ in just one brief line in Matthew, but here in John, Jesus has covered more ground, and as we will see, he has quite a bit more to say.

In the Upper Room Discourse, John writes that Judas asked Jesus, "But, Lord, why do you intend to show yourself to us and not to the world?" (v. 22).[9] He answers Judas by saying that if a person loves him, that person will demonstrate their love by following his teaching; his Father will love that person, and together Father and Son will come to that person and "make our home with him" (v. 23), a phrase that is the basis for human flourishing. When God makes his home with us, we cannot help but experience flourishing.

In John 14, then, union with Christ that leads to flourishing has been described in numerous ways, corporately and individually. In vv. 15–21, Jesus speaks corporately, evidenced by plural pronouns anytime he refers to the disciples as "you," describing the gift of the Spirit to those who show their love for him by pursuing him. He also speaks individually, using singular pronouns in v. 21 and vv. 23–24, carrying the same message that loving discipleship on the part of the Christian will result in union with Christ, which enables flourishing because Father and Son will have made their home in the life of the Christian.

Still Jesus is not done. He goes on to make a surprising comment in v. 28, stating that if they loved him, the disciples would be glad that he is going to the Father, for the Father is greater than he. Given his description of how his departure will lead to a new experience of union with him, this makes sense. Up until this time the disciples experienced an external relationship with Jesus, but they will soon realize an inward relationship with him, both individually and corporately. Jesus' Trinitarian theology in this passage, Father, Son, and Spirit together uniting with the Christian, shows that this new inner relationship, this union with Christ, should be seen as superior to the purely external relationship the disciples currently have with him.

---

9. For purposes of clarification, John specifies "not Iscariot," thus signifying it was the other Judas who spoke.

Jesus continues his teaching on union with Christ and how it leads to flourishing in John 15 when in vv. 4–11 he refers to the principle of "remaining" or "abiding"—they in him and he in them. In fact, using the illustration of a branch broken off from the life-giving power of the vine, no longer able to produce fruit, Jesus says that unless the disciples remain in him and he in them, they will have no power to bear fruit for him (v. 4). Jesus' metaphor is rife with the imagery of flourishing when he continues in v. 5, "I am the vine; you are the branches. If you remain in me and I in you, you will bear much fruit." Importantly, this evidence of fruit-bearing shows that they are truly his disciples (v. 8).

In John 15, then, Jesus is very much in keeping with what he just said in John 14. Union with Christ is essential to the flourishing Christian life, both corporately and individually. Further, it is not only possible but it is also necessary to practice acts of dependence on him if an individual or community is to experience flourishing. Jesus, in summary, teaches union with Christ as applicable to individuals and groups, and he further teaches that a contemplative dependence on this union is required for human flourishing. If this is as important a teaching as I am suggesting, we should be able to observe Jesus' disciples practicing contemplation of union with Christ in their lives, leading to flourishing. Did Jesus' disciples understand and practice this teaching, even after he left them?

The New Testament writers describe for us how Jesus' promise of individual and corporate union with him comes to fruition quickly in his disciples' lives. His arrest, crucifixion, and resurrection take place in rapid succession in three days time, after the events of John 13–17. Another month passes and the risen Jesus brings his disciples to the Mount of Olives where Luke tells us in Acts 1 that Jesus instructs them to wait in Jerusalem until they receive power from on high. He then ascends to his Father, and now he has left them just as he said he would in John 14.

The disciples follow his instructions, returning to Jerusalem, where they engage in prayer. About ten days later when they are together, the Spirit arrives, filling the "whole house"[10] and "all of them were filled with the Holy Spirit" (Acts 2:1–4), who then empowers them to speak other languages and preach boldly. On that day, about three thousand join their group of 120 followers of Jesus (Acts 1:15, 2:41). Once again Luke describes for us both a corporate and individual filling of the Spirit. As Jesus promised, he came and made his home within them.

10. Here Luke uses the word *oikos*, which is generally translated "house" but can be used to refer to "a building consisting of one or more rooms and normally serving as a dwelling place (*oikos* also includes certain public buildings, for example, a temple)." Louw and Nida, *Greek-English*, 80.

For the first time, the disciples were experiencing inward union with Christ, and as Acts 2:42–47 describes, these earliest followers of Jesus flourished: "Everyone was filled with awe. . . . All the believers were together and had everything in common. . . . They gave to anyone as he had need. . . . Every day they continued to meet together . . . with glad and sincere hearts, praising God and enjoying the favor of all the people." Notice the emphasis on togetherness in the words "everyone," "all," and "gave to anyone." This is one of the many beautiful pictures of flourishing-producing togetherness in Scripture.

But there are other scriptural passages we can examine to learn about the connection of union with Christ, contemplation, communities, and human flourishing. In Acts 4, for example, we read of another filling of the Spirit after the apostles Peter and John endured persecution for proclaiming Jesus. Luke reports that Peter and John, having been detained by the authorities, were released and returned to the group of believers, and the group "raised their voices together in prayer to God" (v. 24). In this action of contemplative dependence on Jesus, they asked for God's enabling to proclaim the story of good news in Jesus as well as empowerment for miraculous ministry (vv. 23–30). Luke tells us that "after they prayed, the place where they were meeting was shaken. And they were all filled with the Holy Spirit and spoke the word of God boldly" (v. 31). What follows is another summary of how the believers experienced communal flourishing, particularly emphasizing selfless sharing with those in need.

The early church, then, serves as an example of how a Christian community, through contemplation, draws on union with Christ for the purpose of human flourishing. One major figure in the early church, however, was not at these seminal events. Yet, Paul, after his own powerful experience with Christ, would go on to write numerous letters, providing a solid theological foundation for communal union with Christ leading to flourishing, which the church had already experienced. It is to his letters that we now turn.

First, Paul says that Christians are people who are filled with the Spirit of Christ. In 1 Cor 6:19 he writes, "Your body is a temple of the Holy Spirit, who is in you, whom you have received from God" (NASB).[11] Then in Eph

11. Here the plural "you" refers to the group of believers Paul was writing to in Corinth, so we must question whether Paul is talking about individual bodies or the corporate body, which he refers to in 1 Cor 12, "the body of Christ." In 6:19, the word "body" is in the singular, which could indicate that he is talking about one corporate body. Earlier in the passage, however, he refers to an individual's singular body (vv. 13–14, 16) and to a collective of singular bodies (v. 15). So it would seem unlikely in v. 19 that he would move from the individual to the corporate, especially given his flow of thought, which stated that sexual promiscuity in the individual body is unacceptable,

5:18 Paul cautions believers to avoid becoming drunk with alcohol but instead encourages them to be filled with the Spirit. While the descriptions of the Holy Spirit's filling of the early church in Acts 2 and 4 seemed corporate, Paul's teaching in 1 Cor 6 and Eph 5 lean toward an individualistic understanding of union with Christ.

Rather than the concept of the filling of the Spirit, it is Paul's specific teaching about union with Christ that is more clearly corporate. In Gal 2:20 he writes, "I have been crucified with Christ and I no longer live, but Christ lives in me. The life I now live in the body, I live by faith in the Son of God." How can Paul say that he has been crucified with Christ, that he, Paul, no longer lives, but Christ lives in him? The phrase "Christ lives in me," is a reference to union with Christ, but to understand the logic that brings Paul to that place of union, we need to survey his flow of thought.

Paul precedes this statement by talking about how the disciple Peter was making legalistic concessions to the Judaizers (who believed Christians must keep the Mosaic law), and thus he, Paul, confronted Peter (see Gal 2:11–14). Paul refers to "the truth of the gospel" in v. 14, and then in v. 16 he says this truth comes not by observing the Old Testament law, but by "faith in Jesus Christ." He states that he placed his faith in Christ and was justified by that faith (vv. 15–16). For Paul, this concept of placing faith in Christ means that Christ has become the focus of his hope and salvation.

Previously, Paul placed that hope and salvation on his own observance of the law. There was for Paul, and he wanted there to also be for the Galatians and Peter, a movement of faith away from the law and toward Christ. Paul refers to what happens in this process of placing one's faith in Christ as justification, or as Rutledge describes it, "rectification,"[12] being made right. God makes things right as we place our faith in Jesus who is now our hope.

For faith to be justifying faith, however, Paul clarifies in vv. 17–19 that he is not simply talking about faith in terms of mental assent. Instead Jesus becomes our King when we pledge allegiance to him and him only and then live accordingly. Or as Paul says, "I died to the law so that I might live for God" (v. 19). Here Paul plays the opposites of death and life off each other. He died to the law, which is no longer the bringer of life, and his death to law brings about the conditions for him to be alive to God.

But now Paul has a surprise. In v. 20, the death he referred to in v. 19 is being "crucified with Christ," and he, Paul, no longer lives. A new reality is alive in him, "Christ lives in me." For those who place their faith in Jesus, faith that is both assent and allegiance, Jesus now lives in them, and they

---

a claim he supports with the evidence that one's body is a temple of the Holy Spirit.

12. Rutledge, *Crucifixion*, 296.

have union with Christ. Observance of law, or performance-based faith, is superseded by the life of Christ within the person.

Paul makes this point clear when he talks about how he lives life now. He no longer practices a performance-based observance of the law, as if he could be so good that God is required to bless Paul. There is no earning God's favor. Instead Christ has made union within him by faith. Paul's phrase, "I live by faith *in* the son of God" (NIV, NASB, and ESV), can also be translated "by faith *of* the son of God" (KJV), which has potential ramifications for how union with Christ relates to flourishing.

Is Paul saying that we live by our faith or by Christ's? Biblical commentators Hendriksen and Kistemaker suggest that Paul could be saying "that (life) which I now live in flesh I live in faith, (the faith) which is in the Son of God."[13] Rutledge translates the phrase similarly, "I live by [the faithfulness of] the Son of God."[14] She goes on to quote Morna Hooker. "It seems to be a case of Christ taking over our lives and living in our place."[15] Rutledge explains, "In other words, the acting subject is Christ, not the faithful person per se. Hooker in elaborating, repeats the 'takeover' theme in a vivid way: 'In some mysterious sense, the whole of humanity died on Calvary.... He dies for us, but that means we die with him. He was raised, and raised with such power that our lives are now taken over by him.'"[16]

What's more, we observe that Christ initiated this new life through his loving self-sacrifice, and thus it was a gift from God to Paul. This is a radical departure from the old concept of observance of law. Now Christ's life is literally embodied in us. Paul describes this further in his Letter to the Galatians when he says, "Because you are his sons, God sent the Spirit of his Son into our hearts, the Spirit who calls out, '*Abba*, Father'" (4:6).

When Paul teaches union with Christ, then, he interchangeably uses the idea of "Christ lives in us" with the idea of "the Spirit of Christ in us." Paul is best understood as discussing union with Christ primarily individually, but as we have seen previously, his teaching also aligns with a corporate understanding of union with Christ. We see Paul return to this theme in Eph 3:14–19 when he prays "that Christ may dwell in your hearts through faith" (v. 17). Here Paul is praying for a group, but when he mentions "hearts" it seems best to understand him as referring to Christ dwelling in individual hearts. Paul, in summary, while teaching the necessity of the union of Christ

---

13. Hendriksen and Kistemaker, *Galatians*, 106 (parentheses original).
14. Rutledge, *Crucifixion*, 543n17 (brackets original).
15. Rutledge, *Crucifixion*, 555.
16. Hooker, *Not Ashamed*, 30, quoted in Rutledge, *Crucifixion*, 555–56.

in the life of the believer, is primarily individualistic in his approach yet leaves the door open for a corporate application.

To attempt a synthesis of the theological principles in these passages, we see numerous aspects of union with Christ. First, Christ makes union with the individual believer possible through his Spirit inhabiting that person. Second, union with Christ can be experienced corporately. Third, contemplative connection with this union is vital for human flourishing. Thus any communities composed of Christians have a pathway for their community to practice union with Christ together, and if they want to experience human flourishing, they would do well to devote time to habitual communal contemplation on that union.

CONNECTING THEOLOGY TO PRACTICE

Having built a scriptural foundation for Christian communities to practice contemplation on union with Christ for human flourishing, we can examine some questions that will lead to application. Our first question is this: Is the practice of contemplation on union with Christ applicable only to churches? While our primary, and perhaps only, example in the New Testament of a community practicing contemplative union with Christ was the early church, it seems best to keep the scope of application broad, especially considering Jesus' teaching, "Where two or three gather in my name, there am I with them" (Matt 18:20).

Wright and Roberts are, therefore, correct in applying union with Christ to marriage. In a world filled with parachurch communities, both formal and informal, Jesus' teaching can be understood as applicable in the sense that he meant it, where at least two people come together under the banner of his name. Thus the practice of contemplation toward union with Christ is applicable to any community that has gathered in the name of Christ.

The next three questions follow from the first: How do we know if a community is Christian? Must a community formally claim Christianity to qualify as Christian? Does a community qualify as Christian only if it is composed completely of people who identify as Christian?

As we have seen in Jesus' *teaching*, in the example of the early church, and in the writings of Paul, a community must be Christian for it to have union with Christ. It may be difficult to know, however, if a community is explicitly Christian. In the realm of art, for example, debate has raged for decades as to whether a performer is giving a Christian performance or if an artifact of their work is Christian. Some performers say they prefer to identify as an individual Christian rather than identify their community (e.g., a rock band) as Christian. The result is that they see themselves as a Christian who performs, rather than as a person or group giving a distinctly Christian performance.

Speaking more generally about any community, then, determining Christian identity is up to the community itself. Do they want to identify as nonsectarian, perhaps composed of individual Christians, or do they prefer to intentionally identify their community as Christian? If they claim the latter, it would seem prudent, given the theology of union with Christ, that they take steps to regularly practice contemplation toward deeper union with Christ together, in order to access the power Christ promises for human flourishing.

If they claim the former, we could ask a corollary question: Can a community benefit from union with Christ if that community is not formally Christian but all or some of the members of the community are still Christian?

The answer is a resounding *yes*, as each individual Christian is indwelt with the Spirit of Christ, and through a hearty practice of contemplation, they can access the life-giving power of Jesus that is necessary for human flourishing. Those Spirit-filled Christians, Jesus taught, "will bear much fruit" (John 15:5; see vv. 1–10), which can only help the larger Christian community flourish.

Whether Jesus, when referring to fruit, meant multiplication, as seed-bearing fruit naturally does, or whether he meant something like the character qualities called "the fruit of the Spirit" that Paul would later describe in Gal 5:22–23,[17] the result is in both cases, human flourishing. All Christians can flourish by practicing contemplation of their union with Christ. Because our focus is on Christian communities, how can Christian communities practice such contemplation together?

As we saw in Acts 2 and 4, the church of Jesus is the first Christian community that experiences union with Christ, so we must begin by examining how churches can practice corporate union with Christ. Acts is a historical account that is not necessarily prescriptive and is best read as descriptive, but churches can still choose to follow the lead of the early church by being praying churches. How they pray and when they pray are matters they can decide, but what is essential is that they pray. Their practice of prayer, further, needs to be examined, so that it includes a contemplative

---

17. "But the fruit of the Spirit is love, joy, peace, forbearance, kindness, goodness, faithfulness, gentleness and self-control." As I wrote earlier, imagine the impact when such fruit flows out of the life of the Christian into their community, both inside and outside the church.

habit, such that churches gather people together to "be still and know" (Ps 46:10) that God is God.

Theologian Barbara Holmes describes how the African American church practices corporate union with Christ when she says, "Africana worship experiences are contemplative because they create an atmosphere for communal listening and responsiveness to the manifestations of God."[18] She goes on to describe corporate contemplation in the Black Church as, "hypnotic humming during baptism and the faithful circle of believers around the sick and dying."[19] It is prayers that are "danced and sung."[20]

Echoing Paul's teaching about the necessity of unity in the church, which was grounded in Jesus' teaching on unity in John 17,[21] Holmes also suggests that unity is vital for contemplation in a church. She writes, "All must be on one accord [sic].... This is the contemplative moment, the recognition that each and every member of the congregation shares the same angst over the troubles of the world and the need for reunion."[22]

The practice of Eucharist is another important communal contemplative act and one that exemplifies this unity. Paul teaches that the worshipful ritual of the Lord's Supper is not only for remembrance and proclamation (1 Cor 11:23–26) but also for participation in Christ when he says, "Is not the cup of thanksgiving for which we give thanks a participation in the blood of Christ? And is not the bread that we break a participation in the body of Christ?" (1 Cor 10:16).

This echoes Jesus' own teaching in John 6:53–56 when he concludes, "Whoever eats my flesh and drinks my blood remains in me and I in them," a contemplative statement that is nearly identical to the vital concept of "remaining in the vine," which he teaches in John 15. Therefore Brandt concludes, "Union with Christ is part and parcel with communion; communion implies a real substantial connection with the Triune God in Christ."[23]

Churches must gather not just for the ritual of communion but also for the purpose of contemplative practice, certainly in their regular weekly worship gathering but also in smaller groupings. Far too many local churches pack their schedules with experiential-based programming that simply appropriates cultural norms of entertainment into the church setting.

---

18. Holmes, *Joy Unspeakable*, 68.
19. Holmes, *Joy Unspeakable*, 71.
20. Holmes, *Joy Unspeakable*, 72; see also 75–78.
21. This was noted above in discussion of 1 Cor 12 and is in keeping with Jesus' prayer in John 17:11 that his disciples may be one as he and the Father are one.
22. Holmes, *Joy Unspeakable*, 84.
23. Brandt, "Gospel-Centered Contemplation?," 189.

Corporate worship often emphasizes participants expressing themselves. Churches can consider, rather, how to include corporate contemplation specifically focusing on their union with Christ and this will involve time and space "to gaze upon the beauty of the Lord" (Ps 27:4) and listen for his voice, two practices best led by a seasoned contemplative practitioner.

One way Christians can practice communal contemplation on their corporate union with Christ is through corporate lament, which is an act of together reaching out to God in holy complaint. The Psalms are filled with lyrical laments intended to be used in a corporate setting. In Ps 88, for example, the psalm's title tells us that it was written for the director of music.[24] Together Israelites would cry out to God, yearning for union with the God who seems to have hidden his face from them. Even if the individuals in a particular gathering were not experiencing what the words describe, by joining together they affirm and support those in their congregation who are experiencing loss and pain.

My own congregation has experimented with what we call Silent Sunday. Taking inspiration from Quaker and Taizé worship, we dispense with all audible elements of our standard worship service, with the exception of a few congregational songs using only a softly played piano as instrumentation. The entire service is guided by words and images projected on a screen for all to see. We still include prayer and even a sermon, all via silent words on screen.

Throughout the service we include a handful of three- to five-minute-long periods of total quiet, asking people to contemplate, listen for God, and we give them a notepad and pen if they would like to record anything. Congregants have expressed deep appreciation for these Sundays. Churches would do well to experiment with other forms of corporate contemplation, thus assisting their congregations with developing a practice of together connecting with the Spirit of Christ for the purpose of human flourishing.

In addition to congregational practices of contemplation, how might Christian communities practice contemplation in other ways? First, the Christian community must be intentional about identifying as Christian—to the point of recognizing and claiming their union with Christ—keeping in mind that the goal of the community is flourishing-producing togetherness, no matter what other business or purpose the community undertakes.

This step can take place with language enshrined in formal documents of incorporation. All individuals who seek to join and participate in the community could be made aware of its foundational claims, agreeing to

---

24. Some other examples of laments sung in community are Pss 4, 6, 13, 22, 39, 77, 109, and 140. We will discuss corporate lament further in ch. 16, as it is particularly applicable to racial reconciliation.

unite themselves not only to the community but also to the claim of union with Christ and the goal of human flourishing.

Second, the community can take steps to consistently draw their community's attention to its foundational tenets. Perhaps the best practical way to do so is through regular communal contemplation on the tenets. This practice of contemplation can occur through regular community-wide gatherings, dependent, of course, on the size of the community. Community leaders can serve as guides, or better, a community can hire or appoint a person or team with the role of guiding the community to maintain a regular practice of contemplation.

Finally, communities can have contemplative practice by gathering corporately or in smaller groupings to gaze on the beauty of the Lord, perhaps aided by reading of Scripture, then including a time for listening for the Spirit, and concluding with group debriefing. In so doing, Paul's comment to the church in Corinth, when he says, "What then shall we say, brothers and sisters? When you come together, each of you has . . ." (1 Cor 14:26), may be instructional. That word, "each one" places value on each person in the community.

In that passage, Paul is referring to a corporate gathering of a church, but the principle holds for any Christian community that practices contemplation toward union with Christ. Christ may choose to speak corporately or through any member of the community, and thus a community, in its practice of contemplation, must carry itself with humility to be open to the input of all. Certainly, the contribution of one or a few would need to be brought to the community at large for examination and consensus. As with churches, Christian communities can seek to experiment with corporate contemplation, breaking new ground for deeper union with Christ that leads to human flourishing.

An area for further reflection is the possibility that contemplation for union with Christ might be applicable to all communities, including those that are not Christian. While union with Christ is a specifically Christian theology, consider how it contains principles that could encourage the flourishing of communities that are not Christian? A nonsectarian community could include, for example, a moment of grateful silence in its regular gatherings, as a collaborative ritual. Christian philosopher J. P. Moreland, in his book *Finding Quiet*, suggests numerous such practices, including starting each day by listing four to five things we can be grateful for, even something as mundane as coffee.[25] This practice of ritual thankfulness helps

---

25. Moreland, *Finding Quiet*, 111–18.

the individual contemplate, with a grateful heart, the beauty of God, thus reshaping their world.

I recently suggested that a parishioner begin this practice, as she was deeply struggling with the loss of her husband and other family difficulties. A week later she phoned me to say that though it was such a short time since she began following the practice of daily gratefulness, she already noticed that she carried a more positive attitude. The Scriptures certainly call Christians to be thankful, but they do not specify starting the day by keeping a thankfulness journal.

Moreland was simply observing a theological truth—one that is affirmed by contemporary psychology—and creating a ritual practice based on it. In addition to individuals, Christian communities would do well to observe a consistent ritual of corporate thankfulness when they gather. Any community can do the same, whether they are Christian or otherwise. My local ministerium has a community Thanksgiving service every year that includes a time where anyone can step up to the mic and share publicly what they are grateful for. This is but one potential way any community could benefit from considering how theology of togetherness can help them implement flourishing-producing togetherness.

CONCLUSION

We have seen that a practice of contemplation on union with Christ is not only viable but essential for Christian communities to make progress in flourishing-producing togetherness. Jesus' words in Matt 18:20—"there am I with them"—and Paul's explanation in Gal 2:20—"Christ lives in me"—remind us of the astounding love and grace of God, through which he desires to dwell in the midst of his people. Further, Jesus' beautiful metaphor in John 15 of the flourishing vine swells our hearts with the knowledge that we can abide in him, as he and his Father, through the Spirit, have made their home with us and as, through contemplative connection, he empowers us to flourish, bearing fruit for his kingdom in the world. In other words, our union with Christ together helps us to share flourishing with others in the community. As we will see, when we are in union with Christ, we are in an excellent position to be in solidarity with others.

11

Solidarity with Others

THE TWIN TOWERS WERE still smoking in the days after September 11, 2001, when US President George W. Bush encouraged the nation to respond to the tragedy by going shopping. What might seem to be a terribly inappropriate suggestion had an ulterior motive. Because the terrorists flew airliners into the World Trade Center towers, resulting in horrible physical and human carnage, the American economy and financial markets were also in shambles. By urging the nation to go shopping, the president was at least in part hoping to avoid a further market decline.

But his words betrayed a deeper and darker reality. Americans are consumers, as shopping is for some a kind of national pastime. American Christians, too, bring a consumer mentality to their participation in church families. If a person does not get what they want out of the church, they feel free to "church hop." Some theologians observe that American Christians have been discipled more by our consumerist culture than by Christ. We are so susceptible to consumerism, in part, because of individualism.

In chapter 2, we learned that since its inception, the American psyche has prided itself on individualism. Undoubtedly, our ingenuity and frontier entrepreneurial spirit has achieved much. We also learned that this individualistic streak has been evaluated in a negative light, from the perspective of isolationism, arrogance, and pride. One danger of individualism is that it can erode the community necessary for human flourishing.

To counter that unhealthy side of individualism, we have been seeking a robust understanding and application of the community necessary for human flourishing, a community rooted in our earlier study of the

Trinitarian nature of God. This Trinitarian-shaped community guides us in the formation and practice of human brotherhood and sisterhood critical for establishing flourishing no matter the people or culture. We learned that flourishing-producing togetherness is found within the covenant community of the kingdom of God. But as long as individualism remains, how does flourishing-producing togetherness respond to it?

Responding to the negative aspects of individualism, a Christian observer can point out that the various fellowships of religious believers, such as local church families, small groups, or classes, might include the kind of brotherhood and sisterhood needed to be an antidote to individualism. While true in part, other Christians have raised a yellow flag of caution, suggesting that individualism has infiltrated the church. How has individualism infiltrated the church, thus undermining its ability to promote flourishing? One way individualism has infiltrated the church is through consumerism.

Consumerism is the idea that fulfilling the wants of the individual consumer is primary. Individual consumers come to believe that they will experience flourishing when they obtain what they feel they need. In a shopping mall, consumerism is everywhere, giving individuals untold choice, marketing to them the idea that their lives will flourish when they have bountiful choices and when they consume.

What can a theology of togetherness do to combat individualistic consumerism in Christian communities? First, for flourishing-producing togetherness to occur, a theology of togetherness suggests that Christian communities must recover solidarity. We start this recovery by mentioning two German concepts that provide unique descriptions of solidarity: *gemeinschaft*, which is defined as "social relations between individuals, based on close personal and family ties; community,"[1] and similarly, *gemeinschaftlich*, which is defined as "a collaborative piece of work that is done by two or more people or groups working together."[2]

Notice how these terms align with a theology of togetherness. Their definitions are important: "close personal and family ties" and "a collaboration of people together." *Gemeinschaft* and *gemeinschaftlich* give us a picture of deep connection. Because of the depth with which they depict relationships, they are apt terms with far-reaching application beyond ecclesiology (the theology of the church). Yes, churches, because they promote the kingdom of God, are places where deep connection should be the norm. As Jesus said in John 13:34–35, "By this everyone will know that you are my disciples, if you love one another."

---

1. Soanes and Stevenson, *Concise Oxford English Dictionary*, "Gemeinschaft."
2. *Cambridge German-English Dictionary*, "Gemeinschaftlich."

But *gemeinschaft* and *gemeinshaftlich* can apply in the broader sense to all communities seeking flourishing-producing togetherness. In this way, a theology of togetherness is the antidote to individualistic theology because it directs humans to work together toward flourishing in community as embodied by *gemeinschaft* and *gemeinschaftlich*. But these German terms might have difficulty exciting the hearts and minds of most English-speakers. Thankfully there is an English word that carries the same idea: solidarity.

Pope Francis wrote about solidarity during the COVID pandemic, which started in 2019, and spread across the globe in 2020. He wrote, "Once this health crisis passes, our worst response would be to plunge even more deeply into feverish consumerism and new forms of egotistic self-preservation. God willing, after all this, we will think no longer in terms of 'them' and 'those,' but only 'us.'"[3] In this comment, Francis suggests a theology of togetherness that aligns with *gemeinschaft* and *gemeinschaftlich*. The "us" he encourages us to consider is rooted in the concept of solidarity.

Solidarity conveys the image of that which is not fragmented but that which is together and connected. It is solid. Rauschenbusch comments, "Our solidarity is a beneficent part of human life. It is the basis for our greatest good."[4] When speaking of the "greatest good," Rauschenbusch projects a vision of flourishing, and further, he observes that solidarity is the foundation for flourishing. A theology of togetherness that promotes flourishing must be grounded in the mutual concepts of *gemeinschaft* and *gemeinschaftlich*, thus guided by the connectionism of solidarity.

Like Pope Francis, Sacks remarks, "For the sake of the future 'You,' we should strengthen the future of 'Us.' . . . Ours is an age where there is too much 'I' and too little 'We.'"[5] But how do we help the "I" become "we" in a world that has been swimming in the waters of individualism, consumerism, and ubiquitous screens? Phone screens, computer screens, and television screens give us an electronic connection that enables a fully audio-visual relationship. In fact, because we do not need to be in-person, digital communication promises to connect us with far more people online than ever before. But are we experiencing flourishing-producing togetherness because of all that connection?

Opinions abound as to whether this new age of telecommunication, videoconferencing, and social media can provide flourishing-producing togetherness. Throughout the COVID pandemic, in which live video

---

3. Francis, *Fratelli Tutti*, 10.
4. Rauschenbusch, *Social Gospel*, 182.
5. Sacks, *Morality*, xiii.

teleconferencing became commonplace, observers noted a decreased sense of people being present with one another. Even still, from screen to screen people connected relationally and with significant meaning, building covenantal communities to encourage flourishing. It seems we can, even if only in part, experience solidarity through a disembodied connection.

Others have suggested that disembodied connection severely weakens our ability to have solidarity. Tish Harrison Warren, an Anglican priest, nearly two years after the onset of the pandemic, wrote an article suggesting that churches should abandon pandemic-era online gatherings and only hold in-person gatherings.[6] Her theological rationale was that ours is an embodied faith, and thus solidarity requires presence. Our faith is present, and we are unable to reach the standards of *gemeinschaft* and *gemeinschaftlich* by gathering online.

Response to Warren's article was swift, especially from those who have disabilities that make it difficult or impossible to be in-person.[7] Their point is well-taken. The church, to have flourishing-producing togetherness, must embrace all people, bringing all into solidarity, even if it means sacrificial outreach to be in-person to the homebound. While Warren's article could have been more nuanced to provide a robust solidarity, her general argument is sound. Flourishing-producing togetherness requires an embodied solidarity for all, and that solidarity is applicable to communities beyond the church.

Rauschenbusch describes, for example, a nation-state that seeks fully embodied solidarity, "a State which asks only for an open door and keeps its own door open in return, and which speaks as courteously to a backward State as to one with a big fleet, is to that extent a Christian community."[8] To clarify, the state he describes is behaving in a manner consistent with the ideals of Christian community, but that does not necessarily make it a Christian community. Rauschenbusch is not saying that a nation needs to become a Christian nation to have solidarity.

Instead he is saying that when a nation embraces flourishing-producing togetherness, it is behaving in a way that is consistent with a Christian understanding of a theology of togetherness. This is an important way to view how a theology of togetherness can benefit communities of all kinds, without requiring that community to be explicitly Christian in any way. In the example Rauschenbusch raises, we see a state that applies Christ-like

---

6. Warren, "Online Service," 17.
7. Warren, "Reader Responses," paras. 16–18.
8. Rauschenbusch, *Social Gospel*, 114.

humility, love for the stranger, and kindness. Solidarity, then, is broadly applicable to all communities.

Organizational thinkers Jane Wei-Skillern and Nora Silver offer four principles for how any community can practice solidarity: (1) focus on the mission before the community; (2) build partnerships based on trust, not control; (3) promote others rather than yourself; and finally, (4) build constellations rather than lone stars.[9] These principles are very much in line with the theology of togetherness. Yet, Wei-Skillern and Silver go on to say that "the number that live and breathe these principles in practice is rather small."[10] When communities embrace flourishing-producing togetherness, however, they will make embodied solidarity their goal. How do communities achieve solidarity, especially in a fractured world? As we will see in the next part of the book, we must act. What does it mean to put flourishing-producing togetherness into action?

---

9 Wie-Skillern and Silver, "Four Network Principles," 121–29.
10. Wie-Skillern and Silver, "Four Network Principles," 128.

Part 3

Practices of Togetherness in Christian Communities

12

How a Theology of Togetherness Leads to Practices of Togetherness

BECAUSE COMMUNITIES ARE THE fundamental building blocks of societies across the globe, they have unparalleled influence. It is, however, a common human tendency to idolize solitary individuals such as governmental leaders or celebrities, believing they primarily have the influence or power to effect change.

Yet solo influencers are the exception rather than the rule. It only is the rare person who orchestrates sweeping reform or wields widely influential dynamism by themselves. The rule is that people working together have the most common and pervasive impact, for ill or for good. People working together in community are the greatest impetus for human suffering or for human flourishing precisely because of the power of togetherness.

Therefore, each Christian community would do well to investigate just what is guiding its programs and practices, so that flourishing is both the community mission and outcome. Because such an investigation requires evaluation, we must ask upon what standard should Christian communities base this kind of evaluation? In the previous seven chapters, we learned how a theology of togetherness provides such a standard—flourishing-producing togetherness.

This view of togetherness sees people, working together in Christian communities of all kinds, as the most frequent and best means for accomplishing what this book and others suggest is the goal of theology—human flourishing. We have followed a theology of togetherness as our guide, mining the wisdom of the biblical Scriptures for theological principles.

Our theology of togetherness helped us discover patterns of thinking and behavior that can guide people as they work together to pursue human flourishing.

We now seek to delve into corporate practices and rituals based on and flowing from a theology of togetherness. Traditionally, spiritual practices (or disciplines) are taught as individual or personal habits by which a person can train themselves in a life of faith, demonstrated in the teaching and example of Jesus. Fasting, prayer, and Scripture memorization are but a few such practices, and much excellent work has been done describing their value and encouraging their consistent use.

When observed consistently and persistently, a healthy diet of personal spiritual discipline leads to personal flourishing. Given the near ubiquity of human communities in our world, might it be possible that spiritual habits can be practiced together by groups of people? A theology of togetherness can help us recast the disciplines as corporate practices. Just as individual practices lead to individual flourishing, so corporate practices lead to human flourishing, having impact both individually and corporately.

In contemporary society, even nonreligious businesses express the need for such corporate practices. Journalist Nellie Bowles writes that "divinity consultants are designing sacred rituals for corporations and their spiritually depleted employees."[1] After describing how workplaces became like spiritual deserts during the 2020–21 COVID pandemic, forcing many to work from home, Bowles notes how companies are now hiring people with master of divinity degrees as spiritual consultants for their employees. Some consultants have even started their own companies seeking to help businesses by instituting spiritual practices, "borrowing from religious tradition to bring spiritual richness to corporate America."[2]

Ritualist is one such community. The founder of Ritualist, Ezra Bookman, writes, "Our lives are filled with bland and ineffective rituals—from graduations to product launches to onboarding new employees. By intentionally designing these transitions, leaders can build cultures of wellbeing, communities can grow shared purpose, individuals can find belonging, and communities can thrive."[3] In this purpose statement, Bookman describes the application of corporate practices designed to promote human

---

1. Bowles, "Doing God's Work," 1.
2. Bowles, "Doing God's Work," 1.
3. Bookman, Ritualist (website). Since the time of writing, Bookman has updated the Ritualist purpose statement, now noting "rituals make the intangible tangible, creating spaces for the shared experience and expression of our values. Rituals combat loneliness by connecting us to ideas and communities bigger than ourselves. Rituals connect us with the past, root us in the present, and help us vision the future."

flourishing. While this is an encouraging development, what do scriptural and theological principles tell us about how rituals in a variety of corporate settings can best promote human flourishing?

Bowles goes on to mention the nonprofit Sacred Design Labs and the insights on one of its founding partners, Casper ter Kuile. Kulie remarks, "The question we ask is: 'How do you translate the ancient traditions that have given people access to meaning-making practices, but in a context that is not centered around the congregation?'"[4] Answering this question is the goal of the next few chapters. Because of the vast number and influence of communities of people in our world, Christian communities must provide a solid grounding for their pursuit of practices that lead to human flourishing. A theology of togetherness trains Christian communities, inside and outside the church, toward human flourishing through a regimen of collaborative practices. We get started by exploring ritual from a togetherness perspective.

---

4. Bowles, "Doing God's Work," 1.

13

Practicing Ritual Together for Flourishing

IF THERE IS ONE thing Christians have done together frequently throughout the centuries, it is practicing rituals. From the earliest days of the first church in Jerusalem, which was rooted in the Jewish ritual tradition, Christians have employed corporate ritual in a variety of ways.

First, they observed the ritual of gathering. In Acts 1:12–14, after Jesus ascended to heaven, the Christians "joined together constantly in prayer" (v. 14). Then, about two weeks later, the Holy Spirit fills the Christians who have been together praying, and those first Christians launch the church. The first description of the church, Acts 2:42–47, tell us that the Christians "every day . . . continued to meet together" (v. 46). From that first day of the church, and throughout the next two millennial, Christian ritual is primarily practiced by Christians gathering regularly, primarily for worship services, but also for a variety of other purposes. Christians are people who spend time together.

Second, Acts 2:42–47 describes that even in those early days, Christians included other ritual observances in their worship gatherings, "broke bread in their homes and ate together" (v. 46). This description of their worship included the ritual meal of the Lord's Supper, one of the two rituals Jesus himself taught them to observe. Finally, they practiced baptism, the second ritual Jesus taught them (Acts 2:40–41).

The Christians observed gathering, communion, and baptism, but why do we classify these as rituals? Furthermore, some have rightly criticized ritual. What makes an action a ritual, and how does ritual inform and benefit flourishing-producing togetherness? Are there any dangers to be aware of in the practice of ritual? Might there be ways the practice of ritual could hamper flourishing-producing togetherness?

First of all, what is ritual? Ritual is a repetitive action that points to another reality beyond the ritual itself. We observe of ritual for a purpose. When groups of people together practice ritual, they involve their bodies in doing and acting, sometimes including the act of speaking.

While we are focused on Christian communities, consider how this could be applied outside of a church setting. When the people in a company or nonprofit gather for a weekly staff meeting and that staff meeting always begins with the entire group quoting in unison the company's vision statement, they are using their bodies for speech in a collaborative ritual that can guide their work. The purpose is not to gather people to say the same words out loud at the same time. That is a description of the ritual itself, but there is something more important toward which the ritual points.

People in the company had previously created the vision statement, which included the company's guiding principles, and those people want its employees to be unified, living out those principles in their work together. If the company's vision statement includes a desire for human flourishing, and we hope it does, then the ritual of repeating the vision statement can help everyone in the company not only remember but more importantly be motivated to work in such a way that they are promoting human flourishing. In this way, the repetitive action of ritual points beyond itself to another reality.

Clearly there is a sense of mystery about ritual, as there is with anything that points beyond itself. There is a danger in symbolic mystery; if the symbolism is too vague or ill-defined, it results in those performing the ritual having little understanding of what the ritual is pointing to beyond itself. The result is that people can practice the ritual for ritual's sake rather than for what it symbolizes, and they often quickly find the ritual to be a nuisance.

In the Hebrew Bible we learn that the people of God made this very mistake about ritual when God, through his prophets, tells his people that he desires mercy, not sacrifice. God asked the prophets to communicate the message of "mercy, not sacrifice" (Hos 6:6), because the people had an improper view of ritual sacrifice. The people believed that if they simply performed the ritual, they had satisfied God's purpose, and thus they could live their lives however they wanted.

God, through his prophets, tells the people that the ritual sacrifice itself was never his goal. God's goal was for his people to engage in the ritual so that they might learn the important reality the ritual pointed to, which is God's heart of mercy. The sacrifice of a lamb, for example, was a ritual designed to symbolize that the sin of the people was atoned for. In this sacrifice we see God's mercy in full view, as the people were not slain for their sin. The ritual was intended to point at the reality beyond. When we practice ritual, therefore, we do not do so for ritual's sake but for what its symbolism points to.

If the Jewish sacrificial system feels a bit gruesome or ancient, perhaps the Christian ritual of the Lord's Supper will help us understand how ritual helps us see beyond our world and envision a new world. In Acts 2:42–47, we learned that the earliest Christians, following Jesus' teaching, observed the ritual of the Lord's Supper in their gatherings.

I have participated in or observed the Lord's Supper in an Orthodox Church, a Roman Catholic Church, an Episcopal church, and in a variety of evangelical churches. Each church's practice of the supper has its nuances, but they all include the two elements of bread and wine or grape juice, following the example of Jesus in the Gospels (e.g., Matt 26:26–29). These two actions, eating and drinking, are everyday components of eating meals or snacking, and in and of themselves they carry no symbolic significance. When we eat and drink, we are satisfying the normal nutritional requirements of the human body. But when Jesus holds the bread and cup and says, "Take and eat; this is my body," and "Drink from it, all of you. This is my blood of the covenant" (Matt 26:26–28) he creates a ritual that gives those common actions of eating and drinking a whole new meaning. Jesus said that the bread represents his body and the juice or wine represents his blood, both given for the forgiveness of sins. Jesus' gift of his body and blood was the world-shaping act that makes it possible for the kingdom of God to transform the world.

When Christians practice the ritual of the Lord's Supper, they remember the truth of who Jesus was and what he sought to accomplish so that they might join him in his mission. It is essential, then, that for ritual to inspire flourishing-producing togetherness, the ritual must point beyond itself to the new world it seeks to create. In their book *Ritual and Its Consequences*, the theologians Seligman et al. suggest that ritual brings flourishing through what they call the subjunctive. What do they mean by the subjunctive? As I mentioned above, ritual is the means for envisioning a new world for human flourishing. Seligman et al. explain, "We claim that ritual creates a subjunctive, an 'as if' or 'could be,' universe."[1] The subjunctive is a vision of a better world; the subjunctive is a flourishing world.

To help us understand how ritual creates a subjunctive, Seligman et al. contrast the subjunctive view with what they call the sincere view: "Sincere

---

1. Seligman et al., *Ritual*, 7.

views are focused not on the creation of an 'as if' or a shared subjunctive universe of human beings in the world. Instead, they project an 'as is' vision of what often becomes a totalistic, unambiguous vision of reality 'as it really is.'"[2] What they mean by the "sincere view" is the belief some people have that the world cannot change, or that it can barely change at all, and therefore we should accept the reality of it "as is." When you sell a vehicle, "as is," you are saying to the buyer, "I am not willing to make any effort to repair what is broken. You buy it as it is." But the sincere view takes the "as is" a bit further. While the buyer of an "as is" vehicle could fix that vehicle, the sincere view suggests that we are better off embracing the world "as is."

Which is right? The subjunctive view that hopes for a new world or the sincere view that says we should focus on the real world, as is? If we answer that it is best to focus on the real world, then ritual, because it points symbolically to a new world, is a waste of time. If we answer that we should seek to create a new world, then ritual is important. The connection to flourishing is clear. Flourishing is counter to the "sincere world" because flourishing envisions a new world where God's kingdom advances as more and more people, more and more communities come under his rule and reign.

Seligman et al. importantly note that individualism is a threat to any practice of ritual that will lead to flourishing. "We are often too concerned with exploring the different forms of self-expression and of individual authenticity to appreciate the rhythmic structure of the shared subjunctive that is the deepest work of ritual."[3] In order to counter anti-flourishing individualism, Christian communities can employ flourishing-producing togetherness by practicing rituals that create the flourishing world as it could be. Though we might not currently live in that world, rituals help us envision what that new world could look like. Ritual, then, consistently practiced, forms us and helps us create flourishing in the world.

Seligman et al. describe this picture of flourishing as a community of empathy.[4] Empathy is a particularly helpful word for a study on togetherness because it goes beyond simply having an emotion of care for the other (sympathy). Empathy surpasses sympathy because empathy includes personal comprehension of and sharing in the feelings of the other, usually because one has experienced something similar to what the other is going through.

Likewise, we can develop a community of empathy through the practice of ritual. Ritual is needed, theologically-speaking, to combat the effects of sin, especially when we consider what we learned from a theology of

2. Seligman et al., *Ritual*, 8.
3. Seligman et al., *Ritual*, 10.
4. Seligman et al., *Ritual*, 23.

togetherness about sin. Sin, corporately defined, is selfishness. Christian theology, and its description of human nature, sin, and free will, reminds us that we live in a broken, fallen world, one in which selfishness is rampant. Ritual, performed together in community, can repair the effects of selfishness by helping us see a new world filled with communities of empathy that will produce flourishing.

At the risk of getting lost in heady ideas, let's look at practical applications of corporate ritual. A ritual of corporate repentance, for example, can have the goal of repairing the brokenness one community has caused to others. We need the ritual of celebration to reinform our vision of flourishing. We need the ritual of creativity to inspire us to strive beyond what we think is possible to make the subjunctive become the realized world.

We see, then, how ritual is enhanced by togetherness. We also see how togetherness is amplified by ritual. The two are in a symbiotic, life-giving relationship. Religion, as it is often rife with ritual, helps provide togetherness, especially when many of us can feel lost or alone, though we live amid larger groups such as neighborhoods, schools, or business. When individuals connect themselves to a ritual community, they find meaning and togetherness.

The power of ritual community goes beyond simply survival in the world. By repeating a ritual, the goal is to look beyond to the expanding rule and reign of God's kingdom, which brings transformation to individuals and communities. Think about how this might work in parenting. Parents hope that a child's heart, by requiring them to say thank you, will be formed in such a way that their children become grateful. In other words, by expressing politeness, children become polite. By expressing thanks, they become grateful.

Similarly, the audible expression "I love you" can shape one's heart. What of the person who never says "I love you" but lives out that love, so that it is obvious that they love their beloved? Or what of the person who says "I love you" on a regular basis but does not live out that love, so it is obvious that they do not love their beloved. What then, does the ritual expression of "I love you" matter? The phrase "actions speak louder than words" holds true—that what is best is an active love rather than a verbal one.

Or put another way, ritual could still be viable if it is a ritual of active love, even without speaking any words. This is because ritual, rightly practiced, is aspirational, meaning that it desires the subjunctive, the world as it should be. When practiced by any community, ritual of word or deed has the potential for powerfully shaping the heart of a community. Imagine, then, the power for flourishing that occurs as ritual shapes the heart of a community.

A community practicing ritual together creates a temporary subjunctive world in the midst of the world as it is, so that when that community concludes the ritual and reenters the world as it is, the members of the community continue to live ritualistically in the world. They have been so shaped by ritual that they bring ritual with them, remaking the world as it is into a world of greater flourishing. Ritual holds great hope for the possibility of re-creation, thus we need to see ritual as a formative practice for any community that wants to pursue flourishing-producing togetherness.

Ritual also requires time. But what of John Wesley's teaching of instantaneous Christian perfection?[5] Also known as entire sanctification, Wesley believed Christians could receive a gift of God whereby God had instantaneously perfected them in this life. If Wesley was right, then people could experience flourishing quite fast. Though I respect Wesley's view and wish that he was correct, it seems best to understand the formation of the person as gradual. In the same way, ritual's formation of the community necessitates consistent determined practice over time. Just as a person needs time to gain a proficiency, say, to play a musical instrument, to speak a new language, or to successfully learn most any skill, a community needs repeated practice of ritual to be formed for flourishing.

Very similarly, in Christian theology, the concept of imitating Christ,[6] or in Paul's words, "follow my example, as I follow the example of Christ" (1 Cor 11:1), speaks of a time-consuming process. Ritual says that we become what we imitate, but only after the investment of much-repeated practice. Therefore, we should be life-long practitioners of Christ-like ritual if we want to be like Christ. This concept carries over to any community in that, if we want our community to promote flourishing, then our community should imitate flourishing, and we should do so again and again.

To imitate flourishing, our community should carry out a sustained practice of collaborative rituals that help us envision flourishing. That said, ritual in and of itself neither guarantees the creation of a subjunctive world nor the creation of flourishing in the real world. Years ago my congregation's worship committee discussed how often we should celebrate communion. For years we offered communion once per quarter. Worship theologian Robert Webber, in his book *Ancient-Future Worship*, makes the case that Christians should consider practicing the ritual of communion more frequently.[7] Webber and others suggest that communion is so vital, Christians should consider practicing it weekly. We were concerned some in our

---

5. Wesley, *Plain Account*.
6. See for example, the classic work of á Kempis, *Imitation of Christ*, 433–554.
7. Weber, *Ancient-Future Worship*, 147–48.

congregation might have a hard time with that frequency. This is precisely the claim that is made by people who balk at ritual recitation of the Lord's Prayer and the Apostle's Creed every week during worship services. "Empty ritual," they call it, specifically because it occurs so frequently. This can be a helpful caution, reminding us of the need for balance, because we want ritual to be meaningful and world-shaping. So we decided to have monthly communion.

The idea of imitation of Christ goes deeper than support for ritual practice. Rauschenbusch notes that "the [concern] of the social gospel is how the divine life of Christ can get control of human society."[8] One might read that as "Christianity must be in power," and that is neither what Rauschenbusch meant nor what God desires for his kingdom. While there have been many examples of disastrous Christian power grabs through the centuries, the rule and reign of the kingdom of God must be distinguished from human political power and government.

Therefore, we could say that Jesus' mystical practice fueled his approach to justice. Jesus spent vast quantities of time in solitude, communing with the Father, which was a decidedly individualistic practice. What makes Jesus' practice striking is the presence of massive crowds yearning for his attention. He had no shortage, together with his disciples, for opportunities of collaborative ministry to people who, it could be argued, desperately needed their help. Yet he would regularly leave the crowds—and his disciples—behind so that he could be alone.

A theology of togetherness, then, does not preclude the need for individual experiences, particularly those of a mystical nature. Rauschenbusch points to this when he writes that Jesus' "communion with God and his devotion to the kingdom of God set Jesus free and also bound him."[9] Jesus' practice of individual ritual set him free from the constraints of the straightjacket legalism of the religious community in first-century Palestinian Judaism, and yet ritual empowered Jesus for a life of loving sacrifice for his community and ultimately for the flourishing of the world. In turn this enabled him to create the very community this study envisions, a community of flourishing-producing togetherness guided by sustained ritual practice that advances the rule and reign of the kingdom of God.

As people practice ritual together, following the example of Jesus, they can also envision and embody Christian communities that transcend the ever-deepening political and racial divides in our country.

---

8. Rauschenbusch, *Social Gospel*, 148.
9. Rauschenbusch, *Social Gospel*, 159.

14

Purple Church
Practicing Togetherness to Bring Political Unity in the Church

ONCE PER QUARTER, I pause my sermon series and preach a current events sermon. On the Monday prior to the Sunday I am to preach the current events sermon, I scan through local, national, and international headlines seeking what people are talking about that could become the topic for the sermon. My goal is to bring biblical theology to bear on a topic that is currently affecting our lives, thus helping the congregation learn to think Christianly about the world around us.

Because I watch or read the news almost daily, when it came time for the summer 2021 current events sermon, before I searched the word "headlines" online, I was fairly certain that the main topics of the day were ones I had recently preached. Sure enough, I keyed in the search terms and the results confirmed what I suspected was true. The headlines that summer had been dominating the news nonstop for months: the COVID pandemic, partisan politics, racial injustice, and natural disasters. Even after narrowing my search to local news media, I found little that would work for the sermon.

I decided to ask four people who are not a part of my congregation what they thought I should talk about. I asked these four people specifically because their jobs put them in communication with a wide cross-section of the community. Thus, all four had a unique vantage point in our community, and I was hoping they might give me ideas about local issues. One is a detective in our township's police force. Next was the former principal of the elementary school my kids attended. Third is a local TV news reporter. Each of those three live in my community and have kids who attend my school district.

Finally, I asked my barber what he thought I should preach about. He quipped, "Tell 'em to come to the barber shop!" As my barber cut my hair, we discussed current events. I started to think he might have the most interesting conversations of the four. He admitted that a wide variety of people sit in his chair, giving him the opportunity to have fascinating discussions with numerous people.

Each of the four people responded with a variety of ideas, many of which were the familiar headlines I mentioned above. Some of their ideas were a bit more philosophical or theological, such as personal responsibility, sexual identity, and ethics. These are very important topics that certainly deserve theological treatment. As I reflected on their suggestions, however, a different thought formed in my mind. Perhaps my congregation needed to see the forest for the trees.

The four members of my local community gave me excellent ideas, each of which we could say is an individual tree, a singular issue in society. Though the people in my church family already have opinions about those issues, it would be helpful to examine what Scripture says about each one. Still, I thought it might be better to use a wide angle, trying to see the forest. What I mean is this: What are the larger societal or cultural forces that influence how we have already formed our opinions about those issues? We first need to examine those widely influential forces before we evaluate the singular issues. That led me to a sermon topic: Why We Are a Purple Church.

Before I explain the meaning of that topic, I need to back up nearly one year prior to November 2020, specifically the first Tuesday of November 2020, the date of the United States' presidential election. Earlier that year, as I was planning my upcoming preaching schedule, it seemed wise to preach one of the quarterly current events sermons the Sunday prior to what was shaping up to be a major political event. Of course, presidential elections are *always* major political events. Every fourth year the political parties and candidates claim that year's presidential election is the most consequential in American history, warning that we had better vote for them because the other party and candidate is destroying America.

Whether you roll your eyes at bold predictions like that or whether you believe them, we Americans have heard those apocalyptic sentiments every four years for our entire lives, and America is still here. Presidents come; presidents go. One party has a majority, then the other, and actual change in our country happens very incrementally. As a result, we can become jaded about our governmental system, with many Americans frustrated about voting for "the lesser of two evils," and many choosing not to vote at all.[1] Despite that, the 2020 election had a different tone, an intensity, a bitter rhetoric flowing from the ever-deepening political divide in our nation. For that November quarterly current events sermon, I knew I had to preach about the 2020 election. We were all thinking about it. But what should I preach about that politically divisive situation?

I was not going to preach a sermon telling people who to vote for. My wife, Michelle, and I talked about it, and she suggested that I preach on the "one another" statements in the New Testament.[2] The context of those "one another" statements is the relationships that people have in Christian communities, both inside and outside the church. Christians are called to treat one another with kindness, even if they disagree with one another's political views. In other words, my goal for the sermon was to help the congregation rise above partisan politics.

As I mentioned, I was intentionally *not* telling anyone how to vote, and I wasn't even trying to apply biblical principles to politics. I believe that biblical theology has a lot to say about politics and voting, but that was not what I was going for in that sermon. Instead my goal was to let biblical teaching guide our church family's interaction with one another and with others in our community.

We knew that some in our church family would be voting toward the red side, some toward the blue side, some for third parties, and some wouldn't vote at all. The point of the sermon was that we should love one another no matter what we do with our vote. We should express kindness and graciousness in our relationships, knowing that we disagree about politics and social issues. I thought I was preaching a fairly safe sermon. "Be kind; love one another." That's Togetherness 101. In the intensity of our political climate, however, there is almost no safe sermon, as I was soon to discover.

Later that week I received two emails from people that had heard the sermon. One email was from a family essentially saying my preaching was too theologically progressive, and they never came back. The other email was from another family saying my preaching was too theologically conservative, and they also never came back.

I reached out to both families, responding to their concerns, expressing that rather than focus on conservative or progressive ideology, I believe it is better by far to be part of a church family where we can disagree graciously and still love one another. It is better to practice the kind of solidarity

---

1. DeSilver notes that among developed nations, the United States' voter turnout in 2020, at 62.8 percent, was quite low. DeSilver, "Past Elections," para. 5.

2. See chapter 4, fn. 5.

embodied in flourishing-producing togetherness. In both cases, each of those families chose not to be together with our church family any longer.

Should they have practiced togetherness? Is there a biblical rationale that could have led each of those families to stay? I thought so in 2020, and that is what led to my summer 2021 sermon, titled "Why We Are A Purple Church." We are a culture that is so divided on so many issues. Does that mean the church has to divide too? Church and denominational splits are frequent in our nation's history. Some splits happen for justifiable reasons, some don't. The practice of splitting continues to this day. The Mennonite church broke apart in 2018.[3] The United Methodist Church has followed suit.[4]

We Christians don't seem to do very well at agreeing to disagree and remaining in fellowship. Instead we draw battle lines, and we go to war. How does our divisiveness mesh with what Jesus taught his disciples in John 17:11 on the night of the Last Supper, just before he was arrested in the garden? At that time he prayed to God his Father that his disciples and those who would become his followers in the years to come, would be "one as we are one." Just as the Trinity is three persons in community, Father, Son, and Spirit, but totally unified, Jesus wanted his disciples to practice unity and togetherness.

In other words, there can be different denominations, so long as they work together in unity.[5] I see this happening in my local ministerium. I see it happening within my own denomination, which includes both conservative pastors and churches and progressive pastors and churches. No doubt we disagree with one another and sometimes get really frustrated with one another, but we can still practice unity. Jesus' principle of oneness should also be very evident in any Christian community. We can be one as our three-personed Trinitarian God is one.

Therefore, the church I serve has intentionally tried to be a "purple" church, meaning that it is a place for the politically red (conservative) and blue (progressive) because we believe a church family's primary focus should be on God and the mission of his kingdom. Any Christian community is composed of many individuals who have varied political beliefs, and it is to be expected that we will disagree with each other about many of those beliefs. But we don't stop there.

---

3. Shellnut, "Biggest Mennonite Conference."

4. Adams, "New Denomination."

5. Armstrong makes a strong case for what he calls "the missional-ecumenical church," in which Christians lay down divisions to work together. Armstrong, *Church Too Small*, 153.

Together we make it very clear that our passion and our allegiance is not to a political ideology or to a nation; our allegiance is to Christ our King and to his Spirit who lives within each of us and who enlivens us to be unified. We hold to the ideal and pattern of togetherness, and then we choose the actions of loving and respecting one another as brothers and sisters in Christ. In short, though not perfectly, we strive to practice flourishing-producing togetherness.

What that has meant for Faith Church is that some people in our community who strongly believe church should be red think we're too blue, and the people who strongly believe church should be blue think we're too red. That leaves a group of people who believe that church should be purple, no matter which side they personally lean toward.

This is not just a Faith Church issue. Similar sentiments are reflected in many Christian communities nationwide. In the last thirty years we have seen what some social scientist researchers are calling a sorting.[6] Thirty years ago the nation was very similar to what it is today in that there were people who believed in red or conservative political ideology and there were people who believed in blue or progressive ideology. What is different is that thirty years ago the two sides were more enmeshed, more willing to interact with others of the opposing view. They were part of a large middle of people who might lean one way or the other but had moderate views that overlapped significantly. Yes, there were people on the extremes, on the poles, but those on the extremes were a relatively small group.

As the years went by, however, more and more people in our country started drifting ideologically to the poles. Those at the extreme right and those at the extreme left saw their numbers swell, while the moderate middle slowly shrank.[7] Now thirty years later, we see polarization on the news every day. Political views at the poles have become more extreme. That "middle listening" space within politics, within the media, and within the average person is barely discernible.[8]

From the perspective of the poles, everyone else, including those in the middle, seem so distant, so different, and most damaging and divisive of all, they seem wrong, even evil. If you are standing at the poles, you can hear a

---

6. See for example, Dalrymple, "Splintering," para. 26; Dreher, "Great Christian Sorting," para. 13; Graham and Flowers, "Six Way Fracturing," para. 12.

7. Pew, "Political Polarization," para. 2.

8. "An overwhelming majority (86 percent) of Americans say conflicts between Democrats and Republicans are either strong or very strong, according to a new Pew Research Center survey. By comparison, 65 percent of Americans see strong or very strong conflicts between blacks and whites, and 60 percent see them between the rich and the poor." Gramlich, "Strong Conflict," para 2.

sermon about being kind to one another, loving one another, and you can think "I need to leave this place!"

Across the country, then, churches are becoming less and less purple, and more and more blue or red. If we are to practice the flourishing-producing togetherness that Jesus prayed for that night before he was arrested, we need to be a purple church. In a polarized culture we need to be ready for the probability that people, including many Christians who believe they are holding to what some call a biblical worldview, will see the idea of a purple church as wrong. We're too blue for the reds and we're too red for the blues.

We press on, though, because the church is not blue or red and because the church is not a political party. The church is not American. The church of Jesus is global. The church is focused on the mission of the kingdom of God; it thus cannot not fit into any political party. That's why I'm calling it purple church.

Lancaster County, Pennsylvania, where I live, is an interesting example of how political ideology affects the church. Though it has a slowly growing blue side, Lancaster County is majority red, while Lancaster City is majority blue.[9] Many suburban/rural and urban communities across our nation follow a similar pattern.[10] Simple math tells us that if a church wants to attract people, that church should either become a whole lot redder or a whole lot bluer depending on where they are located. My church is in a red suburban/rural area, so if we want to reach people, the math tells us we should be a red church.

What do the teachings of Jesus and the other New Testament writers tell us? As we learned in previous chapters, we are to be kingdom minded. We are to practice flourishing-producing togetherness and, in the realm of political ideology, that means Christian communities will be purple. What the apostle Paul writes in Gal 3 will help us understand how to practice flourishing-producing togetherness in a culture where Christians seem to allow political ideology to take precedence over biblical theology.

In Gal 3:26 Paul writes, "In Christ Jesus you are all children of God through faith." Being a son and daughter of God is an astounding thought. Humans can become members of the family of God. This is one reason why some Christian communities call themselves families. We need to remember, however, that God's family is international. It is diverse. It cannot be contained by a local church or denomination, and it cannot be contained by any political party. The family of God includes all who have genuine faith in Christ Jesus.

---

9. Walker, "Lancaster County," para. 4.
10. Liu and Berube, "Big Cities," para. 1.

Paul continues this familial thought in v. 27, when he writes that baptism is the symbol of entrance into the family. When we are baptized, we are practicing a ritual symbol of new birth. The old you dips under the water, figuratively following the pattern of Jesus' death, and the new you rises out of the water, figuratively following the pattern of Jesus' resurrection. No matter which mode of baptism a Christian community practices, the symbolism is that of rebirth, new life, resurrection, and cleansing. Baptism depicts the reality that a person has entered a new family, God's family.

Additionally, Paul writes, when you enter God's family, God gives you new clothes. Paul clarifies in v. 27 that Christians are people clothed with Christ. We are not given Jesus' clothes. We are given Jesus *himself* as our clothing. This surprising wardrobe change occurs through the gift of the Holy Spirit living with us. Notice, then, who is clothed with Christ.

Look over Gal 3:26–29, seeking the repeated words in each verse. Other than the name "Christ" or "Christ Jesus," the repeated word is "all." Paul's point is to say that *all* who believe are now sons and daughters of the king. *All* who are baptized are baptized into Christ, and *all* receive Christ as their clothing. Then he writes in v. 28, *all* are one in Christ Jesus, which is his main point. When it comes to the family of God, the many categories of the human experience find unity in Christ. Paul mentions three of these categories: ethnicity, class, and gender.

First, all ethnicities are equally valued in God's eyes. Because God loves all, we follow his lead and we view all humanity equally. Interestingly, the Human Genome Project, twenty-five years ago, proved this from a scientific perspective.[11] Race, from a DNA perspective, must be seen as a social construct. Humans are humans, biologically speaking. Any person from any ethnicity has the same blood, the same DNA. Because humans, both inside and outside Christian communities see race as a reality via the social construct, we would do well explore how flourishing-producing togetherness can help bridge racial division. We will explore how flourishing-producing togetherness addresses race in chapter 18.

But maybe Paul, in writing that "there is neither Jew nor Gentile" (v. 28) means that God wants those of us in Christian communities to ignore ethnicity and race? We can answer that question with an unmitigated negative. God created the many varieties of human appearance, and we need to see racial and ethnic variance as good. Along with affirming the biological research that there is one human race, we can appreciate ethnic variations in skin color, hair, height, build, eyes, and all our other human differences as a

---

11. All human beings are 99.9 percent identical in their genetic makeup. See National Human Genome Research Institute, "Genetics vs. Genomics Fact Sheet," para 6.

beautiful diversity. We celebrate our ethnic differences not by ignoring them but by pointing out that God made each and every one. It was the Creator's artistic design—all made in his image (Gen 1:26–27).

So am I saying that Paul is wrong when he says that there is neither Jew nor gentile? No, the key point Paul makes when he says that in Christ there is neither Jew nor gentile is that we're all equally loved and valued in God's eyes, no matter how different we look. A purple church celebrates and includes diversity. Churches that practice flourishing-producing togetherness embrace all ethnicities. But Paul is not done describing the kind of togetherness Christians are to practice.

Second, the next phrase Paul uses to describe the purple church is that it is neither slave nor free. Slavery was a massive institution in the Greco-Roman Empire.[12] Slavery, therefore, affected nearly every local Christian community in the Roman Empire. In those church communities, Paul writes in his Letter to Philemon, slaves were becoming Christians, as were their owners. What then? Paul teaches Philemon and here in Galatians that because class distinction in God's eyes is false, so Christian communities must treat class distinction likewise. There is no social distinction in Christ, as if some people are lower and others are higher. We are all equally loved and valued in God's eyes, no matter what social class the world creates and uses to try to segment and divide us.

Are you upper class, lower class, or middle class? Class should not matter in a church family because we are all one in Christ. This is one reason I love how Faith Church traditionally celebrates communion, with rows of people kneeling together at the communion rail, taking the elements in unison, as a visual reminder that before Christ we are the same.[13]

In the USA, our class system is primarily economic, with upper class, middle class, and lower class distinguished by income. But in Christian communities, we should not abide by the class system.[14] We read in the

---

12. "Despite the inadequacy of evidence, some scholars estimate that in urban areas of Roman imperial society slaves made up one-third of the population, but others place the figure lower, within the range of 16.6 to 20 percent." Harrill, "Slavery," 1126.

13. Paul seems to address unchecked classism when the Corinthian Christian community gathered to observe the ritual of communion, such that, at their love feasts, the rich had their fill, while the poor remained hungry (1 Cor 11:17–34). See also Jude 12 and 2 Pet 2:13, which describe the communion meal as a love feast, during which, ironically, some could be unloving. What was meant to be a ritual of togetherness could turn into that which divided the church. McGowan writes that Paul's intention in 1 Cor 11 was "to shame a divided community at Corinth with the example of Jesus' humility and self-offering (vv. 27–30)." McGowan, *Ancient Christian Worship*, 33.

14. James writes that there should be no favoritism in Christian communities based on economic class (Jas 2:17).

book of Acts how some in the earliest Christian community in Jerusalem who owned extra properties and possessions sold them to help those in the church in need. ("All the believers were one in heart and mind. No one claimed that any of their possessions was their own, but they shared everything they had," Acts 4:32; see also 2:42–47, 4:33–37.) In a purple church, all social distinctions disappear into one family.

The third and final phrase Paul uses to describe the purple church in Gal 3:26–28 continues this theme of flourishing-producing togetherness when he writes that "nor is there male and female . . . in Christ" (v. 28). Paul's comment could be construed as curious because we can look around and see the males and females among us. Biology makes it obvious. What, then, is Paul talking about when he says in Christ there is neither male nor female?

Is Paul suggesting that when our bodies are resurrected, they become androgynous? Certainly not, as the difference between genders, like the difference between ethnicities, is rooted in God's creative goodness. Both maleness and femaleness are wonderful in God's eyes, and yet society is bent on emphasizing the distinctions between the genders,[15] often to the detriment of women.[16] This is equally true in Christian communities, despite the biblical teaching about gender equality.[17] Just because there are differences between the two genders doesn't mean that one is better or worse, no matter how much society tries to tell us that. What Paul states clearly is that we are equally loved by God, and thus James writes that in Christian communities men and women should forge "a Blessed Alliance that would become

---

15. See for example Kristof and WuDunn, *Half the Sky*.

16. Gebara provides a helpful corrective, noting that "gender is not just the biological fact of being a man or a woman: gender is a social construct, a way of being in the world—a way of being educated and also a way of being perceived—that conditions our existence and action." As a result, she notes that these constructs can lead to the subordination of some people to others. She also warns that "theology has been complicit in accentuating the inferiority of women." Gebara, *Out of the Depths*, 63.

17. Lederleitner, in her award-winning book *Women in God's Mission*, interviews women in ministry across the globe. One North American leader, Jacqueline, remarked that, unlike men who are often assumed to have credibility in ministry, "women are given their job, and then they have to prove their credibility. Earning credibility for women is hard, and they can lose it very quickly." Lederleitner, *Women in God's Mission*, 9; see also 24–25. Lederleitner explains that for women to experience flourishing-producing togetherness in leadership in Christian communities, they can pursue becoming what she terms "the Faithful Connected Leader." Lederleitner, *Women in God's Mission*, 53. See also ch. 5, Lederleitner, *Women in God's Mission*, 69–86.

an unstoppable force for good in the world,"[18] one that "results in mutual flourishing."[19]

When it comes to ethnic, social, and gender distinctions, then, all Christians are one in Christ. This equality and communality in Christ are essential principles that undergird Christian communities of all kinds in their pursuit of flourishing-producing togetherness, especially in a culture that emphasizes distinctions between people. Paul chose three category distinctions that were very much hot topics in his day—as he would, because he is writing to people in his day. We strive to apply Paul's principle of togetherness to the category distinctions that are prevalent in our day.

How, then, do we apply this principle of togetherness to our contemporary situation? What is dividing Christian communities across America? Many factors, of course, as we have already seen how Paul's teaching about ethnicity, gender, and class is applicable today, but another reality that seems divisive, at least in the USA, is political ideology. There is red and there is blue, conservative and progressive. We often allow our political ideology to color how we view a great many things: racial justice, sexual ethics, economics, and foreign policy, to name a few.

Christian communities, then, to express oneness in Christ and that all are equally loved by God, should be neither red nor blue. They should be communities of which it can be said, "There is neither red nor blue, but all are one in Christ. There is neither Republican nor Democrat, but all are one in Christ. There is neither conservative nor progressive, but all are one in Christ." In Christian communities red and blue can mix. Purple church is a figurative way of remembering that no political party or nation can lay claim to Jesus.[20] His kingdom does not fit into those boxes. Purple church is a way of depicting flourishing-producing togetherness in the political realm.

As we learned in chapter 9, Christian communities of all kinds are to train their focus and passion on the kingdom of God. As a result, biblical teaching will line up on different sides of the current American political

---

18. James, *Half the Church*, 137.

19. James, *Half the Church*, 148.

20. Some go so far as to say that the Bible, and therefore the church, is not political, and thus Christian communities should remain outside of politics. These Christians abstain from voting and from participating in political office or process. N. T. Wright begs to differ however, noting that "the New Testament is a wonderfully, gloriously rich political book. Read the Book of Acts. Paul and the others are always telling the magistrates they are getting things wrong." Wright, quoted in Green, "Crisis," para 25. Mennonite theologian Yoder writes that "Jesus is, according to the biblical witness, a model of radical political action." Yoder, *Politics of Jesus*, 2. Progressive evangelical theologian Jim Wallis suggests that "the politics of God calls all the rest of our politics into question." Wallis, *God's Politics*, 32.

aisle. Yet no one side should claim they have the right ideology for all issues. Instead, our focus remains squarely on the kingdom of God, as Jesus once taught, "Seek first his kingdom" (Matt 6:33). Let us not focus on being "red" or being "blue." Let our focus be one other phrase that Jesus taught his disciples: "By this everyone will know that you are my disciples, if you love one another" (John 13:34–35), even when we see things differently. Christians who practice flourishing-producing togetherness will love one another no matter their political ideology.

Why, then, have so many Christians chosen differently? Why did people hear my November 2020 sermon about loving one another and respond by leaving the church?[21] Given their feedback about progressivism and conservatism in my preaching, it is possible that they placed political ideology above their commitment to flourishing-producing togetherness.[22] What should Christians do when we see things differently from one another? Some of the people that left Faith Church did so because of their viewpoint about one of the most divisive social and political issues of our day: sexual ethics.

A few years ago I listened to a podcast about sexual ethics that seemed to demonstrate this divisiveness.[23] The speaker is a Christian, and they proclaimed that if your church doesn't agree with your view of sexual ethics, then you have three options: (1) stay at the church and say nothing about your disagreement; just be quiet, don't rock the boat, but know that if you choose option 1 then you are a coward and wrong; (2) stay at the church but express your disagreement and work to change the church; (3) leave the church to find a church that agrees with you.

I find difficulties in each of those options. Let's examine each one, and then I will propose an option of my own, in which I attempt to apply flourishing-producing togetherness. I start by examining the two options I believe we can disagree with.

Option 1: Just stay quiet. I think the podcast host is correct to disagree with this option. The biblical writers consistently teach us to lovingly express ourselves, sharing differing ideas and opinions with humility and grace, while at the same time practicing quiet listening. Some people are simply too quick to speak. James 1:19 says, "Be quick to listen, slow to speak

---

21. People have a variety of reasons for leaving a church, of course. As cultural sociologist Penny Becker's study reveals, church conflict and its results must be seen as complex. Becker, *Congregations in Conflict.*

22. Journalists Ruth Graham and Elizabeth Dias reported that "many believers are importing their worship of God, with all its intensity, emotion and ambitions, to their political life." Dias and Graham, "Growing Religious Fervor," para. 5.

23. Doyle, "Queer Freedom."

and slow to become angry." But even if we are slow to speak, as the writer of Ecclesiastes taught with his ancient wisdom, there is "a time to be silent and a time to speak" (3:7). So I mostly agree with the podcaster that option number 1 doesn't fit with biblical teaching. We can and should speak the truth in love (see also Eph 4:15).

Option 3: Leave. As of this writing, my wife and I are in our twenty-second year in pastoral ministry at Faith Church, and option 3, in our experience, is what most people do when they are struggling in their relationship with a church family. They just leave. They disagree with something, and rather than choose to stay and speak and work through a situation, they leave.

This is in large part what is occurring in the sorting between red and blue in our culture. Red or conservative-leaning people are leaving churches they feel are blue or purple, and blue or progressive-leaning people are leaving churches they feel are red or purple. I almost always disagree with this option. You might ask, "But doesn't there come a time when a person should leave a church?" Yes. If heresy is being preached. If sin is not being dealt with. If the mission of God is not being pursued. But, in my view, those conditions occur in churches exceedingly rarely. Why, then, are people sometimes quick to leave a church?

When people leave a church, often it is because they believe their personal preferences aren't being met. In leaving for personal preferences, like red or blue political ideology, they are practicing a consumer Christianity, which is something that very few Christians in other countries can practice. Consumer Christianity is a significant problem in American Christianity.[24] Many Christians around the world do not have the option to engage in that type of consumerism within their community. In many locales, there is one church family to join with and that's it. Participants in that church must make community work, no matter their differences of opinion.

Across most of the USA, however, what is true in communities such as Lancaster County, where I live, with our plethora of churches, is that people can choose to align their political ideology with biblical teaching. If a particular church doesn't agree with their political views, they accuse

---

24. Sociologist Peter Mundey writes about this when he describes the goal of his recent book *Sacred Consumption: The Religions of Christianity and Consumerism in America*: "I explore how modern American Christians do consume (or claim to consume) and interpret the relationship between their Christian faith and what is, in many cases, their other faith: consumerism. In doing so, I answer questions like: What, if anything, do American Christians believe material possessions, managing money, and shopping have to do with their faith? And why is it the case that although Jesus told his followers, 'You cannot serve both God and money,' many of his disciples end up doing precisely that?" Mundey, *Sacred Consumption*, 3.

that church of practicing heresy and they leave. The red-leaning people look for a red-leaning church and blue-leaning people look for a blue-leaning church. It is astounding to me how quick people are to leave a church and how often they leave without saying much about the thoughts and feelings that led them to leave.

What does Jesus say to those who would leave? Christ bids us come and die to ourselves, to give sacrificially of ourselves for his kingdom (Luke 9:23–26). Does Jesus mean that, in order to preserve unity in Christian communities, we should abandon our personal political opinions if they differ from others in the church community? No, but Jesus also does not mean that we should only work for the kingdom and worship alongside those who believe in and value the same things in the same way as we do. We are called to unity, not uniformity. In Christ, there is neither red nor blue.

What should you do when you disagree with your church, or with the people in your church? To summarize, the podcast episode listed three options: (1) stay, but don't speak up; (2) stay and work for change; (3) leave. Simply put, I think both 1 and 3 are mostly poor choices. In the Christian community, we should speak the truth in love (Eph 4:15), thus voiding option 1. We are also people who, as much as possible, remain as we are (1 Cor 7:20–26), thus voiding option 3. Therefore, I want to attempt an evaluation of option 2 and then propose a new option.

Option 2: Stay and work for a change. Option 2 suggests that when you are frustrated with your Christian community, stay and work for change. That option, I submit, is far better than options 1 or 3. But does the idea of "staying and working for change" align with what Paul is teaching in Gal 3? Option number 2 presumes that something is broken, that the person who disagrees has the right answer to fix what is broken, and they must tirelessly work to change it because everyone else is wrong and they are right. Because of those presumptions, option 2 has some difficulties.

First of all, there is a potential arrogance in that kind of thinking. Note that I say *potential*. It could be that the disagreeing person is right, and those they disagree with are truly wrong. Even if so, the disagreeing person should take great pains to avoid arrogance and pride in how they interact. Even when we are convinced we are right, we should still hold out the possibility that we could be wrong, that we could yet learn from the other perspective, that maybe we don't have it all figured out.

Second, consider the toll it can take to bring change within a Christian community. I have been a part of my church for more than twenty years, admittedly seeking to be a change agent in my role as pastor. What I have noticed is that if the change one is looking for doesn't come quickly, or if the change agent feels they are not being taken seriously, working for change becomes tiresome. How long do you keep pursuing change when change doesn't seem to be occurring? How long can you do so with grace, love, peace, joy, and the other fruit of the Spirit? (Gal 5:22–23). The labor of working for change, though valuable, can feel hopeless, and what often happens is that people become exasperated, give up working for change, and believe their only viable option is to leave their community. My conclusion, therefore, is that option 2, to stay and work for change, is mostly right, but because it is often so difficult, we need another option.

Option 4: Beginning and ending with union in Christ. I propose a new option that the people in the podcast didn't talk about, an option that I think is more faithful to what Paul talks about in Gal 3, that all are one in Christ. Paul's vision is for a Christian community including many kinds of people, who are together, not agreeing about everything—even disagreeing about seemingly important things—all while remaining in loving relationships with one another. How is my option 4 different from option 2? Maybe it could be said that my option 4 is a variation of option 2, in that it puts love, agreement, and unity as the focus, rather than working for change.

Christian communities must self-identify as people who are unified in Christ. This is what Paul was getting at when he wrote, "Be completely humble and gentle; be patient, bearing with one another in love. Make every effort to keep the unity of the Spirit through the bond of peace. There is one body and one Spirit, just as you were called to one hope when you were called; one Lord, one faith, one baptism; one God and Father of all, who is over all and through all and in all" (Eph 4:2–6).

When it comes to the ideologies of red and blue politics, then, Christian communities should focus on being kingdom-minded, by practicing flourishing-producing togetherness. The kingdom does not fit into any human political party. Especially in America with our two-party system, we Christians should see our Christian communities as purple. We can be red-leaning people who love blue-leaning people. We can be blue-leaning people who love red-leaning people. We can talk about why we are red-leaning or blue-leaning, and we can disagree with one another, but we do so in a gracious, loving way that keeps Christ as our center. Red and blue will pass away. *Purple* will pass away, because God's kingdom is not based on and does not fit within any American political party. But the kingdom of Jesus will remain.

My evaluation of my own congregation, Faith Church, is that while we do not do this perfectly, I think we do it well. Over the years, in many conversations with people in the church family, I've discovered that there is a wide range of views on all sorts of topics. Evaluate your own community. I suspect that your Christian community is very similar. Though the presence of disagreement in your community could be the perfect storm for divisiveness, I urge you to keep working at a loving willingness to agree to disagree. Grow even deeper at letting Christ be your common focus.

Can Christ be our common focus when we have deeply held differences? I mentioned that the podcast above is about sexual ethics. Can people who hold to a traditional sexual ethic and people who hold to an open and affirming ethic experience flourishing-producing togetherness while maintaining their differing viewpoints about sexual ethics? I believe we can.[25]

About ten years ago a gay man visited my congregation, and after the first worship service, he contacted me to let me know that he is a gay Christian, open and affirming, though not currently dating. My denomination, the Evangelical Congregational Church holds to a traditional sexual ethic—namely, that sexual expression should be contained to marriage between one man and one woman. I deeply appreciated his authenticity, and I tried to share the same with him, letting him know that he is welcome in our church family.

Over the course of the next three years, there were multiple times when I thought for sure he would leave the church. One was after a men's group where some of the men were sharing their negative opinions about open and affirming sexual ethics. Another was during a sermon series through 1 Corinthians,[26] during which I tried to walk a fine line between holding to a traditional sexual ethic but doing so with sensitivity and love. During these instances and others, my friend never left the church. Instead he got more involved, and people reached out to him, welcoming him.

At the same time, though, somewhat unbeknownst to me, he was really struggling. He talked about his struggles with his therapist, and the therapist strongly suggested that my friend leave the church. At issue was that our denomination's doctrine disagreed with his core identity as a gay man. My friend's therapist believed this disagreement was negatively affecting my friend's mental well-being; my friend agreed and he left the church.

When he came to talk with me about this decision, I was saddened and asked him, "Did anyone harm you or mistreat you?" He responded no. So I asked if he felt loved in our church family and he said yes. I was disheartened. If he was not mistreated and he felt loved, why did he have to leave? I

---

25. An excellent example of Christians who differ in their view of sexual ethics but who work together to produce a thoughtful guide for navigating the way forward in unity is the compilation volume *Two Views on Homosexuality, the Bible, and the Church*. In the volume, four theologians and biblical scholars have a conversation that includes responses and rejoinder, in a civil tone, from each side of the debate, the traditional view and the affirming view. DeFranza et al., *Two Views on Homosexuality*.

26. Kime, "1 Corinthians 6:9–11."

felt he should stay, yet I do not know what it feels like to try to be part of a church family whose theology disagrees with my core identity. We hugged and parted amicably.

About six months later, he reached out to me saying that he had recently attended a conference on Christianity and homosexuality. There he met gay Christians who hold to the traditional view, such that Christians who are attracted to the same gender should practice abstinence. My friend and I had previously talked about Wesley Hill's work on the abstinence view,[27] but until that conference my friend believed that the traditional view was unnecessary at best and incorrect at worst. After having met fulfilled gay Christians who practice abstinence, he had a new appreciation for that view. Still he did not return to our church family.

When it comes to Christians and sexuality, we can implement the principle of unity described by the flourishing-producing togetherness of the purple church. Richard Beck writes about the difference between zero sum and non-zero sum approaches.[28] A zero sum approach refers to a game that has a winner and a loser. A non-zero sum game can have a variety of outcomes. Christian communities desiring to be purple can practice a non-zero sum approach to the sharp divide in our culture around politics and sexual ethics. Beck suggests that "the game isn't zero-sum; it's non-zero-sum. Fighting doesn't have to be the only thing we have in common. There are significant areas of mutual concern, locations where we can drop our fists and partner together on important Kingdom work."[29]

For example, one of my Christian friends recently made a post on his social media account, using the guise of humor, to disparage transgender persons who made the news in the past year. Another Christian friend quickly and lovingly confronted the person who posted the disparaging comment, noting that transgender persons have some of the highest rates of suicidal ideation[30] and that Christians should not deepen the problem. Instead, Beck writes, Christians should provide loving protection for all, even those we disagree with.

Christians are all clothed with Christ, as Paul wrote in Gal 3:26–28, and that clothing is what we should see as we view one another. We should not make red or blue clothing our banner. The idea that a Christian community

---

27. Hill, *Washed and Waiting*; Hill, *Spiritual Friendship*. For another viewpoint see Rivera, *Heavy Burdens*.

28. Beck, "Non-Zero Sum."

29. Beck, "Non-Zero Sum," para. 14.

30. Austin et al. write that "82% of transgender individuals have considered killing themselves and 40% have attempted suicide, with suicidality highest among transgender youth." Austin et al., "Suicidality."

isn't conservative enough or progressive enough, so a person must leave it, is opposed to the flourishing-producing togetherness that God desires for his people. Let the peace of Christ rule. Be kingdom-minded. Sort all ideas and values through the values of the kingdom, not through any one political party. Continue to love each other. Continue to worship together. Keep working toward bringing more of heaven here to earth side by side with those who may see things from a different perspective. Simply put, flourishing-producing togetherness guides us to be purple.[31]

It is possible to find common ground, even when a group has significant political diversity. Researchers have found that people can practice "purple" habits such as the following: (1) intentionally discussing politics with those you disagree with, specifically doing so with a motivation to learn; and (2) strive to get along with people in your community with whom you disagree.[32] In other words, flourishing-producing togetherness emphasizes engaging our differences rather than avoiding them.

When we pursue practices of seeking unity above political ideology, those practices will help Christian communities create what some have called "Beloved Community,"[33] thus overcoming the second major division in many communities, race. In the next chapter, we explore how flourishing-producing togetherness can lead to the creation of beloved community, bridging the racial divide in Christian communities.

---

31. For a similar argument using the image of a salad bowl, see McKnight, *Fellowship of Differents*, 14–25.

32. Overgaard and Masullo, "Finding Common Ground," para. 2.

33. Where did the idea of the "Beloved Community" originate? It turns out that Josiah Royce, a philosophy professor at Harvard, developed the idea. See Pollack, "Idea," para. 2.

15

Beloved Community
Practicing Togetherness to Bring Racial Unity in the Church

THE NEARLY ONE HUNDRED people of Faith Church, where I pastor, represent a wide variety in demographics of gender, age, socioeconomics, and political and theological viewpoints. But attend a regular Sunday morning worship service of Faith Church and one will easily see that we are not ethnically diverse. Stated statistically, Faith Church is about 90 percent white. Our local school district, however, is only 52 percent white.[1] In other words, Faith Church's ethnic diversity is not reflective of its local community.

Over the years we've had persons of color attend our congregation's worship services, but few have decided to become a part of our church family. I have been at Faith Church nearly twenty years, and this ethnic disparity has always been the case. In fact, during those years, Faith Church's percentage of diversity has not kept pace with our community's growing rate of diversity.

I have often wondered why Faith Church, in terms of ethnic diversity, does not resemble our community. We say that we welcome all people into our fellowship, and this is a genuine assertion. While we are not perfectly welcoming and loving, I have seen time and time again how people are warmly welcomed. Yet people of color either do not step through our doors,

---

1. This figure represents data from the 2024–25 school year. Conestoga Valley School District, "At a Glance," see sidebar.

or if they do visit, they have rarely stayed, even after we have welcomed them.

There are African American churches located nearby in the city of Lancaster, as well as Hispanic churches in our school district, so perhaps Christian people of color from our community attend those congregations. In recent years Faith Church has rented our space to an Ethiopian Church, a Burmese (Myanmar) Church, a Haitian Church, a Honduran Church, and a Hispanic Church. We value each wonderful partnership within Christian communities of color, but the family of Faith Church has remained majority white. For years I have been curious about Christian ethnic disparity, because it seems to represent a serious failure of American Christianity. How can we have flourishing-producing togetherness if we remain ethnically segregated?

On January 1, 2018, I went on sabbatical. With more time on my hands and being a lover of podcasts, I searched online for high-rated podcasts, and the search returned results including the *Scene on Radio* podcast series *Seeing White*.[2] I eagerly listened as I washed dishes, split wood, and drove in my car.

Episode after episode slowly opened my blind eyes to a reality I had not known: *Seeing White* helped me see my whiteness, perhaps for the first time. Because I had for years wondered why people of color rarely attend Faith Church, the question of why was already on my heart and mind. *Seeing White* confronted me with historical evidence and contemporary viewpoints that started forming an answer to my question. As the series continued, I realized I was operating on some false assumptions about Faith Church.

First, I wrongly assumed Faith Church was neutral when it comes to ethnicity. Sure our congregation is mostly white, but from a theological, philosophical, and anthropological perspective, we are not racist or white supremacist, at least not in the overt sense. Instead we believe that we are a church for all people of any color. Yet, I remember listening to *Seeing White* in my car, when the idea first occurred to me: Faith Church is *not* neutral; we are *white*. Just as I was so accustomed to labeling African American churches as "black" and Latino churches as "Hispanic" because of their unique ethnic features, I should likewise label Faith Church as "white" because of our unique ethnic features.

For example, as pastor, I am not only ethnically white, but I preach in a typically white style. I have been educated by white professors and mentors

---

2. For other stories of white evangelicals describing having their eyes opened to racism in the church, see Wilson-Hartgrove, *Reconstructing the Gospel*, 41–56, 107–119; Vroegop, *Weep With Me*, 31–32; Welch et al., *Plantation Jesus*.

who required me to read and study books by white theologians and biblical scholars, from whom I learned to think and minister in historically white ways. In Faith Church's worship services, we sing songs written by white people using a style of music white people generally enjoy. Also our congregation is organized by principles and bylaws that are in keeping with a traditionally white expressions of Christianity. We have a history of nothing but white thinking, perspective, and practice.[3]

As a result of this realization, the idea dawned on me that it made sense why people of color might not attend or come back to Faith Church after one visit. If people are looking for a truly multicultural, neutral church, we are not it. We are not fertile ground for racial flourishing-producing togetherness because of our whiteness.[4] Writing in 1970, Christian scholars Columbus Salley and Ronald Behm suggested that "the inability of the white Christian church to demonstrate values which oppose racist forces has canceled the church as a viable force in aiding black people (and others) in their quest for survival."[5] Fifty years later, has the relationships between the black, Hispanic, or Asian churches and the white church improved? Has the white church taken initiative?

One family of color who has stayed with Faith Church for about the last ten years is Egyptian, and they have had to sacrifice their culture to participate in ours. They could, and sometimes do, attend an Egyptian Christian fellowship that meets locally in Lancaster, but they have persisted in participating in our white congregation. Faith Church has made no cultural accommodation to them, and all the while they have acclimated to us. To

---

3. Admittedly, the definition of whiteness I have described here is not anthropological or sociological. Instead it is based on my anecdotal experience as a white person in a majority white culture. For a beginning study of what whiteness is, I suggest the podcast I mentioned above, *Seeing White*. When my wife and I lived for a year in Kingston, Jamaica, we experienced our whiteness in a new way, as the minority. I'll never forget the first time a Jamaican man on the street called out to me, "Hey whitey!" Immediately, I felt a hot flash of irritation rise up in me, assuming he was being rude or disrespectful to me. My emotion interpreted the situation incorrectly, though, as the man was getting my attention using a cultural norm. As the weeks and months passed, while it didn't occur all that often, I started to get used to being called by my skin color. The reality, though, for nearly all whites in Jamaica is that our skin color indicated not only that we were part of the minority but also that we were part of the wealthy minority. In Jamaica, as in much of the rest of the world, white meant power and privilege. But it took living in Jamaica for me to begin to see it.

4. I am grateful to my dissertation reader, A. Brian Leander, who wrote, "When people of color walk into a Sunday morning service at a majority White church do they see evidence of togetherness and flourishing to encourage them that they will receive the same benefits?" Leander, pers. comm., Jan. 2021.

5. Salley and Behm, *Too White*, 102–3.

summarize, we are white through and through, and though unstated, it is assumed that all people of color will assimilate to our whiteness if they are to become part of the family of Faith Church.

Second, as I mentioned above, Faith Church assumes that our theological and philosophical perspective is neutral, biblical even, and that we are not racist. As I listened to *Seeing White*, this assumption, too, began to fall apart. Northern white evangelical Christians, though we have a much longer history of abolition and societal integration than our southern American Christian brothers and sisters, we are complicit in racism and white supremacy as well.

While northern states, historically, did not participate in slavery, lynching, or segregation to the degree of southern states, we did all those things, and we have been racist in many subtle ways. We have been silent. We have held tightly to our positions of power and privilege, watching our neighbors, who are people of color, suffer. In the north we have been aghast at the racist conflicts around our country in recent years, as if we are witnessing something that had been dealt with decades ago.

All we need to do is look around our sanctuaries on Sunday mornings, and we should have known better. Martin Luther King Jr. said in 1968, "We must face the sad fact that at eleven o'clock on Sunday morning when we stand to sing 'In Christ There Is No East or West,' we stand in the most segregated hour of America."[6] Fifty-four years later, this situation has not changed, even in the north. Our worship services show us that we have a problem. We are not together, and as a result we have severely hampered our ability to experience the flourishing God desires.

In this chapter, therefore, I endeavor to uncover reasons why some northern American Christian churches are less diverse than their surrounding communities in which they are located, providing some suggestions for congregations that want to pursue greater inclusivity and diversity, which are crucial for flourishing-producing togetherness. We will see that a prophetic approach to church leadership, one that creates an alternative beloved community which engages in persistent conversations and leads to Christlike divestiture, is the beginning step for white churches to move toward more diversity and inclusion of people of color required for flourishing-producing togetherness.

---

6. King, "Visit to Cornell College," para. 20.

EXAMINING ASSUMPTIONS

My claim assumes that church families or congregations should be composed of a multiethnic demographic that approximates the ethnic diversity of the community in which the church is located. Because that is a value judgment, it is admittedly subjective and thus must find grounding in some kind of ethical framework. Christian ethics finds that grounding in Scripture, and thus it will be necessary to discover what the biblical text says about ethnic diversity in the church. We will turn to that biblical study after surveying further assumptions. There is admittedly an aspirational nature in this assumption, driving us to seek biblical depictions of diversity in the church and thus helping us envision what a multiethnic togetherness could look like.

Next, my claim assumes that while our American society has eradicated slavery and fought for equality of civil rights for all ethnicities, there is still a divide between whites who hold positions of privilege and people of color who do not. Furthermore, whites have worked actively to maintain this divide, even in the north where abolition and civil rights were granted long before the south.

Biblical scholar Walter Brueggemann helps us examine this assumption when he suggests that "the contemporary American church is so largely enculturated to the American ethos of consumerism that it has little power to believe or act."[7] He goes on to say that "we need to ask if our consciousness and imagination have been so assaulted and co-opted by the royal consciousness that we have been robbed of the courage or power to think an alternative thought."[8] In his assessment, royal consciousness is described as the dominant culture, which includes affluence, oppressive social policy, and static religion, "in which God and his temple have become part of the royal landscape."[9]

In other words, I am working under the assumption that northern American white Christianity has been co-opted by our culture of white privilege and affluence, leading us to support practices of oppressive social policy to keep segregation alive through our confluence with politics. I intend this to be a serious claim, and therefore it needs to be supported. I will endeavor to do so after surveying the biblical rationale for an ethnic diversity in Christian communities that more closely approximates the diversity of the wider communities in which they are located. What does the

---

7. Brueggemann, *Prophetic Imagination*, 1.
8. Brueggemann, *Prophetic Imagination*, 39.
9. Brueggemann, *Prophetic Imagination*, 26–29.

Bible have to say about how we can practice flourishing-producing togetherness toward more inclusive expressions within the ethnic demographics of Christian communities?

EXAMINING THE BIBLE'S TEACHING ABOUT DIVERSITY

As mentioned above, the kingdom of God is for all people. This assumption can first be rooted in the Creation account, where God says in Gen 1:26, "Let us make humankind in our image according to our likeness" (NRSV). While it goes beyond the purpose of this study to delineate the meaning of "image and likeness," suffice it to say that this passage teaches that God has imbued all humanity with some form of divine intentionality. There are no essential theological differences between people or between God's approaches to people. But Christians have not always believed this.

To our modern sensibilities, it may be shocking to hear that even as recently as fifty years ago, *homo sapiens* was posited as being split into three to five major races. One northern white American Christian scholar wrote in 1973, "Usually the whole gamut of humanity is divided into Caucasoid, Negroid, and Mongoloid."[10] But in the 1990s, at the completion of the Human Genome Project, humanity finally had scientific evidence to support what the Genesis story (and creation accounts of other world religions) long taught, that all humans are biologically equal.[11] So not only theologically but also scientifically, there is strong evidence that all humans are equal in God's eyes.[12]

Yet, the biblical text teaches that one family, one nation, Israel, was specially chosen by God. Perhaps God has favorites? To address this question, we turn to one of the earliest biblical statements of God's mission for humanity—Gen 12:1–3, where God revealed himself to one man, Abram. There he told Abram, "I will make you into a great nation, and I will bless you" (v. 2). Clearly, God singled out one man to spearhead his purposes.

---

10. Figart, *Race Problem*, 21.

11. Biewen and Kumanyika, "How Race Was Made," 4:20–5:20.

12. There is an extensive literature on how race was created, and thus how the Western European and American mindset became racialized, placing whiteness above and all other ethnicities below. I recommend "How Race Was Made," ep. 2 of *Seeing White*, as a starting point for further study. See also Painter, *History of White People*; and Kendi, *Stamped*.

This choice must be set in relief with God's larger trajectory for Abram's family, that "all peoples on earth will be blessed through you" (v. 3).[13] God repeats this mission of global blessing to Abraham's son Isaac in Gen 26:2–4 and then to Isaac's son Jacob in Gen 28:13–15. God eventually gave Jacob the name Israel, which became the name of the nation Jacob's family grew into over the next few centuries. Thus the purpose of Israel was to be a blessing to the whole world.

As the story of the people of Israel moves from the book of Genesis into the book of Exodus, it could seem that God's focus on Israel is to the neglect of the rest of humanity and is thus in contradiction to his promise to Abraham. Biblical scholar Christopher J. H. Wright, in his expansive work *The Mission of God*, thoroughly counters this possibility, describing in detail how God's mission to reach the whole world is solidly entrenched in the biblical narrative from start to finish. Wright notes that "the election of Israel does not imply the rejection of other nations. On the contrary, from the very beginning it is portrayed as for their benefit. God did not call Abraham from among the nations to accomplish their rejection but to initiate the process of their redemption."[14]

Wright's claim is supported by Ps 72, attributed to Israel's King Solomon, which states that through Israel's monarchical line "all nations will be blessed" (Ps 72:17). Yet throughout the history of ancient Israel, the nation rarely pursued, let alone fulfilled, this mission to convey God's blessing to the whole world, thus effectively keeping most people out of covenant relationship with God. Israel actively insulated themselves against their neighbors, holding tightly to their status as God's chosen people, viewing outsiders as unclean. Nonetheless, God embedded in his chosen people the mission to be a blessing to all.

This theme of global blessing was reaffirmed by the early church because they saw in Jesus not only the theological fulfillment of the mission as Messiah, that of the royal line of David through whom all would be blessed, but also the early church saw Jesus live out the practical implications of the mission. For example, they watched Jesus regularly interact missionally with non-Jews like Samaritans and Gentiles. Brueggemann notes that "the way of [Jesus'] ultimate criticism is his decisive solidarity with marginal people and the accompanying vulnerability required by that solidarity."[15]

---

13. See also Gen 18:18, 22:18, and 26:4, where God reaffirms this promise to Abram/Abraham.

14. Wright, *Mission of God*, 263.

15. Brueggemann, *Prophetic Imagination*, 82.

This speaks to Jesus' own statement of mission when he read from Isa 61:1–2, as recorded in Luke 4:18–19, and where he proclaimed that Scripture was fulfilled in him. In so doing, he describes his heart for the poor, the prisoner, the blind, and the oppressed, who represent all those who are marginal people. Furthermore, Brueggemann's "accompanying vulnerability" refers to Jesus' teaching of discipleship that is founded on the idea of "death to self." It is this self-giving vulnerability that he himself not only taught but also lived out among his disciples and ultimately demonstrated in his death. Jesus, in other words, embodies God's mission to bless all humanity.

When Jesus' followers decided how to apply Jesus' mission to their context, they were attempting to implement the ideas and life patterns of their master, to be a people of self-giving love for the salvation of all humankind. Once Jesus ascends to his Father, though, he leaves them with the astounding blessing of the Holy Spirit who energizes their mission. As we see in Acts 3:25 for example, Peter, quoting Gen 12, appropriates God's global mission to the church, which was inaugurated at Pentecost, an event in which the Spirit of God was poured out on people from many nations of the world. The church had become the carrier of God's blessing to all humanity.

Tracking the movement of the Spirit throughout the account of the early church in the book of Acts, we see the Spirit's intentional expansion to include all people in the new blessed community. The Spirit moves the apostles beyond people of Jewish descent, to those in Samaria (8:4–25), to an Ethiopian eunuch (8:26–39), and finally to all people groups, as Peter receives a vision from God declaring all food clean (10:9–16), symbolizing God's intent to reach all with the message of good news in Christ (10:34–35). Peter's first action after seeing this shocking vision is to proclaim the good news to a gentile Roman (10:24–48). God's heart, therefore, was not just for the family of Abram, or later the nation of Israel, whom he called his chosen nation, but God's heart is always a desire that all people would be included in this blessed community.

The apostle Paul provides additional theological foundation for this inclusive mission. In his Letter to the Galatians, Paul is making a larger argument that faith in Christ need not require adherence to the law, and therefore he taught gentile Christians not to perform the act of circumcision that was necessary for Jews under the old covenant. Instead, quoting that original promise of God to Abram from Gen 12, Paul says, in Gal 3:8 and following, that all nations will be blessed because those who have faith in Christ are blessed.

Paul summarizes in v. 14, "He redeemed us in order that the blessing given to Abraham might come to the Gentiles through Christ Jesus, so that by faith we might receive the promise of the Spirit." It is obvious to Paul, then, that all are "children of God through faith, for all of you who were baptized into Christ have clothed yourselves with Christ. There is neither Jew nor Gentile, neither slave nor free, nor is there male and female, for you are all one in Christ Jesus" (vv. 26–28).

Furthermore, Paul expands on this theme in Eph 2:11–22, when he writes that Jesus has broken down the dividing wall of hostility between Jews and gentiles, through his death on the cross, so the two might become one. In this Jesus brings peace between all humans. Paul goes on to say in 1 Cor 9:22, "To the weak I became weak, to win the weak. I have become all things to all people so that by all possible means I might save some." In his mission to the whole world, Paul says, he is following the method and mission of Jesus to reach all, even at the cost of his own life.

Finally, in the vision God gave John, which we read in Revelation, we once again see God's heart for all humanity, as the vision describes his kingdom as including people from "every nation, tribe, people and language" (Rev 7:9). Figart concludes that "since Scripture provides no basis for considering black peoples or any others inferior to white races, there is no Biblical reason to sanction the inequality . . . to which many have been restricted. Obviously, then, there are areas of change essential to proper integration."[16]

Sadly, it seems some American Christian churches have utterly failed to integrate as the church for all humanity, much like the nation of Israel failed to be a blessing to the world. Why is the northern American church still segregated, when it is central to the mission of God's kingdom for all peoples to be reached, and at any cost? As mentioned above, Brueggemann calls this failure a "capitulation to royal consciousness," but what does he mean? We now examine our American Christian history for further evidence to attempt to uncover answers to this question.

A BRIEF HISTORY OF THE SEGREGATED NORTHERN WHITE CHURCH

Just as *Seeing White* opened my eyes to my own whiteness, scholars and historians revealed to me an American social and ecclesiological history I was unaware of. I knew that southern Christian slave owners incorrectly used the biblical text to justify not only the owning of human slaves but also the mistreatment of them. As Powery and Sadler report, "Many began to turn to

---

16. Figart, *Race Problem*, 170.

the Bible to buttress their cultural perspectives on race, even as they utilized the holy book to justify the tradition of holding other humans in bondage."[17]

But that seemed a distant southern epoch that had little, if anything, to do with northern white Christians in the post-civil rights era. One look at white Christian sanctuaries on Sunday mornings should have provided a hint that something else was wrong. Why would Christians segregate themselves when the mission of God's kingdom is clearly for all people? Why would we choose to abandon the pursuit of Revelation's vision of a multicultural church? Why would we avoid flourishing-producing togetherness and remain separate?

To attempt to answer these questions, Hart suggests that the "white church never owned its whiteness, and never repented. In the black church, therefore, the impulse was withdrawal, a critique of white supremacy."[18] Pickett further explains, "There is a desire over the last twenty to thirty years for racial reconciliation in many white Christian churches. But what that doesn't recognize is that black people didn't decide to leave churches because they didn't like white people. They didn't decide to leave white churches in general. They were actually kicked out from the very beginning."[19]

What does Pickett mean? He goes on to raise the very question at the heart of this book about togetherness: "Why aren't white and black people and other people of color worshiping under the same roof? It's not because black people said, 'We're outta here; we're going to do our own thing because we were enslaved.' It's actually because white people said, 'We don't want you here.'"[20] Thus the invisible black practice of religion became the visible black church."

Pickett is right. In America, white and black churches have not been together. Can we point to specific instances in the north where white people kicked persons of color out of their churches? Certainly Pickett's claim has ample evidence in the south in the post-abolition era. But as this chapter is concerned with northern Christianity, what evidence can we point to?

Tisby notes that "the struggle for black freedom took place everywhere throughout the country, not just in the south."[21] He points to Catholic schools that excluded blacks or segregated them. Born a slave in 1854, Augustus Tolton felt called to the priesthood, but no American Catholic

---

17. Powery and Sadler, *Genesis of Liberation*, 83.
18. Drew Hart, pers. comm., Feb. 27, 2019.
19. Pickett, "White Christian America," 35:30–35:57.
20. Pickett, "White Christian America," 35:58—36:15.
21. Tisby, *Color of Compromise*, 112.

seminary would accept him as a student, and thus he studied in Rome. He became the first black priest in America, serving a black parish in Chicago.

Tisby records similar stories from the Pentecostal church where, as recently as 1948, when the Pentecostal Fellowship of North America was formed, "not a single predominantly black Pentecostal denomination was invited to join."[22] Pickett describes what amounts to a purposeful ecclesiological segregation: "What we mean by 'racism' is more than interpersonal prejudice. It is a set of larger cultural practices, including an investment and commitment to whiteness. For example, European immigrants were allowed to be declared ethnically 'white'. It wasn't until 1978 that blacks could be ordained in the Mormon Church."[23]

Tisby further details this hidden racism in the evangelical church. Fundamentalism, an extreme version of evangelical Christianity that impacted many denominations, "neglected to place black ministers on the list of recipients" of volumes of its source documents, *The Fundamentals*.[24] Furthermore the theology of *The Fundamentals* excluded a focus on racial progress and social justice.[25]

Also, in what could be an example supporting Pickett's claim above—that blacks were kicked out the church—in the early and mid-twentieth century, when people of color moved *en masse* into cities in search of affordable housing, instead of integrating and welcoming them, whites moved out. Called "white flight" this led to governmental policies of redlining and blockbusting, which further segregated neighborhoods.[26]

Sadly, "over the course of the 1960s and 1970s, as neighborhood demographics changed, these churches relocated to the suburbs where there was a higher population of white people."[27] Tisby quotes Mulder who suggests that Congregationalist polity, where churches are self-governing and own their own property, only exacerbated this undercurrent of racism. When blacks arrived in our neighborhoods, we whites packed up and left town.

In response to all this, northern white Christians remained silent, which can be described as a hidden racism. Silence is unacceptable for Christians who are seeing injustice around us. For example, Cone recounts the different approaches taken by eminent white theologians, Bonhoeffer and Niebuhr. Where the German Bonhoeffer made great strides to

---

22. Tisby, *Color of Compromise*, 115.
23. Pickett, "White Christian America," 34:55—35:25.
24. Orr et al., *Fundamentals*.
25. Tisby, *Color of Compromise*, 116.
26. Rothstein, *Color of Law*, 125.
27. Rothstein, *Color of Law*, 127.

assimilate with black Christians in the mid-1900s, "the nightmare in black life continued to deepen as progressive whites like Niebuhr remained silent about lynching."[28] Thus perhaps we northern white Christians practiced a more overt racism than we might assume.

The preceding examples provide evidence that we allowed our American ecclesiology, as Brueggemann noted above, to be co-opted by "royal consciousness" when we allowed it to be subsumed into the political realm. There, too, we see the racism of silence and sometimes outright segregation. Given the sheer numbers of Christians in our land and the fact that certain segregationist policies were being enacted while Christians were participating in all levels of the government approving those policies, it is necessary to see American Christians as complicit in racist and white supremacist action.

This racism was not just governmental, it was also personal, even in the north. For example, John Biewen interviews people about the difference between northern and southern racism. One person, Liz Phillips, says that "Boston was the most segregated place I'd ever lived."[29] When Bill Clinton was campaigning in Pennsylvania, his campaign strategist, James Carville, described it as "Pittsburgh and Philadelphia with Alabama in between."[30] Living in central Pennsylvania all my life, while this is certainly a generalization, my experience is that Carville is not far off in his assessment.[31] One does not have to drive far on the back roads of "Pennsyltucky," as it is sometimes referred to, to observe the flags and bumper stickers that one would expect to see in the American south. The presence of Confederate flags in the North is another example of a not-so-hidden white racism. Martin Luther King Jr., at a Chicago rally in 1966, Tisby reports, was faced with death threats by Confederate flag-waving counter-protestors. King told reporters, "I have never seen such hate. Not in Mississippi or Alabama. This is a terrible thing."[32]

Yet we northerners are proud of our heritage of opposition to slavery and segregation, especially demonstrated in our historical sacrifices and victory in the Civil War. As a result we can still look down on southerners,

---

28. Cone, *Cross and the Lynching Tree*, 49.

29. Biewen and Kumanyika, "That's Not Us," 9:00–9:10.

30. Rusakoff, "Pa. Governor's Race," para. 12.

31. Perhaps this situation is changing for "Pennsyltucky." An editorial in the *Harrisburg Patriot News* in 2016, "The End of Alabama In-Between," reported evidence for change in Pennsylvania fly-over country. Just a few months after this article was published, however, conservative Republican Donald J. Trump won Pennsylvania in the 2016 presidential election.

32. Tisby, *Color of Compromise*, 128.

as if they are horrible racists. Hidden (or in some, not so hidden) in many of us northerners, however, is our own racist tendency.

Biewen explains an epithet that might shed light on our racism: "Northern whites love the race but hate the people. Southern whites hate the race but love the people. Racism or white domination—has a different style, north vs. south. But the fundamentals are not that dissimilar. People of color put it like this, 'In the north they don't care how high you get as long as you don't get too close, and in the south they don't care how close you get as long as you don't get too high.'"[33] Biewen further explains in an interview with Shannon Sullivan,

> In her newest book, *Good White People*, Sullivan explores strategies that some white folk use to distance ourselves from white racism.... Sullivan says these strategies are usually unconscious and well-intended. They come from an impulse to not participate in racism, but that doesn't make them helpful. One of the strategies is Colorblindness, insisting, "I don't see race."

Sullivan corroborates,

> It's almost like a pride in being completely clueless about the world in which we live as white people, if we can't see how our own whiteness, along with other races, is operating in it. And that actually allows white supremacy, the other things I've been talking about, to hum along quite happily and unchallenged. If you can't see race, then how in the heck are you going to see racism?

Biewen replies, "And then there's the well-worn 'white trash' strategy. Looking down on poorer white people as the problem, the real racists."[34] As Sullivan mentions in this comment, perhaps you have heard people claiming the following when it comes to race: "We should be colorblind!" When it comes to race and ethnicity, it can seem that being colorblind is what is desirable. Just see the person, not their skin color, right? While that sentiment sounds correct, I have three colorblind sons, each with varying degrees of severity. My boys' colorblindness is manageable, but from time to time they need help identifying a shade of color. Visual color blindness means that something is not as it should be, and the same goes for colorblindness toward ethnicity. In the same way, we humans have different appearances and we can and should appreciate those differences.

---

33. Biewen and Kumanyika, "That's Not Us," 12:20–12:40.
34. Biewen and Kumanyika, "That's Not Us," 13:00—14:25.

That said, the heart behind the colorblindness movement may be motivated by goodness. Those who express a desire for colorblindness toward ethnic variety correctly want us to value personhood and not outward appearance. God himself says that "man looks at the outward appearance, but God looks at the heart" (1 Sam 16:7). Is God saying that he is colorblind and that being colorblind is correct? Yes and no. As we'll see, to pursue flourishing-producing togetherness, especially for unity in Christian communities, we should not ignore human diversity. We should not be colorblind, as if the differences don't exist. Too often northern American Christians have used colorblindness as a means to ignore the realities and ramifications of ethnic and racial injustice. Alexander makes a compelling case against colorblindness, writing that colorblindness has proved "catastrophic for African Americans. It is not an overstatement to say the systemic mass incarceration of people of color in the United States would not have been possible in the post-civil rights era if the nation had not fallen under the spell of a callous colorblindness."[35]

Tisby concludes that "the very conspicuousness of white supremacy in the south has made it easier for racism in other parts of the country to exist in open obscurity."[36] Therefore, though existing in a society where slavery had been abolished, where segregation is illegal, and where civil rights are the law of the land, northern American Christianity has for all intents and purposes remained segregated.

What is so striking about this segregation in churches is that it is antithetical to the vision of the concept of flourishing-producing togetherness in Scripture. Segregation in churches represents a failure of those churches to live out the theology of all humans being made in God's image and equal in his eyes. While there is much good that could be said of the northern American white church, our current practice of segregation must be seen as an abject failure.

Segregation in churches is evidence of our capitulation to the "royal consciousness" of society. We are not able to experience flourishing-producing togetherness because we are not together. There is a rift, stemming from the awful treatment of people of color by the white majority, a sin that has largely been left unconfessed.

---

35. Alexander, *New Jim Crow*, 240–41. See also Delgado and Stefancic, *Critical Race Theory*; Yancey, *Beyond Racial Division*.

36. Tisby, *Color of Compromise*, 129.

LOCAL RESEARCH

But maybe Faith Church is an anomaly in our lack of ethnic diversity? Do other churches in my local school district have a diversity level more closely approximating that of the surrounding community? As I look around the table at my local ministerium meetings, I see almost all white faces. Of the approximately twenty churches actively involved in the ministerium, there is one black pastor, a Kenyan who pastors a predominantly white congregation, and one co-senior pastor who is a Hispanic woman and is married to a white man. In our ministerium, this husband-wife pastoral team leads the church that has the most multicultural congregation.

All the rest of the ministerium pastors are white, meaning that our pastoral representation is not as ethnically diverse as the local community. I wanted to learn more about the demographics of each congregation, so I asked the churches of the ministerium to describe their demographics.[37] Their responses revealed two interesting dynamics. First, the majority of respondents have a demographic much like Faith Church. Second, those that have a demographic more closely resembling that of the larger community have taken specific action that has resulted in increased diversity. It is to these results that we now turn.

First, the demographics show that most churches in the ministerium are predominantly white. A pastor of a non-denominational independent church remarked, "[We] have one black family in our congregation, a couple of Hispanic background, one of Philippine descent and one of Laotian descent. But we are basically a white church." A Lutheran pastor wrote, "Our demographics mirror your own. They do not reflect the diversity of the community." A pastor of a Mennonite church told me that his congregation's demographics were also similar to that of Faith Church, nearly entirely white.

Still another Mennonite pastor (at a different church) reports that his church's "demographics are very similar to yours. We have one Hispanic family, one woman from Pakistan, one exchange student from Nigeria, and one family who has adopted an Afro-American son."

Finally, at a meeting of the ministerium, I publicly asked for further input on demographics, and all but three congregations described a diversity that did not match that of the local community. Summarizing the data, while this is admittedly unscientific, if the representatives of the churches I contacted are accurately presenting their demographic, approximately 85 percent of the churches in our school district are mostly white.

---

37. See appendix 2 for the question format.

But there are three churches in the ministerium who have seen changes, and that leads to the second major result of my inquiry with the ministerium: What specific steps have more diverse churches taken? A pastor of a third Mennonite church notes that "our congregation was at one time very homogenous. [But] we have seen movement. The reason is community involvement. We went out and got to know our neighbors. Did we sit down and say, 'We must become more diverse'? No! We just got to know whoever was in our path and invited them into our lives. We are not a mirror image but are pretty diverse."

I was interested in learning more about what that pastor meant by "pretty diverse," and his associate pastor added some details: "The diversity came from assisting families who are resettling here in the States. We have people from the Congo, Pakistan, Kenya, Somalia, Iraq, and Romania. I don't know that reaching these different people groups was intentional; it seems that God brought them to us and we were willing to help them." As our correspondence continued, the pastor noted the following:

> I would estimate that we currently have about fifteen percent of our congregation who are non-Caucasian. A quick browse through our directory and I see about twelve families that make up this number. As I mentioned previously, we have people who are from a variety of countries of origin. Some of the folks who have resettled here have been with us for eight years. Since 2016 we have seen a dramatic increase in the number of resettlement contacts. My unofficial assessment is that after a few brave people broke the ice and were part of our church, it made it easier for others to come.

Earlier, I mentioned a husband-and-wife pastoral team that lead an ethnically diverse church. They confirmed that their congregational diversity is very much in line with that of the community. I have observed this diversity when I visited their church for community Good Friday services, as well as one Sunday morning when I preached there during a ministerium pulpit exchange.

The wife explained that as a Latina, and a pastor, her presence has encouraged diversity. It is also my personal observation that this church is also quite intentional about ministry to diverse communities such as those transitioning out of incarceration and those struggling with homelessness in the city of Lancaster, ministries that have regularly brought them in connection with diverse ethnicities.

Finally, the missions and community outreach pastor of a large independent church says that "at our church, we have seen some major changes in diversity in the last two to four years. There is a visible difference in African, African American, and Latino people at our services. Our 11 a.m. service can often feel like whites are the minority." These changes, he remarked, stem from the fact that

> other than the God factor . . . we welcomed this change. We talked about it, we prayed about it, we had meetings where we asked our minorities to speak into things and we did not explain, but rather listened. Last year one of our mottos was "no mess no harvest." One of the key factors we identified is having visible minorities in ministry. Worship team, service host, ushers, greeters. Minorities need to see others like them to feel like they can be at home. Our staff has a ways to grow in this, but our volunteer diversity is strong. We do still need a pastoral staff who can speak Spanish—we have not gotten there yet. People worship where they feel comfortable, and they see people like them. Diversity is complicated and messy. Of course we are a large church with a much larger sample. If I could say one thing to start people on this journey, it is you need to welcome this, and it must come from the top.

Clearly there is hope. Yet, the evidence of these three churches could be caricatured as simply applicable to their specific situation. Yes, they have seen forward movement. Churches can and do abandon adherence to royal consciousness, as they seek a multicultural blessed community of the kingdom.

But are their approaches healthy? Are there concerns churches need to be aware of as they seek to move toward more diversity? To answer these questions, I discussed the problem of northern white Christian exclusivity with scholars and dug into their research, seeking their wisdom and guidance as to what theological perspectives and actions would represent a faithful approach to address the ethnic disparity in our churches.

DISCUSSION WITH SCHOLARS

Does the Bible teach any theological principles that might help us achieve flourishing-producing togetherness so that we can have greater ethnic diversity in the church? Multicultural church pastor and author Jamin Bradley writes that a theology of peace is foundational to becoming multicultural. He suggests that the presence of racial tension and difficulty of becoming diverse can lead ethnicities to keep away from each other in order to keep the peace. . . . But that's not peace. Peace isn't ignorance. Peace isn't getting your way. Peace is the man or woman who wears earplugs during the music because they don't like the genre or how loud it is, but still attends the worship service and supports it. That's the kind of person that desires to embrace a people different from themselves. That's the kind of person who is more about others than themselves.[38]

Anabaptist groups like the Amish, Mennonites, and Brethren have long settled in Lancaster County where I live. Anabaptists often remark that peace is their major theological tenet. They are pacifists and thus do not participate in the military. But Anabaptists and, more specifically, Peace churches view peace as far more consequential than simply pacifism toward military conflict. They talk much about reconciliation between offended parties, about peace being a way of life, and about shalom and flourishing. Yet most Anabaptist churches in my school district, as reported by Mennonite pastors above, remain segregated.

Anecdotally, I have heard very little in our ministerium about peace and racial reconciliation or about peace as a foundation for the local church to move toward more diversity. A Mennonite pastor in the ministerium described this when he said, "Historically, Mennonites have had a tight ethnic identity. Family connections are and have been important. Playing the Mennonite game, a term used only half in jest, means identifying the various points of connection, primarily family, but also schooling, voluntary service, communities of residence, etc. While this can foster strong ties of identity and connection, it also significantly increases the barriers for 'outsiders' who begin to attend."

How, then, can peace lead to flourishing-producing togetherness? Bradley suggests that for peace to bridge the ethnic divide and create multiethnic local churches, it must be sacrificial and humble. "If we live this kind of humility out, we will live a life of peace—for this is the kind of life that does not see others as different, strange or stereotyped, but simply as masters to be served—even if they betray us in just a few short hours. These are the eyes that are blinded by the love of Jesus and yet, somehow opened far beyond that of those with 20/20 vision."[39]

As Leander suggests, peace leads to reconciliation, which should be in the church's DNA.[40] In 2 Cor 5:11–19, Paul teaches the principle of recon-

---

38. Bradley, "Just Like You," para. 6.
39. Bradley, "Just Like You," para. 12.
40. Leander, pers. comm., Jan. 2021.

ciliation, saying that, as people whom God reconciled to himself through Christ, Christians have a ministry of reconciliation (v. 18), so that we carry a message of reconciliation (v. 19), which is that all people can be reconciled to God (v. 20). While Paul is primarily concerned with reconciliation between God and humans, the principle of reconciliation applies to all humanity. In other words, because Christians are a reconciled people, we strive for reconciliation first between God and humans, but also between all humans wherever there is brokenness.[41]

Theologian Howard Thurman notes that reconciliation is motivated by and flowing from Jesus' self-giving love.[42] Bradley illustrates this by referring to his own congregation. He himself is white, and he became pastor of a Hispanic church which was, in his words, "falling apart, but had multicultural home groups."[43] Originally it was two separate churches, one Hispanic (including worship services in Spanish language) and one multicultural. To strengthen the church, leadership made the decision to combine the two congregations. Bradley preached a series on Acts, and the subject came up time and time again, "you have to give it away." Give what away?

What he means is that the Jewish Christians in Acts, as we saw above, needed to give away the kingdom to the world. The Jerusalem Council (Acts 15) led to giving up the law, which led to a new outward focus to reach all. So in Bradley's church, they decided not only to combine congregations but also to hire an associate pastor of color.

White applicants, who were more qualified on paper, applied for the position, and though their hiring team never mandated, "We're going to hire a person of color," it was an unwritten intention. It showed the congregation that they were committed to inclusivity by who they hired to be up front. For peace to subvert the royal consciousness and lead to diversity, it had to manifest in a reconciliation that expressed itself in humility and sacrifice.

In addition to practicing reconciling peace as an antidote to royal consciousness, theologian Drew Hart mentioned that white congregations should engage in prophetic lament.[44] He pointed to the work of Soong-Chan Rah, such that lament launches repentance, and then repentance moves to

---

41. See Emerson and Smith, *Divided by Faith*, 115–33. Additionally, author Latasha Morrison notes that reconciliation should not be limited to individual relationships. Reconciliation must include a togetherness of "healing communal relationships and societal connections fractured by government abuses, systems of oppression, and systems of structural privilege." Morrison, *Be the Bridge*, 177

42. Thurman, *Disciplines of the Spirit*, 125.

43. Bradley, pers. comm., Feb. 20, 2019.

44. Hart, pers. comm., Feb. 27, 2019.

action.[45] Following this through, Hart suggested the appropriate resultant action is divestiture.

This movement of lament to repentance to action, he writes, is seen when the church learns "to become attentive to all the diverse experiences within our society. If the church is going to manifest the 'beloved community,' we must keep track of any time someone is deemed less valuable than others. In the spirit of Gal 3:28, we must renounce all social hierarchies if we are truly to become one in Christ."[46]

What does this renouncing, this divestiture, look like? Hart suggested to me that white Christians need to be a constant voice, people who break the rules of whiteness, expose racism, always speak up and say "I defer" when racism is present. He said that we need to be willing to speak up not just in the relative security of social media but more importantly in person.

Actually, he told me, we should flip this tendency, speaking up in person first and foremost rather than online. He illustrated this by telling the story of a man who spoke up to confront his majority white church when the church leaders were considering not giving health insurance to their new black youth pastor. Hart suggested that affluent whites could pool their collective resources and redistribute them to help those of color. For Hart, this prophetic divestiture is the act of truth telling.[47]

In this, Hart demonstrates his agreement with Brueggemann who writes, "The task of prophetic imagination is to cut through the numbness, to penetrate the self-deception, so that the God of endings is confessed as Lord."[48] Brueggemann, too, is describing the work of prophetic truth telling. Another example is Vaclav Havel, who reflected on his career of fighting injustice saying, "I've always understood my mission to speak truth about the world I live in, to bear witness to its terrors and its miseries."[49]

This is how *Seeing White*, and another resource, *An American Lent*, spoke prophetically to me. *An American Lent* is a devotional series intended to align with the Christian season of Lent.[50] I invited our church family to voluntarily sign up for the daily devotional email readings, and a woman from our congregation led a weekly email discussion group for those interested in exploring themes further. Barnes explains how *An American*

45. Rah, *Prophetic Lament*, 171–76.
46. Hart, *Trouble I've Seen*, 30.
47. Hart, pers. comm., Feb. 27, 2019.
48. Brueggemann, *Prophetic Imagination*, 45.
49. Havel, *Disturbing the Peace*, 8, quoted in Ledbetter et al., *Reviewing Leadership*, 59.
50. Barnes, *American Lent*.

Lent carries the same prophetic movement described by Hart: "The aim of this journey is that through the prayers, reflections, and responses, the Holy Spirit will transform us, individually and collectively, to look more like Christ. Our ultimate hope is that we would not only be grieved into repenting (2 Cor 7:8–10), but that we would all leave this experience bearing fruit in keeping with repentance (Matt 3:8). *Because, repentance looks like something.* Tangible evidence of our transformation is broadcast in our words and actions, in our giving and service, in our lives and communities. True repentance *must* produce fruit."[51]

While we study further how communities can practice corporate repentance in chapter 16 this repentance begins with prophetic truth telling. It is only after learning the truth about ourselves and our community that we can move into repentant action which will bear fruit. The fruit is evident when a new community of flourishing-producing togetherness is created. Brueggemann explains that "every act of a minister who would be a prophetic is part of a way of evoking, forming and reforming an alternative community."[52]

For multicultural expression to happen in the local church, therefore, prophetic truth telling must lead to the creation of an alternative community, which is the beloved community described by Hart and others. Brueggemann concludes: "The formation of an alternative community with an alternative consciousness is so that the dominant community may be criticized and finally dismantled. But more than dismantling, the purpose of the alternative community is to enable a new human beginning to be made."[53] Therefore, following the research of these scholars and practitioners, in order to implement flourishing-producing togetherness that leads to the beloved community of unity in Christ among all ethnicities, local churches must take the following action.

STUDY AND CONVERSATION

When I sat down with Hart, he told me, "Go deep first. Do the hard work of theology rather than the easy work of changes on stage."[54] Likewise he writes, "I suggest that Christians from dominant cultures change their reading habits so that those on the margins become the main stage. In the church I suggest intentional reading circles that are racially diverse, where stories can

---

51. Barnes, *American Lent*, iii (italics original).
52. Brueggemann, *Prophetic Imagination*, 4.
53. Brueggemann, *Prophetic Imagination*, 102.
54. Hart, pers. comm., Feb. 27, 2019.

be shared and received."⁵⁵ Pickett agrees, mentioning that whites could read black biblical scholars such as Cain Hope Felder's *Stony The Road We Trod*.⁵⁶ Hart reflects on this saying, "If we would dare yield ourselves through the Spirit while in community with marginalized people, to reading, hearing and living out this story, we would see afresh and with Kingdom insight."⁵⁷

Pickett continues by suggesting that white Christians need to fight the desire to be uninformed, to be ignorant. He refers to black author James Baldwin who said that it is not just that white people don't know about the plight of people of color but that whites are willfully ignorant.⁵⁸ I experienced this willful ignorance as a student when in both my undergraduate degree in biblical studies and in my master of divinity studies, I read not one black theologian. Every bible and theology course, and there were many, maintained a focus on white Western sources. Is my undergraduate and graduate curriculum demonstrating Baldwin's willful ignorance? Perhaps so. I suspect at least some of my professors were cautious or even fearful of exposing their students to scholars who had a reputation for being liberation theologians, like James Cone.

What Pickett suggests, then, rings true, that we must first know the truth before we can act personally and institutionally in a new way. Whites, he says, must examine how we hold our authority and power, in our family, in our workplace, neighborhood, and church, to combat all forms of injustice and practices of domination. Study, observation, and listening to non-white, non-Western sources is essential.

The mission and outreach pastor of the large nondenominational church in my ministerium noted that his church's process of creating the beloved community began with a commitment to study and conversation. Prior to the horrific murder of George Floyd in the summer of 2020, finding non-white, non-Western perspectives, such as books and other studies, was possible but it required an intentional search. In the wake of Floyd's murder and the renewed call for racial justice, those same resources lined the shelves of even Target's book section. Many more people were studying the history and complexity of race in America, and that was a wonderful development. Now just a few years later, those books are no longer easily available in stores like Target. Will white Christian communities persist in this necessary study?

55. Hart, *Trouble I've Seen*, 170.
56. Pickett, "White Christian America," 43:20–43:40.
57. Hart, *Trouble I've Seen*, 173.
58. Pickett, "White Christian America," 44:00–44:20.

LAMENT AND REPENT

Once we begin to do the hard work of theology, of study, leading us to learn the truth, an appropriate response will be for us to own our sin of racism and repent with lament and weeping. Cone notes that "it has always been difficult for white people to empathize fully with the experience of black people. But it has never been impossible."[59] Hart concurs when he says, "Considering all that has gone on in our country, we are delusional if we think that we have not at least partially caught the American racialized disease of white supremacy and anti-black bias. Of course we have. Now is not the time to fall into denial."[60] Rather than deny, we humbly embrace truth through lament.

As a result, Brueggemann teaches that "this kind of prophetic criticism does not lightly offer alternatives, does not mouth assurances, and does not provide redemptive social policy. It knows that only those who mourn can be comforted, and so it first asks about how to mourn seriously and faithfully for the world passing away. Jesus understood and embodied that anguish Jeremiah felt so poignantly."[61] When we learn the truth, as Jesus shows us, the truth should cause us to lament, weep, and repent. Lament can be employed as a corporate holy complaint, demonstrated so pervasively in the Psalms. Because those psalms were the songbook of ancient Israel's worship gatherings, there is a precedent for lamenting together. Some psalms seem to have been written precisely for the purpose of corporate lament.[62]

Psalm 12 is unique among the corporate psalms of lament in its description of the connection between corporate lament and God's response to redress injustice. First, the people cry out together, "Help, LORD, for no one is faithful anymore" (v. 1). The Lord responds, "Because the poor are plundered and the needy groan, I will now arise.... I will protect them from those who malign them" (v. 4). Lament, therefore, can bring transformation not only within the hearts and minds of the collective of people doing the lamenting but also in the situation that led to the lament, as God himself responds to the complaint of the people. Flourishing-producing togetherness, in its movement toward racial reconciliation, therefore, practices corporate lament. But how?

---

59. Cone, *Cross and the Lynching Tree*, 41.
60. Hart, *Trouble I've Seen*, 175.
61. Brueggemann, *Prophetic Imagination*, 99.
62. LaSor et al. suggest the following are corporate psalms of complaint: Pss 12, 44, 60, 74, 79, 80, 83, 85, 90, and 126. LaSor et al., *Old Testament Survey*, 435.

While any Christian community can lament our racist nation's racist past,[63] those from northern American white Christian communities particularly can gather to express anguish, weeping for the injustice perpetrated upon people of color for centuries. Northern American white Christian communities can gather to lament how they have been too silent, or perhaps completely silent, and thus complicit in the injustice. In particular, northern American white Christians can gather with people of color to lament together. This is why after study and lament, the next step is relationship.[64]

PROPHETIC ACTION, PART 1: BUILDING AN ALTERNATIVE BELOVED COMMUNITY

The outflow of lament will be the building of relationship that forms a prophetic alternate community. Some have called this the beloved community.[65] Hart describes this when he says, "Sharing life together means intimately identifying with people who carry the stigma of varying racial meaning in their actual bodies."[66] Bradley's church, mentioned above, launched a practice that seeks to apply the theology of peace to relationships in the church and to the community: Dinner Church. Dinner Church is a Sunday evening gathering that begins with a meal, and it leads to a worship service. When I interviewed him, Bradley described to me a segregation-breaking dynamic that happens around tables.[67]

This is very similar to what Sweet teaches. "That's the power of the table: We lower our guard as we break bread together; we become ourselves, and we become open to one another. We cease being rivals, enemies; and we begin to experience companionship, friendship."[68] One of the contributors to

63. For numerous helpful suggestions for those from both majority and minority cultures who want to practice lament, see Vroegop, *Weep With Me*.

64. I also see repentance as vital at this juncture. In fact, it is so vital that I believe it warrants a longer treatment, and thus the next chapter is about how flourishing-producing togetherness relies on and practices repentance.

65. See Moore, *Dear White Peacemakers*, 92–93. Moore suggests that "agape love is the language of the Beloved Community. It empowers us to actively resist division and violence—in thought, deed, and action toward each other and our enemies." Moore, *Dear White Peacemakers*, 93.

66. Hart, *Trouble I've Seen*, 168

67. Bradley, pers. comm., Feb. 20, 2019.

68. Sweet, *Table to Table*, 141. Welch et al. also suggest that for beloved community to form, we must be intentional about building real relationship with the other. They tell the story of Harrisburg Brethren in Christ Church, for whom "the process began many years ago when the church committed to staying in their city neighborhood even as they outgrew their building. During that time, they made a renewed commitment to

An American Lent reports that "one of the best ways to overcome division is through communion with the 'other.' Presbyterian pastor, Lingon Duncan, explained that racism was not even on his radar until he befriended black pastor and church planter Thabiti Anyabwile. Relationship changed his heart. Allow relationships to continue to transform yours. Invite a colleague or neighbor of a different race to break bread over a meal,"[69] with a heart to listen, understand, and learn a different experience.

Some of the pastoral colleagues in my ministerium described the practices of their congregations that intentionally sought to build relationships with people of color, and the result was greater diversity. Perkins issues what he calls "The Friendship Challenge," in which he describes how people from different races and ethnicities can follow the example of Jesus and cross color lines to form deep relationships.[70] He describes how the Christian Community Development Association applied this principle by relocating to the places "where the brokenness was" because their goal was to "become one with our neighbors until there is no longer an 'us' and 'them,' but only a 'we.'"[71]

PROPHETIC ACTION, PART 2: SACRIFICIAL DIVESTITURE

After building relationships, prophetic divestiture is the next action required for the formation of alternate communities based on equality. Pickett, honestly but sadly, describes divestiture when he says that he is "not very hopeful because racism seems intractable on a macro and micro level. To give up the power and privilege of whiteness is unimaginable. It is a death that requires a rebirthing and resurrection. As James Cone said, 'White people need to become black,' which is to divest oneself of one's whiteness."[72] What does Cone mean?

Hart explains Cone's concept of prophetic divestiture when he says, "Solidarity requires that socially advantaged people realize that their life in this racialized society requires them to use their bodies as a living sacrifice."[73] White churches that are to break down the walls are going to have to sacrifice

---

the ethnically and racially diverse community in which they were located." Welch et al., *Plantation Jesus*, 143–44.

69. Barnes et al., *American Lent*, 101.

70. Perkins and Waddles, *He Calls Me Friend*, 145–54.

71. Perkins and Waddles, *He Calls Me Friend*, 152.

72. Pickett, "White Christian America," 41:20–41:50.

73. Hart, *Trouble I've Seen*, 170.

themselves to create an alternative community to the dominant culture. Prophetic divestiture finds precedence in a theology of togetherness' understanding of salvation, which we studied in chapter 7 when we observed the concept of Jubilee. There we noted that Jubilee flowed from God's heart for equality, so that every fifty years people would divest themselves of property and possession to bring equality to those in need. Jesus noted that he himself was the fulfillment of the Jubilee prophecy of Isa 61:1–2, "The Spirit of the Lord is on me, because he has anointed me . . . to proclaim the year of the Lord's favor" (Luke 4:18–19). Furthermore, Jubilee divestiture is fundamental to discipleship to Jesus, as we see in his teaching that his disciples must "deny themselves and take up their cross daily and follow [him]. For whoever wants to save their life will lose it" (Luke 9:23–24).

The apostle Paul knew how to demonstrate this, as noted above, when he wrote to the Christian community in the city of Corinth that he became "all things to all men" (1 Cor 9:19–27). He would later write them explaining that Christian communities should practice economic equality (2 Cor 8:10–15), by which he meant that Christian communities with abundant financial means should divest themselves generously to other Christian communities in need (2 Cor 9:6–15). What we see in Jesus and Paul is a biblical foundation for divestiture, the giving up of our rights, privileges, and possessions for those who are marginalized. When considering how whites can divest themselves of their whiteness to create a prophetic alternate community, we must first identify the dominant community from which we desire to create an alternate.

In the situation of northern American white segregated churches, the dominant culture is not necessarily the wider American culture, though it may have touch points with that culture too. What I am referring to is the dominant Christian culture of the northern American church, which is white, and which has retained privilege and power for the white majority. The mandate for the church to be a community of equality for all requires us to pursue an alternative Christian community that directly confronts the dominant Christian community. Hart explains it this way:

> This subversive Kingdom life means that everything is up for critique and change. It means that the community's life must yield itself to the concerns of those historically excluded. It means that things like job descriptions, church food and meal choices, book selections, curriculum structures, money allocation, meeting times, and the composition of decision-making groups like the church board must be radically reconfigured. These things must become signposts of faithfulness to the God

who sustains all of life, and whom every tribe, nation, and tongue will one day worship.[74]

Pickett says that "diversity talk is all the rage. But too often . . . all the processes and policies remain the same. We have to give up the showmanship, give up appearances. Get on with the hard work of divestment, making them uncomfortable, and running the risk that the community might not exist anymore."[75] Very similarly, Hart writes,

> some people desire merely to attend a diverse service for an hour or two on Sunday morning, while their lives the rest of the week are just as racialized as everyone else's. Baylor University released a recent study suggesting that black people attending a multiethnic church were more likely to hold views that resemble the perspectives of most white people in society than other black people. My observation is that most multiethnic churches are normed by white, dominant-culture sensibilities, even when diversity is being reflected on stage. And it is a real struggle for communities to break from that stronghold.[76]

We need prophetic imagination to critique our dominant Christian communities, and we need alternative prophetic communities to facilitate this because we want all humanity to flourish through togetherness.[77]

CONCLUSION

In America, when we walk into a church gathering, and we notice that the ethnic demographic does not approximate that of the surrounding culture, we disciples of Jesus need to put on the prophetic mantle and declare that this is not in line with the kingdom of God. Then we need to engage in

---

74. Hart, *Trouble I've Seen*, 171–72. See also Hart, *Who Will Witness?*.

75. Pickett, "White Christian America," 45:35—48:10.

76. Hart, *Trouble I've Seen*, 176–77. For additional studies in multiethnic theory, biblical analysis, and extensive practical suggestions for Christian communities, see DeYmaz, *Building*; DeYmaz and Li, *Leading*; DeYoung et al., *United by Faith*; Garces-Foley, "New Opportunities," 209–24; Garces-Foley, "Multiethnic Congregations"; Rusaw, "God's Children," 229–41; Yancey, *One Body, One Spirit*.

77. Ethicist Reggie Williams details how Dietrich Bonhoeffer learned a Christology of suffering from the African-American church during his tenure in Brooklyn. It was this theology that empowered Bonhoeffer to resist Nazism, even giving his life, when he returned to Germany. Bonhoeffer learned, therefore, the prophetic imagination necessary to critique his dominant Aryan Christian community. See Williams, *Bonhoeffer's Black Jesus*.

prophetic study, lament, relationship, and divestment that leads to the creation of an alternate community, the beloved community.

One final encouragement from Brueggemann might help us: "The essential question for the church is whether or not its prophetic voice has been co-opted into the culture of the day. The community of God's people who are striving to remain faithful to the whole counsel of God's Word will be prophetic voices crying out in the wilderness of the dominant culture of the day."[78] The presence of voluntarily segregated churches should be all the evidence we need that we have been co-opted by our culture. To be faithful to the kingdom of God we must apply a prophetic theology of leadership to our churches.[79] As Cone says, "No gulf between blacks and whites is too great to overcome, for our beauty is more enduring than our brutality. What God joined together, no one can tear apart."[80]

What Cone describes is flourishing-producing togetherness as the beloved community of the church. But what about togetherness outside the church? What we will learn in the next few chapters is that Christians can practice flourishing-producing togetherness in any Christian community, inside or outside the church.

---

78. Brueggemann, *Prophetic Imagination*, 125.

79. For example, Emerson and Smith describe the Pentecostal Fellowship of North America dissolving their community in an effort of reconciliation, and thus creating the Pentecostal/Charismatic Churches of North America, "an interracial community," electing a black bishop in the Church of God in Christ, Ithiel Clemmons, as chairperson. The authors go on to describe the efforts of Promise Keepers to bring reconciliation. Emerson and Smith, *Divided By Faith*, 64. Emerson and Smith, writing in the year 2000 could point to numerous successful efforts. Now more than two decades later, given the racial tension of 2020 and 2021, we Christians, to provide flourishing-producing togetherness, would do well to resurrect the reconciliation movements of the 1990s. See also Tisby, *How To Fight Racism*, 120–38.

80. Cone, *Cross and the Lynching Tree*, 166.

16

Practicing Repentance Together as a Prerequisite for Flourishing

Writing mission statements, vision statements, and identifying core values have long been standard operating procedure for all sorts of communities, companies, and organizations. Those statements cannot guarantee that a community will stay on mission. History is replete with examples of communities of all kinds that slide away, sometimes slowly, sometimes rapidly, from their organizing purposes. This trend has been called "mission drift."[1] While it is possible that a community can change and adapt for healthy purposes, such as when a company strives to stay afloat amid a worldwide pandemic and must reinvent itself, there are other occasions when a company might drift away from its mission into the darker waters of injustice.

To maintain its bottom line, for example, one company might outsource its graphic design to another company that does not pay fair wages to its employees or does not provide safe working conditions. Another company's customers back home are quite happy with its low coffee prices, but they have little knowledge that their coffee was purchased from impoverished farmers who are unable to provide for their families, watching as their mound of debt grows higher each year. Then there is the energy provider harvesting bountiful natural gas through fracking, all the while damaging the ecosystem. Maybe it is a narcissistic senior pastor of a church who rules with an iron fist, perhaps emotionally or sexually abusing his staff, while

---

1. Greer and Horst, *Mission Drift*.

church leadership turns a blind eye because attendance and giving have been on an upward trend.

Situations like those described here are only a small sampling of the ways real communities have allowed themselves to drift into injustice that results in human suffering. When a community has veered onto that pathway of injustice, they would do well to listen to the prophetic voice of theology. In particular, the prophetic voice such drifting communities need to hear is the theology of togetherness as it teaches corporate repentance, which, when implemented as a missional discipline, can restore and promote human flourishing.

To learn to hear that voice, it is imperative that we define repentance, as its application to Christian communities is our central investigation. Before we seek to define repentance, however, it is incumbent upon us to uncover potential assumptions we might hold about the subject of repentance, hopefully clearing the way for a more faithful definition of repentance.

EXAMINING ASSUMPTIONS

First, though often seen as the domain of the individual, is it appropriate for repentance to be applied in the wider sense of togetherness? To this Christopher Wright suggests, "That I should long for others to . . . be saved and forgiven by casting their sins on the crucified Savior in repentance and faith is the most energizing motive for evangelism. . . . But there is more in the biblical theology of the cross than individual salvation, and there is more to biblical mission than evangelism. The gospel is good news for the whole creation."[2] Though Wright has a global view in mind, is his description of salvation sufficiently broad so that we could justify applying repentance to Christian communities? On the one hand, it is possible that Wright is suggesting that, because there is more to the theology of the cross than individual salvation and that the gospel is good news for the whole of creation, repentance, which is a critical element of the gospel, can have a corporate dynamic and application.

On the other hand, it is also possible to understand Wright here as connecting repentance with the individual and not specifically with the wider vision for the gospel. Given those potentialities, we can question: Should not repentance also be applied corporately, especially if we are to view the gospel as good news for the whole creation? I will attempt to demonstrate that we should apply repentance corporately, and thus Christian communities of all kinds can and should practice repentance. Our biblical

---

2. Wright, *Mission of God*, 314.

investigation below will seek to bear this out. Though we will seek to show that repentance can be applied corporately, there is another assumption undergirding this, that of its validity.

Second, an investigation of repentance assumes that repentance has broad social acceptance in the contemporary world. Perhaps, though, repentance is no longer considered necessary or appropriate. Anecdotally, repentance seems not to be in fashion in our national conversation in the USA. If repentance is considered so antiquated that it was only appropriate for cultures long past, then our investigation is moot.

While we can lament the loss of repentance in our national conversation, it remains a vital theological doctrine in the church, and further we will see its value for all communities. Missional theologians Alan Hirsch and Mark Nelson write that repentance is "crucial to cleansing the doors of perception, the key to transformation, and the pathway to the true knowledge of God."[3] With Hirsch and Nelson, as we will see, even when the practice of repentance is belittled or shunned, it remains vital to mission in our world today, especially because our understanding of salvation is predicated on repentance.

Because repentance remains a vital practice, a third assumption needs to be examined and that is the nature of repentance. Repentance must be distinguished from what philosopher and spiritual writer Dallas Willard calls "the Gospel of Sin Management."[4] What Willard is referring to when he uses the phrase "sin management" is a gospel message that is focused on modulating behavior rather than producing the deep inner transformation of the heart taught by Jesus.

In other words, is repentance just trying to get people to change their outward behavior (sin management), or does repentance point to a deeper heart change? As we will see below when we examine the biblical teaching on repentance, it is correct to teach even young children that repentance is a critical element to experience the flourishing life. But Willard's caution remains. To make the concept of repentance understandable to children, is it possible that even adults have a misunderstanding of the nature of repentance?

For years, my congregation has supported a missionary whose primary ministry is open-air preaching. We have traveled to the city of Philadelphia to work with him, both for weeklong trips in the summer and one-day visits in the winter. One feature of those trips has been his Sidewalk Sunday

---

3. Hirsch and Nelson, *Reframation*, 125.
4. Willard, *Divine Conspiracy*, 35–59.

School, for which the missionary uses a variety of creative methods like magic tricks and paint boards to share the good news of Jesus with children.

He teaches them that the definition of repentance is simply, "Stop doing the wrong thing, and start doing the right thing." While certainly easy for children and adults to grasp, is this definition sufficient to meet the biblical standard that we can employ toward a theology of togetherness' conception of repentance? Or is this definition wanting? What is the nature of repentance? Perhaps the missionary's definition is the "milk" that children can take in, but what happens when they never move on to the "meat" of a more mature understanding?

Author Jeremy Treat concurs with Willard when he says that a sin management approach to repentance "inevitably . . . ends up in the spin cycle of failure, guilt, trying harder, and then more failure and deeper guilt, until we reach despair or settle for duplicity."[5] In other words, repentance opens a door for hope. Theologian Jonathan King quotes Blocher who says, "Repentance has a future, it enters the open future; remorse relates only to the past."[6] Therefore, we will see that repentance, to avoid resulting in outward sin management, must be rooted in a heart motivated to restore broken relationships with God and humanity.

As a child and through most of my teen years, I was immaturely unkind to my younger brother. After my freshman year in college, I still had not matured in this area, even as God was at work in my life in a new way. One day my brother expressed his understandable frustration with my meanness, saying, "I can't wait till you go back to college." His words were the truth telling I needed to hear, and I felt his pain in a new way, pain that I had caused for many years. I repented and began to make changes.

Theologian Thomas Oden suggests that a definition of "repentance is incomplete or insincere that does not resolve to lead a new life."[7] Thus we will endeavor to demonstrate a biblical theology of repentance that affirms its corporate application, its vitality for mission, flowing from a deep inner transformation. It is to that definition we now turn.

DEFINING REPENTANCE

What is repentance? To begin to answer that question, it is imperative that we research the use of the term in the biblical languages. First, the word the Hebrew Bible predominantly uses for repentance is the word *shuv*, which

---

5. Treat, *Seek First*, 93.
6. King, *Beauty of the Lord*, 303.
7. Oden, *Systematic Theology*, 86.

means "to turn back." Linguists tell us that it is used "of someone who has shifted direction in a particular way and then shifted back from it in the opposite way. As long as there is no contrary factor the assumption is that such persons or people will turn back and reach the original point from which they departed."[8] Therefore, the most common English translation of *shuv* is the word "turn."

While we have admittedly not yet entertained any further biblical teaching and context, the Sidewalk Sunday School missionary's definition of repentance above seems to align with the lexical understanding of *shuv*—turn away from the wrong thing and turn toward the right thing. As we will see, however, the biblical context adds color, tone, and texture that provides a much more nuanced understanding of the Hebrew conception of repentance, one that leads to human flourishing. Before examining that context, let's first examine the New Testament word most often used for repentance.

The New Testament Greek word most commonly translated "repentance" is the word *metanoia*, and one definition describes it quite similarly to what we learned of the Hebrew *shuv*. *Metanoia* means "to change one's way of life as the result of a complete change of thought and attitude with regard to sin and righteousness. . . . Though in English a focal component of repent is the sorrow or contrition that a person experiences because of sin, the emphasis in [*metanoia*] seems to be more specifically the total change, both in thought and behavior, with respect to how one should both think and act."[9]

In this definition the linguists give us the beginning of the nuance I mentioned above. Repentance is more than turning. For the turning to be sufficient, the linguists suggest, repentance must include a total change of person, both inward (thinking) and outward (acting). As theologian Donald Bloesch suggests, "Sin is not a mistake that can be routinely taken care of by an apology, however sincere, but a willful transgression that calls for confession and absolution."[10] The Sidewalk Sunday School missionary's definition is beginning to show some deficiencies, as it focused only on outward action and did not include any sense of the inner transformation we see in *metanoia*.

Let me attempt to combine what the Hebrew and Greek words teach us about repentance with the following definition: a willful choice that transforms a person internally and thus leads to their external restoration with God and others. But what of the components of corporate repentance

---

8. Koehler et al., *Hebrew and Aramaic*, 1429.
9. Louw and Nida, *Greek-English*, 509.
10. Bloesch, *Jesus Christ*, 52.

and human flourishing? While we have begun to discover the need for a definition of repentance that goes beyond the Sidewalk Sunday School missionary's definition, we have yet to see how repentance could be understood corporately, thus helping us practice a theology of togetherness for human flourishing. Clearly, these definitions must be enhanced by placing the biblical words *shuv* and *metanoia* in biblical contexts. Let's now take a look at that biblical context.

A BRIEF STUDY OF THE BIBLE'S TEACHING ABOUT REPENTANCE

When we examine the context of the use of *shuv* in the Hebrew Bible, the writers provide a much clearer picture of community repentance that not only includes the concept of turning away from sin and turning back to God but also a turning that includes human flourishing.

From its inception, the Lord gave the nation of Israel a means for corporate repentance. As the nation was nearing the conclusion of its sojourn wandering in the wilderness for forty years, the people arrived on the border of the promised land of Canaan. Moses, the great prophet leader of the nation, launches into a kind of fireside chat with the nation. Recorded in the fifth book of the Pentateuch, Deuteronomy, Moses retells the covenantal relationship the people had with the Lord their God.[11] Moses knows that his time is short, that he will soon pass on and die, and he delivers a prophetic speech to the nation, including the concept of *shuv*.

In Deut 4:1–40 Moses sternly warns the people of Israel not to worship any other gods and to obediently practice the ways and laws of the Lord. In this warning he conjures the image of a future day when the people will turn away. Analyzing the literary structure of this chapter, Wright sees repentance at the center of a chiasm.[12]

---

11. Tigay notes, "Deuteronomy has two Hebrew names. The popular name, Sefer Devarim, is short for (Sefer) ve-ʾelleh ha-devarim, "The Book of 'These are the words,'" a name based on the ancient practice of naming books after their key opening word or phrase. A second name, Mishneh Torah, "the Repetition of the Torah," appears frequently in rabbinic literature. Philo and the Septuagint used its Greek translation, Deuteronomion, whence it came to the Latin Vulgate and then to English as "Deuteronomy." Ironically, this name stems from a misunderstanding of Deuteronomy 17:18, where the phrase first appears but actually means "a copy of the Teaching." Nevertheless, it is an apt designation for the book, which recapitulates the teachings of Genesis through Numbers." Tigay, *Deuteronomy*, xi.

12. Wright, *Mission of God*, 376–77. Chiasm is a literary structure in which authors match an opening point with a closing point, a second point with a second-to-last point, and so on, until they reach an unmatched center point. There are a variety of

In Wright's view, vv. 29–31, the second of two matching center points, feature the Hebrew *shuv*, as Moses provides a means of restoration if the nation finds itself in a broken relationship with God: "But if from there you seek the Lord your God, you will find him if you look for him with all your heart and with all your soul. When you are in distress and all these things have happened to you, then in later days you will return [*shuv*] to the Lord your God and obey him." The author of Deuteronomy's focal point of this structure is God's promise of a restored relationship between himself and the people, if, as Wright observes, "there is repentance and a wholehearted loyalty and obedience to their covenant Lord."[13]

It is also apparent that Moses is not simply referring to a personal repentance but to a corporate one. Israel must return to the Lord together, and their return must emanate from a changed heart that leads to obedience. When he says that the nation will seek the Lord with all their heart and with all their soul, Moses specifies that true repentance involves inner transformation. Instilled in the people, corporately, is a vision of repentance that can only be described as flowing from deep heart change.

Potentially hundreds of years later, the Lord issued a similar warning to the people, but this time the nation was in a very different position. In Moses' day, they were a nation of recently freed slaves, wandering, desperate, and seeking a homeland. In the next passage we will examine, 2 Chr 7, the nation's economic fortunes have completely changed. Israel is perhaps at the height of its wealth and power, and King Solomon has just completed the construction of the temple of the Lord.

After an elaborate dedication of the temple, the Lord appeared to Solomon, speaking in v. 13 about a dire future that might include drought, pestilence, and famine. Though natural disasters can occur quite frequently as the result of a broken world, and they often did in the ancient Near East, in this passage the Lord connects at least some potential future disasters to the unfaithfulness of the nation. Describing the nation's potential sin further in vv. 19–20, the Lord pictures Israel's disobedience as a turning away (*shuv*), a forsaking of his commands and a betrayal, should the nation serve and worship other gods.

If the nation chooses this kind of spiritual adultery, this turning away, it is only repentance, a return, that can heal them. Using words very similar to those of Moses in Deut 4, the Lord proclaims to Solomon that, though they have turned away, there remains hope for the nation through repentance,

---

chiastic structures, but the seven-point structure is fairly common especially in Old Testament literature. See for example Dorsey, *Literary Structure*. Dorsey's chs. 1–5 provide an overview of literary structural studies in the Hebrew Bible, including chiasm.

13. Wright, *Mission of God*, 377.

as we read in 2 Chr 7:14: "If my people, who are called by my name, will humble themselves and pray and seek my face and turn [*shuv*] from their wicked ways, then I will hear them from heaven, and I will forgive their sin and will heal their land."

In this warning, God places repentance as the priority for national salvation. He does this precisely because the nation has chosen a wicked pathway, breaking their covenantal bond with the Lord. They have turned away, and now they must return. Noting the plural use of "people," the repentance God has in mind is of a corporate nature, and it leads to human flourishing when he says he will heal their land. Also similar to the conception of repentance that the Lord gave through Moses in Deuteronomy, here in 2 Chronicles the Lord describes a repentance not simply of outward action but one that is rooted in a change of heart. This change of heart is evident in the Lord's comments that this return necessarily stems from humility, an attitude that reveals the status of one's heart.

With two warnings describing a full-orbed repentance, we begin to wonder if Israel will eventually need to employ that kind of repentance. Students of ancient Israel's history are well acquainted with the many instances of their rebellion that predated the events in 2 Chr 7, including rebellious acts prior to Moses' words in Deut 4 and those that take place after Deuteronomy, which are featured prominently in the book of Judges. But it would be many years after God's warning to Solomon that Israel's apostate national and spiritual situation warranted a call to *shuv*, perhaps most acutely.

As we survey the nation of Israel's historical timeline, we travel through eras when Israel had turned away, thus fulfilling God's prophetic warnings to Moses and Solomon. Beginning with the reign of Solomon, who utilized forced slavery and allowed foreign gods within the borders of Israel through his many marriages to foreign royalty, the successive leaders of the nation often failed to restrain apostasy in the nation, and eventually God allowed the people to be exiled. All along, though, God raised up prophets to sound the message of repentance. The Hebrew prophetic writings, speaking to the apostate nation, utilize the image of turn and return.

Jeremiah, for example, says in Jer 4:1–2, "If you, Israel, will return, then return to me." Jeremiah's call for repentance is particularly fascinating not only due to its corporate call to repentance, but also because it connects repentance to the nation's theological headwaters found in the Abrahamic covenant of Gen 12, where God says that through Abraham's family he would bless the whole world. Making this connection, Jeremiah says that Israel will return to the Lord "and no longer go astray, and if in a truthful, just and righteous way you swear, 'As surely as the Lord lives,' then the nations will invoke blessings by him and in him they will boast" (4:1–2). In other words, corporate repentance by Israel will lead to corporate blessing of the world.[14] For Israel, then, corporate repentance was intended to lead to human flourishing.

In the prophetic word of Isa 30:15, we read, "In repentance and rest is your salvation." As the prophecy continues, if Israel walks in God's ways, removing their idols (vv. 21–22), God promises to send rain, food will be rich and plentiful, animals will graze and work the harvest. Even the moon and sun will shine brighter (vv. 23–26). These are pictures of flourishing, premised on the corporate repentance of the people.

Like Isaiah and Jeremiah, the prophet Hosea's unique story features the concept of return. Ordered by God to marry an unfaithful wife, Hosea embodies in his marriage the Lord's relationship to Israel. The nation, the Lord is saying, has become like an adulterous wife. Through Hosea, the Lord gives to his beloved but unfaithful nation a picture of what he desires—repentance. Three times he uses the word "return." "Come let us return to the Lord" (Hos 6:1); and "you must return to your God" (Hos 12:6); and finally he says in Hos 14:1, "Return, Israel, to the Lord your God."

Furthermore, it is a repentance, not just to individual piety, though that is important. In the first declaration of "return" (Hos 6:1) the Lord goes on to implore Israel to a repentance that leads to human flourishing when he says, "for I desire mercy, not sacrifice, and acknowledgment of God rather than burnt offerings" (v. 6). Thus the repentance the Lord had in mind was not leading to an outward practice of religious ritual but flowing from a transformed heart, repentance led to mercy, or *hesed*, which refers to right conduct between humans as well as between humans and God.[15]

Hesed is a loving kindness that leads to actions of love. Israel had been wicked, as the rest of Hos 6 bears out, mentioning priests who lie in ambush, waiting to commit murder and other shameful crimes. "Ephraim is given to prostitution, Israel is defiled" (v. 10). Israel is in desperate need of repentance but sadly "Israel's arrogance testifies against him, but despite all this he does not return to the Lord his God or search for him" (Hos 7:10). In Hos 12:6, the Lord calls out again for repentance that should lead to human flourishing: "You must return to your God; maintain love and justice."

---

14. Wright, *Mission of God*, 240–41. Wright points out that Jer 33:6–9 ("All nations on earth that hear of all the good things I do . . . will be in awe and will tremble at the abundant prosperity and peace I provide for [Jerusalem]," v. 9) and Ezk 36:16–36 ("Then the nations around you that remain will know that I the Lord have rebuilt what was destroyed," v. 36) are similar passages where repentance leads to restoration, which leads to "a corresponding impact on the nations." Wright, *Mission of God*, 241.

15. Koehler et al., *Hebrew and Aramaic*, 337.

As Hosea continues, we learn of the depth of injustice occurring in the nation—fraud (12:7), wealth used to cover sin (v. 8), human sacrifice (13:2). Finally, God calls again for a return in Hos 14:1, a call for repentance that will lead to the nation walking in God's ways of righteousness (14:9), and Hosea poetically paints a picture of flourishing: Israel will "blossom like a lily," "send down . . . roots" like a cedar of Lebanon, and "his splendor will be like an olive tree. . . . People will dwell in his shade; they will flourish like the grain. They will blossom like the vine" (vv. 5–8). A gorgeous invitation to repentance. The people would turn, at least in part, and that leads to return to the land, but Israel would always need repentance, which is where the New Testament begins.

As we move forward in the New Testament to John the Baptist's ministry, we see him calling for the nation to practice repentance into the community of the baptized. In Matt 3:8, the Gospel writer describes John by the Jordan River, preaching to a crowd of people saying, "Produce fruit in keeping with repentance."[16] In Luke 3:10, the people ask John, "What should we do?" Here we observe Luke framing this question as coming from the crowd, a corporate impression of togetherness.

Continuing in v. 11, John goes beyond his idea of baptism for repentance. Instead John depicts repentance in terms of human flourishing. It was not enough to just bank on their ethnicity ("Do not begin to say to yourselves, 'We have Abraham as our father,'" v. 8), they needed to live a new way of the kingdom: "John's baptism invited corporate repentance and readiness to enter the coming new kingdom and community."[17] Thus John suggested that "anyone who has two shirts should share with the one who has none, and anyone who has food should do the same" (Luke 3:11). To tax collectors and soldiers who asked him what they should do, he advocated that the repentant life that leads to human flourishing is marked by fairness and truth (Luke 3:12–14). A genuine repentance, then, is not simply the outward ritual of baptism but an inner transformation of heart that persists in actions that bring about human flourishing.

John's ministry was potentially quite short, as Jesus came along to continue and advance the preaching of repentance John had started. There is a moment of confluence between John's and Jesus' ministries, that of Jesus' baptism by John, which has a striking connection to corporate repentance. Consider the fact that Jesus, though perfect, is baptized by John, who performed baptisms for repentance. While Jesus had no need of repentance, Jonathan King notes, "Jesus shows himself to be obedient to the call to Israel

---

16. See also Luke 3:8.
17. Cummins, "John the Baptist," 437.

for repentance in full compliance with God's righteous requirement. And thus by submitting to John's baptism, Jesus is identifying representatively with his people Israel, and fulfilling all righteousness."[18]

Jesus joins the activity of corporate repentance on behalf of the people, though he himself did not need individual repentance. This example of representative corporate repentance is one we will return to later as we consider how communities can practice repentance together in our day. After the brief meeting between Jesus and John at the Jordan, John falls into the background while the narrative focuses on the up-and-coming ministry of Jesus.

In Mark 1:14–15, we read that after John baptizes Jesus, John is put in prison and Jesus' public ministry commences in Galilee with the proclamation, "The time has come. . . . The kingdom of God has come near. Repent and believe the good news!" (v. 15). Repentance would continue to be a feature of Jesus' preaching, as described in Luke 5:32 when he says, "I have not come to call the righteous, but sinners to repentance." In Luke 13:3–5 he twice says to the people, "Unless you repent, you too will all perish," followed by a parable that carries overtones of corporate repentance.

The parable is about a man who planted a fig tree in his vineyard, but after three years the fig tree did not produce fruit. In frustration the man tells his gardener to cut down the fig tree. But the gardener advocates for one more year of fertilization and care for the tree. Coming as it does on the heels of a teaching about repentance, the parable of the fig tree could very well refer to the nation of Israel's sin, perhaps particularly evidenced in its religious leaders' lack of fruit and need for repentance.

Furthermore, as Jesus' ministry continued, one of his primary tasks was investing in his disciples, raising them up to eventually take over for him. On one occasion, as part of their training, he sent them on a mission trip, and Mark tells us that "they went out and preached that people should repent" (Mark 6:12), just as Jesus had preached.

Later, after his resurrection, we read in Luke 24:45–57, in his conversation with the two disciples on the road to Emmaus, Jesus "opened their minds so they could understand the Scriptures" (v. 45), which had long before predicted that, after the Christ's suffering and resurrection, "repentance for the forgiveness of sins will be preached in his name to all nations" (v. 47). Jesus' theology of repentance was prolific, and it included touches of corporate repentance.

Jesus' focus on repentance would continue long after he ascended, precisely because he had discipled his followers to continue his ministry, including the themes of his preaching. It is no surprise that his apostles'

---

18. King, *Beauty of the Lord*, 183.

ministry included a focus on repentance from the very beginning of the church. In Acts 2:38, Peter's sermon to the Pentecost crowd concludes with "repent and be baptized, every one of you."

To what degree is this a corporate calling to repentance, and to what degree is it a calling to individual repentance? Might Peter conceive of his call to repentance in a corporate way? In the preceding material, he depicts the corporate group as culpable in the death of Christ, and thus it could be argued that they need to make a corporate repentance. In fact, quite a large group does just that, as Luke records in v. 41, "Those who accepted his message were baptized, and about three thousand were added to their number that day."

Shortly after the beginning of the church, we read in Acts 3:19 another sermon by Peter. Here he admonishes the crowd to "repent, then, and turn to God, so that your sins may be wiped out, that times of refreshing may come from the Lord." In that one sentence Peter makes two important statements for a theology of togetherness' conception of corporate repentance that brings flourishing.

First, he hearkens back to the Hebrew idea of *shuv*, mentioning the turn to God that is necessary in repentance. Second, he looks to the future hope that repentance brings, calling it a "time of refreshing from the Lord." This refreshing time is a clear reference to human flourishing that is brought about by a truly repentant heart and truly repentant action. Near the conclusion of this sermon, Peter, in Acts 3:25, further references the ancient Hebrew vision of flourishing, the Abrahamic covenant, in which the Lord says, "Through your offspring all peoples of the earth will be blessed" (Gen 22:18). In other words, there is yet another direct link between repentance and the flourishing of the world.

But is Peter speaking corporately in his sermon in Acts 3? Evidence suggests that he is. Looking back at the beginning of the sermon, Peter addresses the crowd corporately in v. 12, "Fellow Israelites." Then in vv. 13–15, he conceives of them as a group, culpable for the death of Jesus. Peter's approach is fascinating, as clearly not all in the crowd that day could have been personally involved in the death of Jesus.

Peter lumps them together, giving them corporate responsibility for the crucifixion. It follows that we view his call to repentance as a corporate call, if we are to maintain rhetorical consistency throughout his sermon. What we conclude is that the preaching of the early church began with a theology of togetherness that emphasized repentance as essential to human flourishing. But did the preachers and teachers of the early church persist in focusing on repentance?

The apostles' emphasis on repentance continues throughout the book of Acts,[19] including in the preaching of Paul.[20] While Paul did not have a major focus on repentance, he did write about it as integral to the life of the Christian. In his Letter to the Romans, in 2:4, Paul notes that it is God's kindness that leads us to repentance, a helpful corrective to the potential conception of repentance that is simply responding to judgment or punishment from God. We need not fear repentance because God is kind.

Too often repentance is conceived as negative and detestable, which is understandable, as repentance is an admittance that a community has committed an injustice. Like individual people, most communities do not want to admit any wrongdoing. To raise the specter of culpability means that the community could face negative consequences, and generally communities, like individuals, want to avoid consequences.

Paul here reminds Christian communities to view repentance from a positive paradigm, God's kindness. Seeing repentance as motivated or inspired by God's kindness gives us the impression that repentance is a profoundly positive experience, especially when we see its outflow, human flourishing. Though Paul did not often talk about repentance, there is at least one other place we can examine where he writes about it a bit more.

Perhaps Paul's most extensive passage on repentance is found in 2 Cor 7:8–11. Previously he had cause to write a rebuke to the unruly Corinthian church. Now in 2 Corinthians he lauds them for how they received his rebuke, with sorrow that led to repentance. "You became sorrowful as God intended" (v. 9). This sorrow, Paul explains, is vital to true repentance. He goes on to call it a godly sorrow that brings repentance, and that repentance leads to salvation, leaving no regret.

He adds even more to his description of repentance that is produced by godly sorrow in v. 11: "See what this godly sorrow has produced in you: what earnestness, what eagerness to clear yourselves, what indignation, what alarm, what longing, what concern, what readiness to see justice done." For Paul, repentance is rooted in godly sorrow for one's sin, a deep inner transformation, such that one is passionate about moving toward justice, which is another picture of human flourishing. But what of the other writers in the New Testament? Was repentance a part of their preaching?

We already heard Peter include repentance in his preaching in the early sermons of the book of Acts. In 2 Pet 3:9, he continues this theme when he writes that God is patient, "not wanting anyone to perish, but everyone to come to repentance." Like Paul's indication that God's kindness

---

19. Acts 5:31, 8:22, and 11:18.

20. Acts 13:24, 17:30, 19:4, 20:21, and 26:20.

leads to repentance, Peter refers to God's patience as providing opportunity for repentance and furthermore that God wants all to do so, though this is likely not a reference to corporate repentance.

The next writer to mention repentance is the writer of Hebrews, when he refers to it as an elementary and foundational teaching in 6:1–6. As such, we can learn that repentance is critical. Finally, though John does not refer to *metanoia* in his writings, it appears frequently in the vision God gave him. In Rev 2 and 3, which contain letters from Jesus to seven churches, he calls them to repent.

In conclusion, the broad biblical picture of repentance is one of a deep inner godly sorrow that transforms the heart, thus bringing restoration between humans and between God and humans, bursting forth to the new hope and new life of flourishing. Further, Christian communities of all kinds can and should embrace and practice repentance for these same purposes.

In contradiction to theologian Nicholas Perrin's view that repentance is granted by God,[21] the biblical picture is one of repentance as choice. This is in line with theologian George Eldon Ladd's description of repentance, which emphasizes free will: "To change the whole direction of action, to turn and to embrace in decision the Kingdom of God."[22] True repentance springs from a heart disposed to freely express its will. Bloesch summarizes well, "The Bible teaches self-surrender, which sets us free for repentance—turning from our absorption in self—and for obedience—serving God and neighbor in self-giving love."[23]

The implication of free will, therefore, is that not all will choose repentance, as some will freely choose to remain in an unrepentant state. As we noticed above, the Old Testament prophet Isaiah, while pleading with the people to find their salvation in repentance, says, "but you would have none of it" (Isa 30:15). In the New Testament, in Heb 6:6, the author suggests that those who, after having repented and followed the way of flourishing, fall again may not be able to taste repentance anew.

Furthermore, the entire biblical corpus presents a theology of repentance in the context of some people who choose it and some that do not. For flourishing to occur, therefore, it is imperative that Christian communities choose repentance. We now move to the logistics of appropriating the theology of corporate repentance to these communities, seeking practical methods and rituals they can choose to embody repentance together.

21. Perrin, *Kingdom*, 77–78, 127.
22. Ladd, *Gospel of the Kingdom*, 96–100.
23. Bloesch, *Jesus Christ*, 256–57.

HOW TO PRACTICE REPENTANCE TOGETHER

While I am writing for Christian communities, I believe that any community, even those that are nonsectarian, would do well to apply repentance as a practice within their community, as it involves a willingness to move toward restoration to bring about human flourishing. This is more than just the implementation of ethical practices. It is a deep examination of how the community's activities have affected humanity. It asks if there is any brokenness, any harm done in the name of the community. If so, then that community would do well to practice repentance toward restoration for flourishing.

But what could this practice entail given what we have learned about repentance? Surely each individual, or perhaps those culpable for the injustice within the community, can practice personal repentance, thereby forming a representative repentance on behalf of the community, just as Jesus demonstrated for us when he participated in John's baptism of repentance. Symbolically, though Jesus himself had no need to be baptized, he joined with repentance of the larger group, thus affirming the need for national repentance.

It seems, though, that the repentance that biblical theology has in view ought to embody a collective approach in addition to an individualistic or representative approach. This collective approach must also move repentance from the domain of the symbolic toward a realized practice. Christian communities, both inside and outside the church, can participate in the kind of corporate repentance envisioned by God in his warnings to the nation of Israel. What, then, might this look like in practice?

To start, Christian communities need to create a culture that invites the prophetic voice to speak to the possible injustices the community might have committed together and for which they need to repent together. Admittedly, a group might be reluctant to submit themselves to unbiased observers who speak the truth to them, such as the prophets who spoke truth to the nation of Israel. Yet, the humility God requests of his people in 2 Chr 7 is precisely the attitude required for communities to develop a culture of repentance.

One practice that flows from this kind of humility that would lead to repentance is the hiring of an ethics officer or team whose sole job description is to review the entirety of the community for the purposes of best practices. The ethics officer or team could also serve as a consulting body before policies or practices are implemented. Once injustice is observed, these communities would do well to hold a public forum, including everyone in the communities, but also inviting the public and especially those affected by the injustice. The public forum could include at least the following two courses of action.

First, the community would name the injustice, describing in honest terms how they came to the point of practicing the injustice, what the injustice involved, and how the injustice affected humans or the planet. This truth telling is crucial to any genuine repentance, showing that the community has taken the injustice to heart.

Second, they could hold a public declaration of sorrow together. The idea of godly sorrow, which we found in the writings of Paul, and the idea of the nation of Israel humbly praying and seeking God's face, depict for us the model of public declaration of sorrow. The community would publicly declare its apology and its ongoing grief and sorrow. Given that communities consist of individuals, either the entire community or, if it is sufficiently large, perhaps the leadership of the community should express sorrow. It should be, as much as possible, a face-to-face, in person conveyance of grief and apology for all the harm done—not to dredge up pain again and thus make the injustice worse but to convey an apology with sensitivity to cease the injustice.

Third, after the community holds a public forum marked by truth and godly sorrow, reparations are in order for true repentance that leads to flourishing. "Genuine repentance calls for a fitting act of restitution, the restoration of whatever has been wrongly acquired, in which practical amends are made for the injustices inflicted upon others insofar as that is reasonably possible."[24]

When Jesus calls the corrupt tax collector Zacchaeus to repentance, though he was an individual, Zacchaeus responded in a way that a community could use as an example of repentant reparations (Luke 19). He made sure that those upon whom he had committed an injustice were paid back more than the amount he had defrauded them. True repentance that leads to human flourishing will abide by his example. Furthermore, in Jesus' parable of the good Samaritan, the Samaritan paid for health care for the Jewish man who was injured, though the Samaritan had nothing to do with the injury (Luke 15). Communities can seek to bring new hope and new life by abundant reparations.

Finally, an additional word is in order as repentance, certainly for Christian communities, is especially pertinent. Add "God" as the focus; Christian communities should willingly move toward restoration *with God* to bring about human flourishing. This would suggest all the possible applications suggested above but also a worshipful gathering in which the

---

24. Oden, *Systematic Theology*, 97.

community expresses the truth about their sin, as well as their deep sorrow, seeking God's forgiveness then plotting the way forward to correct the injustice and make reparations.

CONCLUSION

Repentance is a vital discipline Christian communities must practice to encourage more justice and human flourishing in the world, a repentance that flows from a theology of togetherness as seen in the Old and New Testaments. But this repentance is not easy. A pastoral colleague in my local ministerium recently told me he felt convicted that his congregation needed to repent for how the church handled the firing of a previous youth minister. The firing took place at the beginning of the pastor's tenure, and in fact the process of firing the youth minister had begun prior to the pastor's arrival. At the time of the firing, the pastor was essentially involved in a decision that had already been made.

Now ten years later, knowing the ongoing reverberations the firing still had in the church family, he proposed a worship service of repentance. Numerous members of his congregation balked harshly at his suggestion, to the point that the church leadership team made the decision to postpone the worship service. The coronavirus pandemic hit in early 2020, leading to a quarantine that made it impossible to hold the worship service. Years later I asked him if they ever held the service, and he said no.

Despite a setback like that, corporate repentance is not only possible, but imperative, to promote human flourishing. White Christian communities in the United States can repent for their racist past. Universities, like Georgetown in Washington, DC, which were built on the backs of slaves, have already repented and now offer reparations in the form of scholarships for students of color.

Companies that produce goods and services by hiring child laborers can repent and not only discontinue their practices, but they can also make changes that ensure future labor is given fair wages, appropriate benefits, and healthy working conditions. The goal of human flourishing, which flows from God's heart for justice, is attainable as communities willingly undergo a stringent self-examination and repentance that leads to deep inner change—the well from which springs new hope and new life.

Once having practiced corporate repentance, Christian communities of all kinds can begin to envision a new future of human flourishing. What, then, can this new future marked by flourishing-producing togetherness look like? All along in our study we have encountered vibrant descriptions of flourishing, of the abundant life—a world marked by justice and thriving, people experiencing shalom in loving covenant community with God, one another, and with the created order. When we practice flourishing-producing togetherness, we create beloved community that transcends political and racial division, with an eagerness to practice corporate repentance.

17

Creating Culture Together for Flourishing

IN THE UNITED STATES of America there is much talk about culture war. This discussion goes back a century or more in America, with roots in the fundamentalist movement. Some Christians dream of the country reverting to what they consider to be a more righteous time. One of their primary methods to bring about cultural change is the use of political power.

Historian Philip Jenkins provides a caution to Christian use of political power when he says that "the modern story of Christian political activism is often an inspiring one, but history suggests that there are potentially disturbing sides of the story."[1] While Dietrich Bonhoeffer in Nazi Germany and Martin Luther King Jr. in the United States are examples of inspiring Christian political activists who sought to or actually did bring about positive cultural change, Jenkins warns that "it is not a vast leap from churches exercising political power to demanding an exclusive right to that power, perhaps within the confines of a theocratic state."[2]

Sadly, Jenkins is not just writing theory, as his corrective is rooted in the human experience. He refers, for example, to the American experiment of repatriating formerly enslaved Africans to their home continent by creating the nation of Liberia. He notes: "One of the rare independent African states to declare its Christian status from the outset was Liberia, in which

---

1. Jenkins, *Next Christendom*, 152.
2. Jenkins, *Next Christendom*, 152.

religion was used to justify the gross corruption of the nation's political elite and the oppression of the country's native people."[3]

Another African example is the Lord's Resistance Army (LRA) in Uganda, which had its roots in a messianic Christian prophetic movement, the Holy Spirit Mobile Force, which sought to change culture via the removal of witchcraft. Disturbingly, rather than changing culture in a beneficial way, the LRA violently abducted children and brainwashed them into becoming child soldiers. Jenkins correctly concludes that this is not an exclusively African trend, "as so often in European history, it is the leaders most convinced of their divine inspiration who carry out the most bloodthirsty actions."[4] How can Christians do better?

Responding to this, in *Culture Making*, Christian journalist Andy Crouch suggests that "the only way to change culture is to create more of it."[5] Crouch goes on to demonstrate that Christians, when they have resorted to condemning, critiquing, copying, or consuming culture, have failed to produce the human flourishing envisioned by Christian theology. He concludes that "the only way to motivate a large enough bloc of consumers to act in a way that really shapes the horizons of possibility and impossibility, in Hollywood or any other massive cultural enterprise, is to create an alternative."[6]

Further, given Christian theological imperatives rooted in the mission of God and other seminal doctrines, such as the Trinitarian nature of God as community, creating this alternative culture requires Christian communities of all kinds who see their theological mandate as creators of culture for the purpose of human flourishing.

All along, we have been defining communities as "people working together." They are Christian communities when, as Jesus taught, two or three come together in his name; he promises to be in their midst (Matt 18:20). Therefore we will see that while individuals can certainly have an important impact, the theological impetus of the biblical narrative is that Christian communities are best suited, and even mandated, to create culture for human flourishing.

---

3. Jenkins, *Next Christendom*, 154.
4. Jenkins, *Next Christendom*, 154–55.
5. Crouch, *Culture Making*, 67.
6. Crouch, *Culture Making*, 72.

DEFINING CREATING CULTURE FOR FLOURISHING

At the outset, we define the primary terms we are using. What is culture? Our approach to understanding culture draws on the rich definitions of culture by anthropologists Brian Howell and Janell Paris, theologian Richard Niebuhr, and Andy Crouch. Howell and Paris, from an anthropological viewpoint, define culture as "an idea created to describe a reality that people experience: the behaviors, values, practices, technologies, and assumptions that distinguish one group from another."[7] In other words, culture is "the total way of life of a group of people."[8]

Moving to a theologian's perspective, Niebuhr defines culture similarly as "the total process of human activity and the total result of such activity."[9] Furthermore, Niebuhr lists some of culture's characteristics. It is social,[10] or relational, and thus is not individual, a point that undergirds the theme of togetherness. Because culture is relational, we will see that the relational aspect of communities is required for creating and thus changing culture.

The next characteristic he points out is that culture is human achievement,[11] and therefore it differs from nature. This characteristic of culture gives a nod to the creative impulse required of people working together to bring cultural change. Finally, combining two more of Niebuhr's characteristics of culture, he says that culture is a "world of values" for the "good of man,"[12] which we will see below is in line with the theology of togetherness for human flourishing.

Last, Crouch brings a journalist's perspective, defining culture as "what we make of the world."[13] Similarly to the other definitions, Crouch believes in a relational element of culture, such that "until an artifact is shared, it is not culture."[14] Taking these three perspectives together, then, culture is human, relational, creative activity for human flourishing. What then is the unique relationship between human flourishing and culture?

To review what we have previously stated, Volf and Croasmun suggest that human flourishing is the goal of theology—that is, "forming human

---

7. Howell and Paris, *Cultural Anthropology*, 27.
8. Howell and Paris, *Cultural Anthropology*, 30.
9. Howell and Paris, *Cultural Anthropology*, 32.
10. Howell and Paris, *Cultural Anthropology*, 33.
11. Howell and Paris, *Cultural Anthropology*, 33.
12. Niebuhr, *Christ and Culture*, 34–35.
13. Crouch, *Culture Making*, 23.
14. Crouch, *Culture Making*, 40.

beings according to the pattern of Christ, such that each person and community is able to improvise the way of Christ in the flow of time in anticipation of becoming, along with the entire creation, the home of God."[15] In this definition we see a connection to Christian communities creating culture through their embodiment of the way of Christ in the world so that people and communities become the home of God.

Missional theologian Alan Hirsch adds a caution for those seeking to create culture: we should never "refuse to bring aspects of our cultures and lives under the lordship of Jesus."[16] Human flourishing is only possible under the lordship of Jesus. Certainly Volf and Croasmun also, rightly, include an individual ("each person") aspect to their definition because the goal of theology must be broad enough to include the individual as well as the entire community. Their definition, then, is sufficient for our purposes to see, through the lens of a theology of togetherness, how Christian communities can be culture creators for the purpose of human flourishing.

REVEALING OUR ASSUMPTIONS

With our definitions in hand, what assumptions could deter us from properly understanding how flourishing-producing togetherness can lead Christian communities to create culture? First, because our focus is on a theology of togetherness, we start by noting that the task of creating culture is often assumed to be the project or the domain of the individual, and especially of the artist. While we believe that individuals can create important cultural artifacts, what we will see is that substantive cultural change occurs best by Christian communities working together for human flourishing.

But to this, our second potential assumption is that it could be said that communities are too nebulous or too large to create culture. In our contemporary era, however, even some of the largest communities like Apple, Meta/Facebook, Google, and Amazon have changed the face of our nation and world. It is precisely their size that enables them to have the greatest potential to change culture for human flourishing.

Third, it could be assumed that Christian communities are normally seen as having different purposes than creating culture. Christian communities often define themselves according to the unique niche they serve, be it spiritual ministry, medical, educational, manufacturing, or other. For-profit companies have the further requirement to make money. To that concern, we will see that it is still possible to view communal purposes through the

15. Volf and Croasmun, *For the World*, 9.
16. Hirsch, *Forgotten Ways*, 108.

lens of a theology of togetherness, so that even for-profit companies can be financially viable and practice flourishing-producing togetherness as they create culture. Christian communities will need to see themselves theologically, and that will require them to evaluate how their community can be a creator of culture for the purpose of human flourishing.

Fourth, another preliminary consideration that could keep us from making progress in creating culture is that Christian communities can resort to being custodians of culture. A custodian of culture sees its mission as maintaining the status quo or tradition. Crouch affirms that this custodial posture can be positive,[17] but only if we are keeping or preserving cultural good that leads to flourishing. Clearly, though, a custodian of culture is not creating culture, and thus Crouch suggests that Christian communities would do well to put creation of culture at a premium if we truly want to effect cultural change.[18]

Fifth, and flowing from the fourth, missiologist Leslie Newbigin wisely cautions that "the content of the revelation in Christ, defined crucially by the twin events of cross and resurrection, provides a basis on which the great diversity of cultures can be welcomed and cherished and the claim of any one culture to dominance can be resisted."[19] This caution is quite important given the destructive history of colonialism perpetrated in the name of Christ over the centuries. Missionaries, under the guise of bringing the gospel to so-called heathens, attempted to transform "heathen" culture into Westernized cultures, often damaging that other culture and hindering Christian witness in the process. In so doing, these missionaries deceived themselves into believing they were successfully creating culture while in fact they soiled the name of Christ.

To counteract this possibility, Christian communities will need to exercise patience and sensitivity during the process of creating culture. There will always be aspects of culture to preserve, but we will see that it is in line with God's heart that Christian communities move beyond a merely custodial posture into a mode whereby they are defined as creators of culture for human flourishing.

17. Crouch, *Culture Making*, 98.

18. Crouch, *Culture Making*, 98. Theologian James Davison Hunter lists the mission statements of several Christian communities that state their desire to be change agents in the world. The reality, Hunter observes, is that "the dominant ways of thinking about culture and cultural change are flawed . . . and will not work." Hunter, *Change the World*, 4–5. I submit that Hunter's claim is true because so many Christian communities, though desiring to effect change, end up not doing so because they revert to a custodial posture.

19. Newbigin, *Pluralist Society*, 197.

Finally, expanding on the third assumption above, Christian communities are usually viewed as serving God's kingdom purposes but rarely as creators of culture. Many church mission statements involve some version of Jesus' quote in Matt 22:34–40 of the greatest commandments of loving God and loving people, or worshiping, fellowshipping, making disciples of Jesus, and reaching out to share the good news of Jesus in word and deed. How many churches, though, would understand their primary mission as a theological mandate to create culture? What we will see is that the scriptural vision for Christian communities, and especially churches, is that they can express and live out their mission as creators of culture, grounded in a theology of flourishing-producing togetherness.

ANTHROPOLOGICAL AND THEOLOGICAL METHODS OF CULTURE CREATION

Having defined terms and addressed some assumptions, we now examine anthropological and theological methods of culture creation. We will ask how these methods help us understand culture, leading to a theology of togetherness that helps us understand how Christian communities create culture for human flourishing.

The first method is communication. Theologically, God is a communicative being. The three persons of the Trinity communicate with one another. God also communicates with his creation in a variety of ways, in nature, through audible speech, the written word, and through inner impression or dreams and visions. God also communicates through his people, and he desires his people to communicate. Flowing from God's communicative nature, there can be no culture without communication.

Communication is not defined by active speaking. Communication involves both speaking and listening. Sociologist Sandhya Jha refers to one church's approach to creating new culture. That church addressed issues of injustice in their neighborhood first by engaging in a healthy dose of listening. "For the people wanting to effect change, it meant listening to the people who would be affected by the changes. For the people in power, it meant listening to the people affected by their decisions."[20]

This is very much in line with the example of Jesus whose communication emphasized asking questions of his conversation partners and listening for their answers. The ramification of the communication motif is that Christian communities, to be culture creators for the purpose of human

---

20. Jha, *Transforming Communities*, 32.

flourishing, will be active listeners and communicators. This central method of communication flows smoothly into the next one.

The second method is relationship. As we have seen above in our definition of culture, there is no culture without relationship. Again we turn to Christian theology's understanding of God as a Trinity. Trinity, a three in one, refers to one God in three coequal persons, a community, working together in unity. "People working together" is part and parcel of Trinitarian theology, thus serving as a foundational doctrine for our discussion of cultural change. In other words, the creative Trinity is a community. My theology mentor Tony Blair writes, "Redemption of the collective/corporate requires action by the collective/corporate. That redemptive activity, understood theologically, is always the work of the group, never the work of the solo individual. God has a people, always a people, who participate with God (who is also plural) in the work of redeeming the world (always plural). The very nature of the Trinity suggests community, collective action, redemption via organizational behavior."[21]

The community of the Trinity is creative; from their deity-culture they created human culture, endowing humanity with the ability to create still more culture. Christian communities, following the Trinitarian pattern, should see themselves as continuing what the Trinity started in the original creation, making more culture.

The third motif is incarnation. To illustrate, Paris recalls her anthropological research while living at Esther House, a Christian house for women in Washington, DC. During that time, she says, she "came to see that the methodology of anthropology—living among people and listening to their stories—could be a Christian practice."[22] What Paris is describing is an incarnational understanding of anthropological research. We cannot fully understand culture without participating in it. As Paris notes, incarnational approaches involve relational listening. Jesus is our model in this practice, as Paul writes in Phil 2:5–8,

> In your relationships with one another, have the same mindset as Christ Jesus: Who, being in very nature God, did not consider equality with God something to be used to his own advantage; rather, he made himself nothing by taking the very nature of a servant, being made in human likeness. And being found in appearance as a man, he humbled himself by becoming obedient to death—even death on a cross!

---

21. Blair, pers. comm., Jan. 2021.
22. Howell and Paris, *Cultural Anthropology*, 2.

In other words, God, in Christ, goes before us, leading the way as an example for us of how to make culture. Before we can change culture by creating an alternative, we first incarnate the culture, which means we sacrificially take on the skin of the receptor culture. As we learn that culture, we must remember that we bring our culture along with us. We cannot remove culture from ourselves. Christians have attempted to posture themselves this way, what Niebuhr calls "Christ above culture,"[23] as if we, because we are Christians, are unaffected by culture.

When my wife and I moved to Kingston, Jamaica, for a year, there was a real sense in which we brought our white affluent American culture with us. We could not shed our culture like clothes just because we hopped on a jet and immigrated to a new culture. When Christian communities strive to create new culture together, therefore, we do well to practice a humble awareness of the ongoing influence of our home culture.

We must also be on-guard against over-enculturation, which can lead to syncretism. Syncretism is an identification so deeply into one culture that leads to the creation of a new culture, blending elements of the old and new. This cultural fusion is not inherently wrong. In Kingston, we loved seeing how the McDonald's fast-food restaurants offered jerk chicken sandwiches, blending an American sandwich with a tasty Jamaican spice.

But syncretism can also be disastrous. Consider Christians seeking to communicate the good news of Jesus to people in a new culture that includes theological beliefs that are inconsistent with the good news of Jesus, perhaps including injustices such as child sacrifice or female genital mutilation. Syncretism occurs when a person attempts to make a mash-up of both belief systems, often changing the doctrine of both or preserving injustice.

To combat syncretism, Hirsch provides a corrective that all those who seek to create culture should heed. He calls the corrective "Christocentric monotheism." Monotheism is the belief that there is one God, which is consistent with the Christian understanding of God as one Trinitarian community. The term "Christocentric," when describing monotheism, views Jesus' birth, life, death, and resurrection as central to one's understanding of God. Hirsch explains, "When the surrounding culture intrudes on the lordship of Jesus and his exclusive claim over all aspects of our lives, then monotheism functions as the defining criterion by which we can distinguish between syncretism and genuinely incarnational expressions of the church."[24] The incarnational model of Jesus reminds Christian communities to remain focused on Jesus while we are planted in any culture. Taken together, there

---

23. Niebuhr, *Christ and Culture*, 116–48.
24. Hirsch, *Forgotten Ways*, 105.

is a rich anthropological and theological foundation upon which to view Christian communities as having a mandate to be culture creators for the purpose of human flourishing. To sustain that, we turn to the story of God in Scripture.

A SCRIPTURAL BASIS FOR CREATING CULTURE TOGETHER FOR FLOURISHING

We begin at the beginning, where Gen 1–2 describe God the Creator, sharing creative ability and mission with his creation, which is the foundation for all creativity. When God says to the humans he created in Gen 1:28, "be fruitful and increase in number; fill the earth and subdue it. Rule over [it]," and then blesses them to do so, he is turning over to them a partial measure of creative rule. Further he places the man in the garden to work it and take care of it (Gen 2:15). While humanity does not have the unlimited creative capability of the Trinitarian God, that same God does give us the ability to co-create with him. Hunter says that "human beings are by divine intent, and their very nature, world-makers."[25]

Furthermore, the text explicitly describes how we are to create in community, together, not alone. This is evident, after God has placed the man in the garden and given him instructions, when God observes, "It is not good for the man to be alone. I will make a helper suitable for him" (Gen 2:18). The account continues to describe the man naming the animals, among whom there is found no suitable helper. God resolves the tension by creating a woman, and the man and woman are married, the first human community (Gen 2:21–25). This small community, then, has a mandate to create culture in line with God's desires for flourishing. But their fall into selfish disobedience (Gen 3) is decidedly anti-flourishing.

Eventually, God creates a new plan to establish a wider community that will create culture for the purpose of human flourishing, an extended family. To another husband and wife, the aged and childless Abram and Sarai, God promises an heir that would lead their family to multiply into a large family. Thus God says that "all peoples on earth will be blessed through you" (Gen 12:3), an expansive statement of flourishing if there ever was one.

God would go on to rename this couple, Abraham and Sarah, and he reaffirmed the promise to their son Isaac (Gen 26:2–4) and then to his son Jacob (Gen 28:13–15), who was later renamed Israel. The extended family was growing, just as God said, and though God continued to grow the family, as many years passed, it remained to be seen exactly how God would

---

25. Hunter, *Change the World*, 3.

fulfill his promise to bless the world through them. For centuries, God's approach of culture creation did not seem to be leading to human flourishing.

The family of Israel grew exponentially, transforming from a family into a nation. Though a nation has many purposes, one purpose for the nation of Israel remained the creation of a new culture for human flourishing. What the biblical narrative describes for us is that the promise of human flourishing that God made to Abraham, Isaac, and Jacob was reaffirmed, though some four hundred years later, to Israel's leader Moses (Exod 6:2–8). It was through a unique law code God gave to Moses that the fulfillment of the promise of human flourishing began to take shape.

What God taught Moses and the nation of Israel was that they were to be, simply put, different. Many times, God tells them that they are set apart to be his chosen people, and thus they are not to live in the manner of other cultures. God establishes and guides the creation of their new culture through a body of language, the law, that he gives the nation of Israel.[26] Numerous passages in Deuteronomy explain how God, through this new language of the law, desires people to work together to create culture for human flourishing.

First, we look at the Ten Commandments (Exod 20; Deut 5). These foundational statements provide a moral code for the creation of the new culture. Israel is to give their allegiance to the Lord God and him alone. They are to honor his ways, which means they will also honor human life, as they together create a new culture marked by justice.

Lest this sound like the whim of a dictatorial god, as in the law codes of the religions of the cultures surrounding Israel, the Lord affirms his love for the people of Israel, and he desires that their formation of the new culture be rooted in their love for him. God promised to bless them richly, to be their God and to protect them among other cultures that would threaten them. Through this covenant he envisioned himself in an ongoing loving relationship with his people that would spill over to the other peoples of the world, producing flourishing for all.

Thus in Deut 6 he asks them to love him with their total being. Their new culture was radically different from the other cultures of the day, as the people of Israel and their God would be in close personal relationship. It was a covenant, a treaty, an agreement of love between the parties—like nothing the world had ever seen. Israel was to be a community that lived out a new theology of togetherness that resulted in the creation of culture for the purpose of human flourishing. As they migrated to and took possession of

---

26. The Sapir-Whorf Hypothesis "posits that language shapes people's perceptions, thoughts and views of reality." Howell and Paris, *Cultural Anthropology*, 66. The Mosaic law has this very effect on the people of Israel.

the promised land of Canaan, Israel was surrounded by people groups and city-states, the cultures of which included practices that were incongruent with the phrase "human flourishing."

Wright suggests that "the historical culture of the Canaanites... was degraded to the point of deserving divine judgment."[27] One evidence of this was the Canaanite practice of human sacrifice. Thus the Lord instructs Israel to avoid syncretism with Canaanite culture. In Deut 12:4 and 31, he repeats to Israel, "You must not worship the LORD your God in their way." Israel's practice of religion would show just how different God wanted his people to be.

God guided Israel to create a new religion that abolished the sacrificing of human life (Deut 18:10). Further, he adds that they must not drink blood, which was a ritual in Canaanite sacrificial worship, based on the false belief that blood is a life force that can give power to the one who drinks it (Deut 12). Similarly, God gave Israel strict regulations on what was clean versus unclean food (Deut 14), and what detestable Canaanite practices to avoid (Deut 18:9). Each of God's stipulations for Israel's new religious culture was designed to promote human flourishing.

Next Israel was to create a culture marked by justice. That meant the eradication of any practice based on a philosophy of "might makes right." In Deut 10:17–19, for example, Israel is told to actively remember their own experience of injustice when they were oppressed as enslaved foreigners for over four hundred years in Egypt. That terrible epoch, the Lord says, should cause them to create a culture free of oppression and instead create a culture noted for justice, especially to the marginalized.

He specifically mentions that they are to take up "the cause of the fatherless and the widow, and loves the foreigner residing among you, giving them food and clothing. And you are to love those who are foreigners, for you yourselves were foreigners in Egypt" (v. 18–19). This new culture is exemplified by the heart of the Lord himself, who embodies justice, which he illustrates by saying that "he shows no partiality and accepts no bribes" (v. 17).

Israel, therefore, will create a culture with checks and balances on power to prevent injustice, which would help them create a flourishing culture utterly differently from that of the surrounding cultures. How they will do this is spelled out in rather specific detail. In Deut 16:18–20 they are to appoint judges in every locality to flesh out the justice of God's heart described above, specifically to judge fairly, show no partiality, and take no bribes.

---

27. Wright, *Mission of God*, 475.

Furthermore, they are to create a kind of supreme court on the national level, as taught in Deut 17. Even due process is embodied in the new culture, which we see in the requirement for witnesses in Deut 19. God also asks Israel to create "cities of refuge," whereby the accused could find safe harbor until due process could be applied to their case. The Lord also established property laws that led to fair treatment, such as the canceling of debts and freeing of servants in Deut 15.

The Mosaic law has numerous examples of how Israel was creating a new culture for the purpose of human flourishing. In establishing an entirely new culture based in the justice of the Lord himself, Israel became a beacon for the cultures around it. In summary, Wright mentions, "The Old Testament is not content to leave the nations in the passive role of spectators of all that God was doing in Israel. The nations will come to see that God's dealings with Israel were to be, for them, not just a matter of alternating admiration or horror. The story was for their ultimate good."[28] Israel's new culture was designed to fulfill God's promise to Abraham that his family would be a blessing to the whole world.

As biblical history progressed, however, Israel would fail to live up to the Lord's ideals. After fits and starts under the leadership of Moses and Joshua, they established their nation in Canaan, but it was not until hundreds of years later, through the reign of King David, that they most fully followed the law to create the culture God intended. Sadly, this high point would devolve rapidly, as Israel rode a roller coaster of human inconsistency, unable to consistently live the culture through which God intended them to be a blessing to the world. Eventually, Israel's apostasy led to their exile.

Observing their slow fade to near oblivion, it seemed God's centuries-old covenant with Abraham would not come to fruition and the whole world would not experience the blessing of God. The prophets of Israel, however, began to point to a new hope, a coming Savior who would restore Israel, so that God's covenant of world-wide blessing would find fulfillment. Following the prophets' trajectory, we cross over into the New Testament in which the earliest Christians found that messianic hope in Jesus Christ, a hope that a new culture based in him was available for the flourishing of all.

As we learned in chapter 9, Jesus described the creation of that culture using the image of the kingdom of God as the ultimate destiny of culture. While God's kingdom had not been fully consummated, Jesus preached that in him the kingdom was near (Mark 1:14) and was working its way surprisingly and mysteriously into the world. In two brief parables in Mark 4, Jesus

---

28. Wright, *Mission of God*, 474.

suggests that the kingdom of God is first like a growing seed (Mark 4:26–29) that thrives, though the planter of the seed knows not how.

In the two millennia since Jesus first told that parable, though scientific research has unraveled the process of the growth of seeds into plants, Jesus' teaching is still helpful. The culture of the kingdom of God, he says, can grow in and among the receptor cultures of the earth. Additionally, Jesus continued, the kingdom of God is like a mustard seed (Mark 4:30–32), an incredibly small seed, and yet it grows into a large plant. Like the parable of the growing seed, here Jesus describes the process of the cultural growth of the kingdom. While by all accounts the kingdom first seems insignificant, yet there is a power deep within it, causing it to grow and bring human flourishing to the world.

But it is Jesus' teaching on prayer, what is commonly called the Lord's Prayer, that perhaps gives us the best understanding of what kind of culture Christian communities should create for human flourishing. In Matt 6:10, Jesus teaches us to pray to the Father that his kingdom would come, that his will would be done "on earth as it is in heaven."

This new culture being ushered onto and through the earth, as Jesus envisioned it, was marked by humans doing the will of God. As the will of God is perfectly obeyed in heaven, so it will be in the new culture. Jesus himself was a living, breathing example of how to live out that new kingdom culture on earth, and furthermore, he shaped a new community that would convey this new culture to the receptor cultures in which the community would live and move.

That new community, enlivened by his Spirit, launched on the day of Pentecost (Acts 2). On that day, Jesus' disciples preached to the descendants of Israel, Jewish pilgrims from many lands who gathered in the city of Jerusalem to celebrate Pentecost. What started as a Christian community of 120 men and women, led by Jesus' eleven disciples, was bolstered by three thousand more on that momentous day (Acts 2:41). We call this community the church, and we will see how it creates the new culture of the kingdom of God. Here again we will see how language, through a body of moral and theological teaching, creates culture just as it did in the Mosaic law for the nation of Israel.

In the account of the beginning of the church (Acts 2–6), we read the earliest references of the first Christians applying Jesus' teaching and language to their lived experience. In Acts 2:42–47, the church quickly became a new culture within an old one, precisely because they were in community with one another. In this passage the writer of Acts describes for us in rich detail what this new culture included.

First, they had a new theology of togetherness from the teaching of the apostles, which was based on the teaching of Jesus.[29] Like the Mosaic law, Jesus' teaching was rich in justice, flowing from love for God and others. Once, when asked what the greatest command of the law was (Matt 22:34–40), Jesus quoted the passage mentioned above on which many churches base their mission statements, a passage from Deut 6:5: "Love the LORD your God with all your heart and with all your soul and with all your strength," after which he noted that the second greatest command is "love your neighbor as yourself," from Lev 19:18.

He would further demonstrate this love through his own ministry of healing the sick, freeing the demon-possessed, and providing food for the hungry. Jesus called his followers to do the same. In Matt 25:31–46, in the parable of the sheep and the goats, he goes so far as to say that when his followers minister to the hungry, thirsty, naked, sick, and the prisoner, they are ministering *to him*. If they do not minister to those in need, they are neglecting him. So much did Jesus want his followers to create culture for human flourishing that he embedded himself in identity with those in need.

Jesus grounded this new theology of togetherness in love when he said, "A new command I give you: Love one another. As I have loved you, so you must love one another. By this everyone will know that you are my disciples, if you love one another" (John 13:34–35). The new culture of the kingdom of God would pursue human flourishing because it would be marked by love for one another, for the least of these among us, as that is the kind of love Jesus himself gave to us.

This was the new theology of togetherness, the new teaching and example that Jesus' followers were promoting as the church began in Acts 2. As theologian David Niringiye states, "What distinguished the disciples from the crowds and the seekers was that the disciples had fashioned their lives along that of Jesus."[30] As their master was so attractive, drawing crowds of thousands to follow him, the new community of the church would do likewise because their lives were so filled with his life of love.

Second, they had a new communal practice based on Jesus' teaching. They called it a fellowship, and it involved being together regularly, meeting daily in the temple's courts and meeting in homes, sharing meals, and worshiping together. Here we see the relational aspect required for Christian communities to create culture. As Jha states, "Building a movement requires

---

29. See also Acts 4:33, where the author of Acts notes that early apostolic teaching was heavily defined by the proclamation of the resurrection of Jesus, the epitome of new life and flourishing.

30. Niringiye, *Church*, 109.

relationship."[31] They were committed to one another, communicating with one another. Creating the new culture could not be accomplished in a solitary way.

Fellowship also affected their weekly calendar. We are accustomed to a work week that begins on Monday, and for many, that work week finishes on Friday or Saturday, leaving Sunday as a day off. Thus worship gatherings most often happen on Sunday. But in the ancient culture of the new community called the church, Sunday was the first day of the week and thus the first day of work. Because Jesus rose from the dead on a Sunday, the earliest Christians commemorated that crucial event weekly by gathering for worship and fellowship on Sundays. This would require many of them to work during the day Sunday and then gather in the evening in their house churches. Fellowship, then, was vital to the creation of the new culture, even when they didn't have a day off from work to make gathering convenient.

Third, they had a new togetherness approach to economy, one that undergirds human flourishing and is consistent with the teaching of Jesus. The author of Acts tells us that the church believed and lived as though they had everything in common. They sold their possessions and goods, giving the proceeds to anyone as they had need. Previously Jesus taught the rich young ruler (Luke 18:18–23) to sell everything he had and give it to the poor, and now the disciples took Jesus' teaching to heart. They did not see possessions as owned by the individual but as owned together, for whoever had need.

As the narrative continues in Acts 4:32–37 the writer of Acts gives us additional stories of Christians selling possessions, thus enabling them to support people in need. Also in Acts 6:1–6, we read that the church had a food distribution ministry for widows, who were extremely vulnerable in that culture. This is the church at work creating culture to make sure the vulnerable are cared for. When there is an ethnic breakdown in the food distribution system, the church addresses the injustice by creating a leadership structure to make sure needs continue to be met equitably. The Christian community created a new culture focused on loving sacrifice together to make human flourishing possible.

Finally, they had a new communal worship, gathering regularly in homes around tables for discussion about the apostles' teaching, for celebrating communion, and for praising God. These were powerful times of language building, which supported the community's creation of new culture. The symbols, signs, and words provided the cultural glue for the church to grow and flourish together, empowered by the Spirit of God, even

---

31. Jha, *Transforming Communities*, 138.

when they faced persecution. An entirely new culture began to emerge out of the Christian community's unique theology and practice of togetherness.

Not long after the church community's beginning, Peter once again preached to a crowd in Jerusalem. In Acts 3:24–26, he makes an astounding observation that has great implications for other Christian communities seeking to create culture for human flourishing. Preaching to a crowd of Jews, Peter grounds the story of Jesus in the earlier story of the nation of Israel. He points out that Israel's prophets had not only foretold this day but also that the descendants of Israel, the people standing before Peter, and in fact all Jews are heirs of the covenant God made with Abraham so long before. That was the covenant stating that through Abraham's offspring all peoples on the earth will be blessed (Gen 12). Peter has brought the theology of God's plan for creating culture full circle, explaining that the human flourishing God intended from the beginning now finds its ultimate fulfillment in the good news of Jesus, as lived in the communal expression of the church.

Paul would carry this new community one step further, breaking it open to the gentiles, when, in Gal 3:7–9, he writes that "those who have faith are children of Abraham. Scripture foresaw that God would justify the Gentiles by faith, and announced the gospel in advance to Abraham: 'All nations will be blessed through you.' So those who rely on faith are blessed along with Abraham, the man of faith."

Paul continues, explaining in v. 14, that Jesus "redeemed us in order that the blessing given to Abraham might come to the Gentiles through Christ Jesus, so that by faith we might receive the promise of the Spirit." Truly, the promise of human flourishing, first given to Abraham, has been fulfilled, through Christ, in the community we call the church, as it creates a new culture, exemplified by the togetherness theology of the kingdom of God.

Wright notes that Paul's "task was not merely to bring the nations to worship the right God and find salvation through faith in the gospel of Jesus Christ. He aimed at ethical transformation as well—a massive challenge in the degraded world of Greco-Roman culture."[32] Paul refers to this in his Letter to the Romans when he says, "Through him we received grace and apostleship to call all the Gentiles to the obedience that comes from faith for his name's sake" (1:5). The idea of seeing all peoples come to obey the culture of Jesus is a concept he will repeat again in Rom 15:18 and 16:25–27, the latter of which is a wonderful summary of his theological connection between the Abrahamic covenant and its fulfillment in Christ: "Now to him

---

32. Wright, *Mission of God*, 527.

who is able to establish you in accordance with my gospel, the message I proclaim about Jesus Christ, in keeping with the revelation of the mystery hidden for long ages past, but now revealed and made known through the prophetic writings by the command of the eternal God, so that all the Gentiles might come to the obedience that comes from faith—to the only wise God be glory forever through Jesus Christ! Amen."

Crouch, referring to sociologist Rodney Stark's book *The Rise of Christianity*, provides a fitting conclusion to this discussion of the scriptural narrative: "The belief of Christians that Jesus of Nazareth had been raised from the dead made them culture makers, and the culture they created was so attractive that by the fourth century AD, an entire empire was on the verge of faith."[33] In summary, the narrative of Scripture is clear: God desires human flourishing, and he has established Christian communities to create culture for that purpose.

CULTURAL CHANGE REQUIRES FLOURISHING-PRODUCING TOGETHERNESS

Scholarly observers also agree with the claim that flourishing-producing togetherness creates culture. First, regarding the necessity of togetherness to create culture, Crouch says, "The only way we can truly create cultural goods is in partnership with others, in a process where power does not so much flow from one participant to another as accrue to the overall creative capacity of a community of people, who become more and more able to contribute new and good things to the world."[34]

Reflecting on Niebuhr's comment that "radical Christianity . . . does something constructive even when it cannot intervene directly with what is going on . . . by building 'cells of those within each nation who . . . unite in a higher loyalty' than loyalty to nation or to class," theologian Charles Scriven writes that this "is nothing less than the prospect of social change through the witness of small groups—cells of Christians, if you please, who by their solidarity with Christ remake the world."[35] We create culture together.

Furthermore, scholars also identify the centrality of love as the foundation for Christian communities to create culture. "Love is the only way we will make it through what is to come. . . . It has to be a kind of love that has been honed and intensified through regular prayer, fasting, and repentance

---

33. Crouch, *Culture Making*, 159.
34. Crouch, *Culture Making*, 230.
35. Niebuhr, "Grace of Doing Nothing," 379, quoted in Scriven, *Transformation of Culture*, 194.

and, for many Christians, through receiving the holy sacraments. And it must be a love that has been refined through suffering."[36]

Or as Crouch writes, "So do you want to make culture? Find a community, a small group who can lovingly fuel your dreams and puncture your illusions."[37] Christian communities, therefore, are rife with potential to create culture, and if they do so in line with flourishing-producing togetherness, they will do so together, guided by love.

HOW CHRISTIAN COMMUNITIES CAN CREATE CULTURE TOGETHER

In conclusion, we have seen that Christian communities of all kinds must create culture for the purpose of human flourishing, and the only way to accomplish this is through love. How does a Christian community go about this momentous task of creating culture? "Culture cannot be Christian," Howell and Paris argue, "because to be a Christian is to follow Christ."[38] This is helpful to understand as we consider the concept of creating culture together. Just what kind of culture are they to create, if it is not Christian culture?

Here again, Howell and Paris guide us to one reason we create culture and thus provide a foundation for how Christian communities can create culture. They write that "God gave us different cultures so that we could understand God more fully." They continue by suggesting that "we need culture in order to learn to love and serve God."[39] If they are right, Christian communities can see their task of creating culture as a practice by which to know, love, and serve God. Because knowing, loving, and serving God is another way to describe the Christian task of discipleship, we could say that discipleship is enculturated. Christian communities, then, must view their purpose through this lens of enculturated discipleship.

Considering concepts like discipleship, the goal of Christian communities creating culture for human flourishing might be misconstrued as relegated only to the church. This is certainly understandable as our primary scriptural example thus far has been a theocracy (the ancient nation of Israel) and the early church. Given a theology of togetherness, our thesis must work for any Christian community, be it a church, business, school, or

---

36. Dreher, *Benedict Option*, 238–39.
37. Crouch, *Culture Making*, 263.
38. Howell and Paris, *Cultural Anthropology*, 38.
39. Howell and Paris, *Cultural Anthropology*, 46–47.

parachurch. Each Christian community, therefore, would do well to seek to apply the thesis of creating culture to its own unique purpose.

If the Christian community is a business, for example, the task of money-making is central to its viability, but that does not preclude the necessity of applying a theology of togetherness to every facet of the community. In other words, every Christian community should be able to answer the question, How are we working together to create culture toward human flourishing? Because this still may seem like a nebulous concept, we turn to some illustrations of Christian communities that have created culture for human flourishing.

ILLUSTRATION #1—AGAPE AND IMAGINE GOODS

In June 2016, I traveled to Cambodia with my wife. Though it was our twentieth anniversary, we were not in Cambodia on vacation, at least not primarily. While we visited the astounding Angkor Wat temples, our main purpose for travel was to work with Imagine Goods (IG).[40] My wife, Michelle, and her business partner, Aiyana, started Imagine Goods in 2008 with a heart to create culture for the purpose of human flourishing.

As a community, though not labeled as nor overtly Christian but composed of Christians, Imagine Goods sought to provide empowerment through opportunity for employment to women in Cambodia who were survivors of trafficking. The Christian ministry Agape provides them opportunity for healing through counseling and then training as seamstresses. The women create beautiful garments and other cloth-made products and are paid a fair wage, all in the hopes to provide needed opportunity to expand the thin margins of their lives, which so often lead to poverty and trafficking. Thus Imagine Goods and Agape sought to upend two injustices, that of trafficking as well as that so often found in the clothing industry.

The Imagine Goods business model involved work in both countries. In the United States Michelle and Aiyana created designs for a variety of handbags, tablecloths, skirts, dresses, and aprons. They traveled to Cambodia where they purchased material from local vendors, and then they worked with women at Agape to make sure the fabrication process was of a quality nature. After Agape shipped completed products to the USA, Michelle and Aiyana sold the products via local boutiques or through their website.

---

40. Due to lack of production resulting from shutdowns during the COVID-19 pandemic, Imagine Goods closed operations in 2021. Agape International Mission continues to operate in Cambodia. See AIM, "49.6."

During that trip in 2016 I helped Michelle select fabric. Well, I held armfuls of fabric while she selected it. I also watched as Michelle participated in meetings with the staff at Agape. The staff members told us the story of how their village just outside Phnom Penh used to be known as a global destination for sex tourism. In the village's many brothels, women and young girls were enslaved, servicing the people who would come to abuse them.

As Agape slowly started rescuing women and girls, introducing them to a new way of life as taught by Jesus, one by one the brothels shut down. In fact a local businessman had purchased a property in town and was in the process of building a hotel for sex tourists. By the time the hotel was completed, the culture in that town had changed dramatically, and sex tourism was nearly eradicated. The man sold the hotel to Agape who converted it into a church and school. Such cultural change required Christian communities working together to create a new culture for human flourishing.[41]

ILLUSTRATION #2—THE TRUTH & RECONCILIATION COMMISSION IN SOUTH AFRICA

Jenkins refers to the temptation churches have, resulting from their involvement in political revolutions that change culture, "to provide uncritical support for the new regime and to judge them by different standards from those applied to the old order."[42] While the revolution swept away oppression in the old culture, the unexamined support of the new regime can simply lead to new forms of oppression.

One impressive example of a Christian community, rooted in the theology of human flourishing, that avoided this temptation, Jenkins observes, was the Truth and Reconciliation Commission (TRC), led by Bishop Tutu in post-apartheid South Africa. The TRC, Jenkins notes, "examined the sins of the revolutionaries as searchingly as those of the government, and recognized both sides as requiring forgiveness."[43] In what could have been a vindictive response by formerly persecuted people groups, the TRC promoted forgiveness, which led to the creation of a new culture and human flourishing.

---

41. See Greer and Horst, *Entrepreneurship*; Perkins, *Beyond Charity*.
42. Jenkins, *Next Christendom*, 154.
43. Jenkins, *Next Christendom*, 154.

CONCLUSION

Cultural change for human flourishing, as we have seen, is not only possible but is the theological mandate of Christian communities, both within and outside the church. To accomplish this grand mandate, Christian communities must create new culture rooted in the theological imperatives flowing from the narrative of Scripture. The imperatives of love and justice must be employed by churches and Christian communities of all kinds to create new culture amid their receptor cultures, and as they pursue this goal, humanity will flourish.

Conclusion
A Vision of Flourishing Together

As we come to the end of this study, perhaps it would be helpful for us to encounter one more biblical picture of what flourishing-producing togetherness can accomplish in the world. To prepare for that encounter, consider a summary of what we have learned from a theology of togetherness.

We began this study by noticing that people use the word "together" and ideas such as "let's get people together," as a panacea for the world's ills. When people express a desire to be "together," they often assume at least three things: (1) that they know what they want the idea of "together" to accomplish, (2) that others also know what "together" should accomplish, and (3) that all involved agree with that goal.

But as we have seen, such a general agreement about the idea of being together is far from reality. Instead, people have often gathered together to do awful things. It begs the question, What kind of "together" do people want? Of course there are many answers to that question, answers that can be very different, or even plainly contradictory. As we saw in chapter 14 for example, some Christians believe that coming together under the banner of a red (politically conservative) church is best, while others believe in the blue (politically progressive or liberal) church. Instead, we learned that we need to ask another question: What kind of "together" *should* we strive for? In other words, what qualities of "together" should we strive for?

The quality of being together is "togetherness." I suggested that the kind of togetherness humans should strive for is encapsulated by the concept of flourishing. Flourishing, or as Jesus called it, the abundant life, is God's desire for his creation to experience life free from injustice, experiencing the bountiful characteristics of the fruit of the Spirit—love, joy, peace, patience, gentleness, kindness, goodness, faithfulness and self-control—all in healthy relationship with God and others. In God's view, therefore, this flourishing is best produced by people in communities working together. Thus the kind of togetherness we should strive for is flourishing-producing togetherness.

At this point in our study we noticed that there is a significant problem that has kept humanity, especially in the American cultural context, from experiencing and producing flourishing in our society. That problem is an unhealthy dependence on individualism. This unchecked individualism has infected not only American culture but also the theology of the Christian church in America, leading Christians to overemphasize the idea of individual salvation to the detriment of flourishing-producing togetherness.

We next learned how a theology of togetherness can counteract individualism, guiding us to become Christian communities, both inside and outside the church, who will pursue flourishing-producing togetherness. Why theology? Theology is a lens through which we can study the Scriptures to help us understand God's desire for his creation. As we looked through that lens, considering how various categories of theology understand the Scriptures, a theology of togetherness emerged.

This theology of togetherness is first rooted in our understanding of God, specifically the traditional Christian view that God is a Trinitarian community. Within his being, God is inherently a community of flourishing-producing togetherness. Therefore God's followers do well to align with God's kind of togetherness, which is a togetherness of self-giving love. Humanity in general and Christians in particular, however, are not always in line with God's heart of self-giving love, which is another way to say that we choose to sin.

We learned that corporate or institutional sin, at its core, is selfishness. To be saved from this selfishness, togetherness theology helps us see salvation as selfless emancipation. When we are saved, we are set free together, freed to covenant together for community flourishing. But this covenant is temporary, whereas God's kingdom of loving togetherness is the ultimate and eternal expression of flourishing-producing togetherness. Jesus himself taught about the kingdom, explaining that he came in love so that all people might experience the flourishing of the kingdom, both for abundant life now and for eternal life after death. Finally a theology of togetherness shows us that to experience the flourishing of the Kingdom, together we pursue union with Christ and solidarity with others.

Having studied a theology of togetherness, we explored how Christian communities, both inside and outside the church, can apply the principles of a theology of togetherness. In other words, what does flourishing-producing togetherness look like in the real world? First of all, we learned that Christian communities can practice ritual together to reframe the world as it ought to be. Christians have long practiced ritual together, even from their earliest days, but we can learn new and different rituals to help us envision together the flourishing of our contemporary world .

Second, we learned how Christian communities can practice flourishing-producing togetherness to bring unity to the political and racial divide in America. Ancient Christians embraced Jesus' teaching about togetherness and solidarity in the kingdom of God, seeking to create a new beloved community marked by equality and diversity for all. We contemporary Christians can practice the same flourishing-producing togetherness in our communities even when we disagree with one another.

Finally, in those divisive areas, especially, it is likely that Christian communities of all kinds will discover that they have not been faithful to the high bar of flourishing-producing togetherness. As a result, the next practice Christian communities need to implement is repentance together as a prerequisite for flourishing. As we conclude, let's consider again what does flourishing-producing togetherness looks like? We've seen examples throughout our study. So perhaps it would be helpful to close this study with one more illustration of flourishing: heaven.

A CONCLUDING VISION OF FLOURISHING-PRODUCING TOGETHERNESS

When you think of heaven, what images come to mind? Maybe a long line of people waiting to enter a celestial city? Does the celestial city have pearly gates connecting jewel-encrusted walls, a castle, golden streets, and angels? In my mind, for some reason, it looks a lot like the castle in Disney World's Magic Kingdom but surrounded by the walls of Jerusalem. The television show *The Good Place* had a unique take on heaven (a.k.a, "the Good Place"): a suburban main street filled with coffee shops, delicatessens, purveyors of frozen yogurt, boutiques, and people sitting outdoors around perfectly landscaped patios—something you might see in the small towns and suburbs dotting America.[1] Will heaven be like suburbia?

There are so many visions of heaven. Maybe your mind conjures bright light filling the sky over green rolling hills? Maybe your preference is a wooded forest, maybe a beach. Sometimes we think of mansions. The theologians and Bible scholars among us long for heaven to include meetings with Jesus where we ask him all sorts of questions we've agonized over. I suspect most of us hope that in heaven we get to be with loved ones who passed on. No matter what you think heaven should or could look like, my guess is that most believe it to be the epitome of flourishing.

1. Schur, *Good Place*.

Maybe you've read accounts of people who claim to die, go to heaven, and then come back to life on earth. They describe heaven somewhat like the celestial city I described above. It is impossible to know, however, if what they say is true. Instead, when we research the one source that seems like it ought to have the answers, the Bible, many find its image of heaven somewhat vague or downright confusing. When it is precise in its description of heaven, those images come mostly in apocalyptic literature like the book of Revelation, and what we read in apocalyptic literature is almost certainly symbolic. What, then, is flourishing in heaven like?

Some theologians and Bible scholars interpret the Scriptures as teaching the new heavens *and the new earth*. The vision in the book of Revelation describes the new Jerusalem as a city that comes down out of heaven to earth (Rev 21–22). Maybe heaven is not pie in the sky in the great by and by. Maybe it is the kingdom of God come to earth. Jesus seemed to have a different view of heaven than the view we Christians often use. He said things like "the kingdom of God has come near" (Mark 1:15) and "the kingdom is in your midst" (Luke 17:21). What did he mean? To take the questions in another direction, perhaps you've heard this phrase: "That person is so heavenly-minded, they are of no earthly good." Can a person be too focused on an other-worldly heaven?

I'm purposefully asking questions that don't have easy answers because I want to get you thinking. We can long for heaven because life on earth is often exceedingly frustrating, difficult, and painful. Life on earth can feel like the opposite of flourishing. When we are having those dark thoughts and feelings, we can start to think about heaven. When a loved one dies, when we're battling an awful disease, when a long-term relationship shatters, or when our finances are in shambles, we think, "Get me out of here." In those moments, we can be so sick of our personal travail on earth, that we yearn for a place like heaven where there is no more pain, sorrow, or tears.

But what if God has other plans? What if heaven isn't what we think it is? What if heaven isn't what we really want? Have you wrestled with the concept of heaven? If heaven means singing worship songs for eternity, won't that get old? I really enjoy singing worship songs, but the longest worship service I've ever participated in was in a small mountain church in Costa Rica, and I was exhausted after two hours of it, which probably had something to do with the dancing involved. Have you had those thoughts about eternity possibly getting tiresome? Have you doubted how good heaven can really be?

In response, maybe you're thinking, "Yeah, but we will be with God the Spirit, Son, and Father, along with all true believers who ever lived. We will be immersed in total perfection, so our earthly, time-bound minds cannot fathom how good heaven will be. We simply need to have faith that whatever heaven will be, it will be better than we could possibly imagine. In heaven we will flourish." Point taken. I'm counting on that, but I must admit that I still have many questions and frustratingly few answers when it comes to heaven. I suspect these kinds of questions have been on the minds of many people throughout history, and that goes for the people of ancient Israel too.

Right around the year 586 BCE,[2] the people of Israel suffered deeply at the hands of the powerful Babylonian military who decimated their nation, their holy city of Jerusalem, and their precious iconic temple. Likely thousands of Jews died, and many others were deported, joining an earlier wave of exiles that had been in Babylon for nearly fourteen years (2 Kgs 25:1–21). They were not flourishing.

Given that desperate situation, we can make an educated guess that those Jews were asking hard questions of God. How could God let this happen to his temple, his city, his people? Will God keep his promises? God had made very clear promises, and as the Jews looked at the smoking rubble of their city, those Israelites could easily be wondering if God's promises were empty. I suspect you know that feeling of fear, doubt, and struggle with faith.

How often do we look around our world and wonder about the promises of God? Are things going on in the world today that make you wonder, "God, where are you?" Your wonderings might stem from fraught international events like rogue nations test-launching hypersonic missiles or from nation mercilessly bombing and invading another nation. Our unsettledness might be due to national events, like the political and racial tension shaking our nation for years.

I would venture a guess that most often we doubt God's promises when we experience difficulty in our personal lives—a health concern, a job loss, a relationship struggle eats at us. As a result, we wonder if God cares. We wonder quietly, Is God real? And we can doubt. Though we might feel guilty about the doubt, if we start talking to people about it, what we find is that it is quite natural to feel doubt, just as it is natural to wonder if God will keep his promises. When we talk about it with others, we realize that many other people doubt. It is a distinctly human experience. Our doubt grows out of lives and a world that are not flourishing.

In Ezek 33, this kind of thinking was going through the minds of the people of Israel. News of the destruction of their beloved hometown, Jerusalem, reached the ten thousand Jewish exiles living in Babylon, including the prophet, Ezekiel. God tells Ezekiel that his countrymen nine hundred miles away in Israel were saying that since God long before gave possession

---

2. Wiseman, *1 and 2 Kings*, 334.

of the land to one man, their forefather Abraham, then of course he would give them, a nation of millions, *re*possession of the land.

When they speculated about how God should act, the people are doing theology, just as we have been attempting to do theology in this book. In Israel the people were wondering, Will God keep his promises to us? In Ezek 33, God's stern answer to the people is, "You've got to be kidding me, people. This situation you're in has nothing to do with me keeping my promises. Instead, you've gotten yourselves into this non-flourishing situation because of your persistent choice to rebel against me." God is right, of course. Those terms were clear in their covenant with God: if the people rebelled, and they repeatedly rebelled, then they would face the consequences of their behavior. That's precisely what happened when God allowed the city of Jerusalem to be destroyed.

What next? Have the people forfeited the promises of God? Is there any hope? What should they do? By the end of chapter 33, God has not answered those questions. But in chapter 34, God gives Ezekiel a prophetic word that will answer the nervous questions on the hearts and minds of the Jews. In v. 2, God asks Ezekiel to prophesy against the shepherds of Israel. Who are the shepherds of Israel? Is God talking about the many people who had the actual job of shepherding sheep? God's prophecy against the shepherds has everything to do with flourishing-producing togetherness.

I live in a community with flocks of sheep on many of the farms around us. On one local country road, when my dog and I are out running, we regularly pass a flock of sheep that are separated from us by a fencerow. If we're on their side of the road, and sheep are close to the fence, my dog will lunge at them. The sheep jump back in fright. But the threat is not real because my dog is on a leash and the sheep are safe behind the fence. In Lancaster, we have many flocks of sheep, but we have neither a profession of sheepherding nor a class of workers that herd sheep. Instead farmers own flocks of sheep. Our is a very different practice of shepherding than that of Ezekiel's day. It is also very different from shepherding in many parts of the world still today.

When my family lived in Kingston, Jamaica, a man would walk his cattle through the streets of the city looking for grass on which they could graze. Imagine, a herd of animals in the middle of a city! Our neighborhood was located on the side of a fairly steep hill, so the man would herd the cattle up our road and into our lawn where they could eat. Then he would "beg a couple limes" for himself from our lime tree, and once the cattle were finished, he would keep them moving on up the road to find another yard.

In Ezekiel's era sheep herding was like that. It was far more nomadic than the fenced-in sheep my dog and I run by along the country road. In ancient times, as in many places around the world still today, flocks of sheep wander across vast stretches of land in search for grass to eat and water to drink. Shepherds would sometimes follow the sheep, sometimes guide and direct them, and also protect them from theft, predators, and natural pitfalls. Shepherds would bind up wounds and train the sheep how to move and not wander off. When one sheep walked away from the flock, that lone sheep was in exponentially increased danger. A shepherd was to pay close attention, count the sheep, and know the sheep. The sheep were the source of the shepherd's livelihood; the shepherd took care of the sheep so that both they and his family would flourish.

Though God says this prophetic word is for the shepherds of Israel, he's not talking about the sheepherders or sheep. Who is he talking about then? In Ezek 34, vv. 2–10, God says the shepherds of Israel have done a horrible job. They have not cared for the sheep while, at the same time, they have cared for themselves. God calls the sheep "*his* sheep." He had given the shepherds of Israel the task of stewardship of his sheep, but their individualistic selfish streak left the sheep in a position that was the opposite of flourishing. The sheep have been scattered, preyed upon by wild animals. God says that his herd of sheep are now on the verge of being eradicated. But like I said, God is not talking about shepherds and sheep.

God is using shepherds and their sheep as a metaphor to depict exactly what the kings of Israel and Judah allowed to happen to the people of Israel under their watch. A summary of the history of the nation of Israel for centuries before Ezekiel's era is a very, very sad story. Every human king of Israel succumbed to individualistic selfishness, just as we all do. This selfish pattern began after the reign of the great king Solomon, who himself had numerous issues, when the nation split in two. Ten tribes to the north formed the new nation of Israel, and two tribes to the south formed the new nation of Judah (1 Kgs 12:20–21). As noted earlier in the chapter, the kings in the north were one wicked king after the other, choosing to rebel against the way of God.

These wicked kings not only perpetrated individual evil, often motivated by greed and power, but they also allowed evil to be done among God's people. The kings led the people to worship foreign gods and idols, sometimes including child sacrifice, and they committed acts of corporate evil such as slavery and economic injustice (2 Kgs 17:7–23). The kings of Israel were selfish rather than focused on flourishing-producing togetherness. In the end God allowed the foreign superpower Assyria to invade and conquer the northern kingdom of Israel (2 Kgs 17:1–6).

In the south, in the Kingdom of Judah, things were better. It was, however, a bit of a roller coaster ride. Some were wicked like the kings in the north (for example, 1 Kgs 15:23, 34; 16:20, 25, 30; 2 Kgs 13:2), and some were exceedingly good, like Josiah (2 Kgs 21:26—23:30) or Hezekiah (2 Kgs 18–20), who made significant reforms to bring the kingdom back in line with God's heart and way. But eventually, Judah had its own run of bad kings (2 Kgs 23:32, 37; 24:9, 19). Like the kings of the north, the Judean kings were also selfish, and neither they nor the people flourished.

The situation in the south deteriorated in two stages. In the first stage, responding to a string of wicked kings, God allowed another superpower, Babylon, to defeat Judah's capital city, Jerusalem, and to exile ten thousand Jews back to Babylon (2 Kgs 24:10-17), including Ezekiel (Ezek 1:1-3). Stage two involved the events as told in Ezek 33, where Babylon destroyed the city, the temple, and exiled more people.

During Israel and Judah's rebellion, it was not as if God was outside the picture, watching from afar. Whenever a wicked king and the people rebelled, God would send prophets, pleading with the people and the kings to together repent and return to following God's ways. Sometimes the kings and the people heeded the prophet's words. Often they ignored the prophets.

Within that larger story, we now focus on the people mentioned in Ezek 33, the Jews living in Jerusalem. How could they ignore the prophets after Babylon had already defeated them and exiled ten thousand of their countrymen and women? Here's how: After that first wave of exiles was deported to Babylon, the people could still surmise, "At least the temple is still intact." As they sought to answer the question of whether God was keeping his promises rather than consider their role in breaking the covenant, they looked at the temple standing strong as evidence that things must be fine.

As we learned above, that didn't last long. Babylon had installed a Jewish puppet king in Jerusalem, but he was such a terrible shepherd of God's people that he not only chose to ignore God's ways but he also rebelled against Babylon. Babylon's response was to devastate the city. Now exiled in Babylon, you can imagine people wondering, What about the promises of God now? God answers that question in Ezek 34:11–15, with another question: Who is the true king of Israel?

There were plenty of human kings over Israel, but the human monarchy had largely been a disaster. To rectify their situation, Israel needed to see that God was their true king all along. In God's covenant with Israel for centuries past, he said that if the people and kings of Israel would worship, serve, and love God as their true king, and if their earthly kings would lead the people in proclaiming and obeying God as the true king, then God would bless them. That's flourishing, living together in the blessing of God.

But the kings and people did not follow God, so now he proclaims that he is the true king and he will shepherd his people together toward flourishing. This is a theme that pops up in many places in the Bible, perhaps most famously by David in Ps 23—"the Lord is my Shepherd, I lack nothing" (v. 1). In that psalm, though David was the human king, it is the Lord who was his shepherd. David, though he is king, has the right perspective on God. David must submit to God because God is the true leader. The result? "He makes me lie down in green pastures, he leads me beside quiet waters, he refreshes my soul" (vv. 2–3), and on and on David writes, describing a vision of flourishing provided by God the shepherd.

Here also in Ezek 34:16–22, God is attempting to restore the correct understanding of himself as the Shepherd King of the people. He has some rehab work to do because there were so many bad kings, and the people looked to human kings, as well as foreign kings, to save and protect them rather than looking to God.

God starts by noting that he will reach out to rescue and care for the lost, the injured, and the weak. We expect the owner of the flock to do just that. What he does next, though, might sound controversial. God says that the strong and sleek he will destroy. What does God have against the strong and sleek? It can seem that God is biased in favor of the poor and hurting, the marginalized, those who have faced injustice. Here we see God's heart for justice, as he goes on to describe how the strong have committed injustice against the weak. Flourishing requires justice, especially for those on the margins.

The strong have allowed the weak on the margins to live in a world where they are floundering rather than flourishing. In vv. 17–19, we learn that the weak have been beaten down at the hands of the wealthy and powerful. The strong are now compared to sheep who not only have their fill of the lush grass but also stomp on the uneaten grass, thus leaving none for any of the weaker sheep. The strong are like sheep who not only have their thirst quenched by clean water but also muddy the remaining water, making it non-potable for the rest.

Note that God is speaking in general terms. He is not saying that these principles of injustice are at work in every single case. Sometimes the poor are poor because they made bad decisions. Sometimes the poor are poor because they spend their money unwisely or they are lazy or gluttons. But often, far more often, the gap between the rich and poor is widened because the rich have the access and power to control the wealth gap, and they want to keep it that way. This is precisely what happened in ancient Israel. The wealthy powerful kings made sure that they stayed rich and powerful at the expense of the people. The kings allowed selfish individualism to guide their desires rather than God's heart for flourishing-producing togetherness.

In response to this systemic injustice, God declares that he is on the move. This is why he allowed Assyria to defeat Israel to the north, and it is why he allowed Babylon to destroy Jerusalem and Judah to the south. When God gave Ezekiel this prophecy, there was no longer an Israelite monarchy. Not in the north and not in the south. The monarchy was over.

This is what God refers to when he says he will judge between the fat and the lean sheep. The fat ones, the kings of Israel, drove away the lean skinny sheep, the powerless starving people. Now God says that he will shepherd a new flock, a flock made up of the skinny sheep. God will be the shepherd of the skinny sheep. God's heart beats for the downcast, the poor, the hungry, the homeless, the foreigner, the widow, the orphan, the refugee. This is the theological principle of flourishing-producing togetherness we have seen throughout Scripture, in both the Old and New Testaments.

God will create a new flock made up of the marginalized. In fact, in vv. 23–31, God shares a new vision of hope for the people. While God will be the new shepherd for the shepherdless, he will also bring them into a land where they can flourish. Though the people were in exile in Babylon and though it seemed that Babylon was more powerful than God, God will rescue them. He will restore them, and he will give them the land. But the restored, flourishing land won't be like it was before the exile. The wealthy powerful kings will be gone. There will be a new king, a new shepherd king, of the line of David. God will be their God, and this new Davidic king will be a servant prince.

God also promises to make a new covenant of peace. The people had broken the old covenant God had previously made with Moses. Now he will make a better covenant of peace. When we think of a peace deal, we think of a treaty to end armed conflict between nations—a peace accord. God is thinking of something much more than that. That word "peace" (*shalom*) is expansive in meaning. It is the idea of human flourishing, which speaks to a place and a means for people to be fruitful and multiply. No more injustice. Now justice will reign. No more wealthy, powerful kings hoarding the resources and oppressing the marginalized, as now there will be enough for all. They will flourish together. In the covenant of peace, God's vision for his people is that of communal flourishing.

This covenant of peace guided by flourishing-producing togetherness is not socialism or communism. It is the loving generosity of God that flows from God to his people and through his people to the rest of the earth. This new covenant of peace is not coerced. It is the natural outflow of God's heart as his people live in that peace. There is safety. There is food. There is rain. There is freedom. Most of all, God is there among his people. What a vision of flourishing! This is the place where the longings of human hearts are satisfied because God is there.

Best of all, this vision is not just for the ancient people of Israel. This hope for flourishing is for the whole world. In Jesus, we see that God has kept his promises because Jesus also called himself the good shepherd, the fulfillment of the Davidic King God promised would come and shepherd his people for flourishing together. One of the best pieces of advice I ever heard about the hard times in life, the times when God seems absent is to remember the cross. On the cross, the shepherd gives his life for the sheep. Remembering that he gave his life for us doesn't mean the pain or doubt will leave. It means that we have hope in life. Jesus has defeated sin and death and together we can experience the flourishing life now as well as have hope for eternal life.

Is Ezek 34 a vision of heaven? It certainly is that. Heaven is the ultimate expression of the kingdom of God. But remember what Jesus taught us to pray: "your kingdom come, your will be done, on earth as it is in heaven" (Matt 6:10). What we read at the end of Ezek 34 is also attainable now. Jesus said that we, his disciples, together usher in the kingdom. Together, we are to help all people experience human flourishing. Just like a good Father wants his children to flourish, so does our heavenly Father!

So does God keep his promises? It depends what promises you think God has made to us. For example, God has not promised us an easy life. If you think human flourishing and the abundant life means an easy, comfortable, entertaining life full of great health, effortless relationships, and lots of money and possessions, then God will not keep that promise. Because he never made that promise. He promises instead a flourishing, abundant life in his kingdom. We usher in God's kingdom when we practice flourishing-producing togetherness.

Appendix 1
Additional Suggestions for Practicing Ritual, Habits, and Disciplines Together

Given the discussion of the importance of persistent ritual practice to pursue human flourishing, listed below are some additional ideas for practicing flourishing-producing togetherness in Christian communities.

Encounter of the Other: This is the practice of exposing oneself to other cultures or living with those with whom we disagree, using the concept of "argument for the sake of heaven."[1] Purposefully gather one community amidst another community. Short-term mission trips can be a helpful practice. Christian communities can work together to help resettle refugee families in their area.

Sitting with the Grieving: "In the Jewish custom of *shiva*, a bereaved family sits together for a week and is visited by members of the community and by friends."[2] In those periods of loss and pain, periods marked by feelings that seem to be the opposite of flourishing, we can produce flourishing by being together for love and support of those who are grieving.

Shabbat: The biblical concept of Sabbath rest can be recaptured and reframed for twenty-first-century technologically-inundated families. "Thirty-three centuries ago, Moses liberated the Israelites from slavery to Egypt. Now, the same institution is liberating young people from slavery to smartphones."[3]

Baptism: "Contact with the Kingdom of God would restore baptism to its original ethical and spiritual purity."[4] In other words, if we can move our understanding of baptism away from an individualistic theology toward

1. Sacks, *Morality*, 186–87.
2. Sacks, *Morality*, 39.
3. Sacks, *Morality*, 47.
4. Rauschenbusch, *Social Gospel*, 201.

a social one, we will find a ritual embedded with impetus for flourishing. What principles can we learn from the ritual of baptism that might lead to other nonsectarian rituals that could help Christian communities pursue such flourishing? Baptism is rich with the symbolism of washing and rebirth to a new way of thinking that leads to a new life. What other rituals could Christian communities design to celebrate new commitment to a new community?

Communion / Lord's Supper: Where baptism is about consecration and convocation, communion is about ongoing recommitment. First, communion is a symbol and rite of remembrance for the purpose of realignment to the mission (1 Cor 11:23–25). Communion is also about proclamation of the good news of Jesus (1 Cor 11:26) and participation in his flourishing life (1 Cor 10:16). "Within the world of the game, children are superheroes and puppies, just as a wafer is the Body of Christ. Children do not need to be able to fly or wag their tails any more than the wafer needs skin and hair."[5] Jesus said, "This *is* my body" and "this *is* my blood." There is a real sense in which transubstantiation, viewed ritually, is important and formative. Not that the bread itself is changed into the literal body of Christ but that the person enacting the ritual is changed. The economy of communion is "grounded in a social vision of economics as described in Acts 4:32–35 and evident in the Jerusalem Love Community (*social locus of ethical activity*). The following are among the numerous guidelines for business practices that have been developed for this movement: promote initiatives that favor people who are in need (also known as the preferential option for the poor); communal structures should be designed to nurture human relationships among stakeholders because people—not work—are at the center of a business; provide safe, healthy and hospitable workplaces; obey the law; and practice participative decision-making."[6]

Mentoring: "Any leader needs a mentor, a counsel, a wise voice that one trusts, who can look at a situation dispassionately and say, quietly and confidentially, 'Not a good idea.'"[7] I started seeing a spiritual director a year ago. Every month I start to feel uncomfortable when my next spiritual direction appointment is only a few days away. My discomfort stems from the reality that my spiritual director is so good, so helpful. In other words, he asks me difficult questions, probing my relationship with God. I need that. Spiritual direction, whether one-on-one or in groups, can be a practice of flourishing-producing togetherness.

---

5. Seligman et al., *Ritual*, 73.
6. Dyck and Wiebe, "Salvation Across the Centuries," 316.
7. Sacks, *Morality*, 40.

Fair Wages: "In 1965 the ratio of chief executive to worker pay in the United States was twenty to one. Today it is three-hundred-twelve to one."[8] What can Christian communities inside and outside the church do to pursue fair pay? Too often workers feel isolated in their ability to advocate for better working conditions and wages.

Create a morals or ethics governing board, or an accountability board with actual veto power. Every Christian community, but especially those in the business world, could benefit from a board that can evaluate that community's actions.

Story Telling / Witnessing: In particular, stories "of the redemption of suffering"[9] are beneficial. They bring people together, storyteller with listener or reader. A friend of mine is incarcerated, and when he was first sent to prison, he longed for stories about people like him who had committed a crime but who also experienced flourishing. He wanted assurance of hope for a new flourishing life because his choices in life had brought him to the low point of incarceration. When a prison chaplain gave him a book of stories about people who committed similar crimes to his own and who had experienced a life change, my friend devoured the book. We can tell stories of redemption to inspire flourishing. Similarly, a community could create myths for the purpose of engaging the imagination of its people. This is quite in line with Jesus' use of parable. "A mythic conceptualization provides those who would practice emancipation in their respective contexts an opportunity to articulate a contemporary emancipation myth that provides for a greater degree of relief from suffering. . . . Mythic expression, based on deeply rooted archetypes, is capable of providing us with the means to express a different myth that grounds us within our common humanity."[10]

Restorative Justice: What should one Christian community do, corporately, if it sees another community perpetrating injustice? Rather than rely on a system of punitive justice so common in our culture, the community could seek, together, to advocate for restorative justice. This is not easy and should not be taken lightly, as abusers in power often fight hard to retain their power, causing additional harm, especially when they are perceived as successful and can point to results.

Limitations on Individualism: For example, does any one person need to be a billionaire? We can wrestle with questions of the economics of individualism. Should a society limit personal wealth to improve the lives of the society at large? Could a Christian community, and especially a Christian

---

8. Sacks, *Morality*, 90.
9. Sacks, *Morality*, 246.
10. Seligman et al., *Ritual*, 319.

business, handle pay scale differently than the status quo in society? For example, must a chief executive office make ten times the salary of the average employee?

Moral Community: "We can share all kinds of things in the world—subways, soccer teams, grocery stores, fear of the police—without ever coming together as a moral community, much less accepting the existence of other moral communities. Moral communities require sharing empathy, not just spaces, times, and objects."[11]

---

11. Seligman et al., *Ritual*, 97.

Appendix 2
Questions Asked of Ministerium Churches Regarding Diversity[12]

ARE ANY OF YOUR churches more closely aligned with the demographic of our school district?

Have any churches in the last ten to fifteen years seen a demographic movement toward a diversity that is more in line with that of the community, even if the change was miniscule? If so, why did this change happen? Was it intentional on your part? What choices did you and your congregation make to encourage this?

Are any churches similar to Faith Church, meaning that your demographic is fairly different from that of the community? Why do you think this is the case?

If Christian people of color are not attending our churches, where do they worship?

---

12. The responses to these questions are discussed in ch. 18.

Bibliography

Abdelaziz, Salma. "ISIS Publicly Smashes Syrian Artifacts." *CNN*, July 3, 2015. https://www.cnn.com/2015/07/02/world/isis-syrian-artifacts/index.html.

Adams, Liam. "New Denomination Announces May Launch as United Methodist Church Inches Toward Split Over LGBTQ Rights." *Nashville Tennessean*, Mar. 3, 2022. https://www.tennessean.com/story/news/religion/2022/03/03/global-methodist-church-announces-launch-umc-postpones-general-conference-lgbtq-rights/9367534002/.

Agape International Mission (AIM). "49.6." https://aimfree.org/child-trafficking/.

Alexander, Michelle. *The New Jim Crow: Mass Incarceration in the Age of Colorblindness*. New York: New Press, 2012.

American Battlefield Trust. "Civil War Casualties: The Cost of War; Killed, Wounded, Captured, and Missing." Last updated Sept. 15, 2023. https://www.battlefields.org/learn/articles/civil-war-casualties.

———. "Pickett's Charge: That July Afternoon in 1863." https://www.battlefields.org/learn/articles/picketts-charge.

Andersson, Hilary. "Social Media Apps Are 'Deliberately' Addictive to Users." *BBC*, July 3, 2018. https://www.bbc.com/news/technology-44640959.

Aquinas, Thomas. *Summa Theologiae*. 2nd ed. Translated by the Fathers of the English Dominican Province. 1920. Revised and edited by Kevin Knight for New Advent, 2017. https://www.newadvent.org/summa/.

Armstrong, John H. *Your Church Is Too Small: Why Unity in Christ's Mission Is Vital to the Future of the Church*. Grand Rapids: Zondervan, 2010.

Austin, Ashley, et al. "Suicidality Among Transgender Youth: Elucidating the Role of Interpersonal Risk Factors." *Journal of Interpersonal Violence* 37.5–6 (Apr. 2020) NP2696–NP2718. doi:10.1177/0886260520915554.

B Lab. "Make Business a Force for Good." https://www.bcorporation.net/en-us.

Barnes, Jacalyn, et al, eds. *An American Lent Devotional*. Repentance Project, 2019. https://static1.squarespace.com/static/61fc038c685dca1fba1e2b85/t/620a6b63268c723e56954dc3/1644850040665/An-American-Lent-2022.pdf.

Bates, Matthew W. *Salvation by Allegiance Alone: Rethinking Faith, Works and the Gospel of Jesus the King*. Grand Rapids: Baker Academic, 2017.

Bebbington, D. W. *Evangelicalism in Modern Britain: A History From the 1730s to the 1980s*. New York: Routledge, 1989.

Beck, Richard. "A Non-Zero Sum Conversation Between the Traditional Church and the Gay Community." *Rachel Held Evans* (blog), Nov. 11, 2011. https://rachelheldevans.com/blog/richard-beck-traditional-church-gay-community.

Becker, Penny E. *Congregations in Conflict: Cultural Models of Local Religious Life*. New York: Cambridge University Press, 1999.

Bellah, Robert N., et al. *The Good Society*. New York: Alfred A. Knopf, 1991.

Ben & Jerry's. "Ben & Jerry's Joins the B Corp Movement." 2024. https://www.benjerry.com/about-us/b-corp.

Bessey, Sarah. "Only Way We All Keep Going Is Together." Instagram photo, Aug. 11, 2021. https://www.instagram.com/p/CScGVwfFpn2/.

Biewin, John, and Chenjerai Kumanyika. "How Race Was Made." Season 2, episode 1, *Seeing White*. Edited by Loretta Williams. Mar. 1, 2017, on *Scene on Radio*. https://sceneonradio.org/episode-32-how-race-was-made-seeing-white-part-2/.

———. "That's Not Us, So We're Clean." Season 2, episode 6, *Seeing White*. Edited by Loretta Williams. Apr. 26, 2017, on *Scene on Radio*. https://sceneonradio.org/episode-36-thats-not-us-so-were-clean-seeing-white-part-6/.

Bingham, Nathan, and Stephen Nichols. "What Is the Goal of Studying Theology?" Lingonier Ministries, May 4, 2023. https://www.ligonier.org/podcasts/ask-ligonier/what-is-the-goal-of-studying-theology.

Bird, Brad, dir. *The Incredibles*. Emeryville, CA: Disney/Pixar, 2004.

Bloesch, Donald G. *Jesus Christ: Savior and Lord*. Downers Grove, IL: InterVarsity, 1997.

Blomberg, Craig L., et al. *From Pentecost to Patmos: An Introduction to Acts Through Revelation*. 2nd ed. Nashville: B&H Academic, 2021.

Boers, Arthur. *Servants and Fools: A Biblical Theology of Leadership*. Nashville: Abingdon, 2015.

Boersma, Hans. "The Beatific Vision: Contemplating Christ as the Future Present." In *Embracing Contemplation: Reclaiming a Christian Spiritual Practice*, edited by John H. Coe and Kyle C. Strobel, 203–23. Downers Grove, IL: IVP Academic, 2019.

Boff, Leonardo. *Holy Trinity, Perfect Community*. Maryknoll, NY: Orbis, 2000.

Boggs, W. Brady, and Dale L. Fields. "Exploring Organizational Culture and Performance of Christian Churches." *International Journal of Organization Theory and Behavior*. 13.3 (2010) 305–34.

Bonhoeffer, Dietrich. *Life Together: A Discussion Of Christian Fellowship*. San Francisco: Harper, 1954.

Bookman, Ezra. Ritualist (website). https://www.ritualist.life/.

Bowles, Nellie. "Doing God's Work." *New York Times*, Aug. 30, 2020.

Boyd, Gregory. "What Do You Think of Thomas Aquinas' View of God?" *ReKnew*, Dec. 23, 2007. https://reknew.org/2007/12/what-about-thomas-aquinas-view-of-god/.

Bradley, Jamin. "If Everyone in Your Church Is Just Like You, You Have a Problem." *Relevant Magazine*, Aug. 30, 2023. https://relevantmagazine.com/god/church/if-everyone-in-your-church-is-just-like-you-you-have-a-problem/.

Brandt, Ryan A. "Gospel-Centered Contemplation?" In *Embracing Contemplation: Reclaiming a Christian Spiritual Practice*, edited by John H. Coe and Kyle C. Strobel, 185–202. Downers Grove, IL: IVP Academic, 2019.

Brueggemann, Walter. *The Prophetic Imagination*. 40th anniv. ed. Minneapolis: Fortress, 2018.

Budziszewski, J. "The Problem With Communitarianism." *First Things*, March 1995. https://www.firstthings.com/article/1995/03/the-problem-with-communitarianism.

Cambridge German-English Dictionary. "Gemeinschaftlich." 2018. https://dictionary.cambridge.org/us/dictionary/german-english/gemeinschaftlich.

Carson, D. A., and Douglas J. Moo. *An Introduction to the New Testament.* 2nd ed. Grand Rapids: Zondervan, 2005.

Carson, Don, and Michael Reeves. "Studying Theology for the Glory of God." Gospel Coalition, Aug. 22, 2023. https://www.thegospelcoalition.org/sermon/studying-theology-for-the-glory-of-god/.

Carten, Alma. "How the Legacy of Slavery Affects the Mental Health of Black Americans Today." *The Conversation*, July 27, 2015. https://theconversation.com/how-the-legacy-of-slavery-affects-the-mental-health-of-black-americans-today-44642.

CompuServe. "About CompuServe." Yahoo. https://www.compuserve.com/home/about.jsp.

Cone, James. *The Cross and The Lynching Tree.* New York: Orbis, 2011.

Conestoga Valley School District. "Conestoga Valley School District: At a Glance." 2024. https://www.conestogavalley.org/district/homepage.

Corbett, Steve, and Brian Fikkert. *When Helping Hurts: How to Alleviate Poverty Without Hurting the Poor . . . and Yourself.* Chicago: Moody, 2009.

Cornell, Tom. "A Brief Introduction to the Catholic Worker Movement." *Catholic Worker Movement*, Sept. 11, 2005. https://www.catholicworker.org/cornell-history.html.

Crabb, Larry. *Inside Out.* Colorado Springs: Navigators, 2013.

Crouch, Andy. *Culture Making: Recovering Our Creative Calling.* Downers Grove, IL: InterVarsity, 2008.

Cummins, S. A. "John the Baptist." In *Dictionary of Jesus and the Gospels*, edited by Joel B. Green et al., 436–44. 2nd ed. Downers Grove, IL: InterVarsity, 2013.

Dalrymple, Timothy. "The Splintering of the Evangelical Soul." *Christianity Today*, April 16, 2021. https://www.christianitytoday.com/ct/2021/april-web-only/splintering-of-evangelical-soul.html.

Dashort, Patricia, et al. "Intergenerational Consequences of the Holocaust on Offspring Mental Health: A Systematic Review of Associated Factors and Mechanisms." *European Journal of Psychotraumatology* 10.1 (2019) 1–29. https://doi.org/10.1080/20008198.2019.1654065.

DeFranza, Megan K., et al. *Two Views on Homosexuality, the Bible, and the Church.* Edited by Preston Sprinkle. Grand Rapids: Zondervan, 2016.

DeGruy, Joy. *Post Traumatic Slave Syndrome: America's Legacy of Enduring Injury and Healing.* Rev. ed. N.p.: Joy DeGruy, 2017.

Delgado, Richard, and Jean Stefancic. *Critical Race Theory: An Introduction.* 3rd ed. New York: New York University Press, 2017.

DeSilver, Drew. "Turnout in U.S. Has Soared in Recent Elections but by Some Measures Still Trails That of Many Other Countries." *Pew Research Center*, Nov. 1, 2022. https://www.pewresearch.org/fact-tank/2020/11/03/in-past-elections-u-s-trailed-most-developed-countries-in-voter-turnout/.

DeYmaz, Mark. *Building a Healthy Multi-Ethnic Church: Mandate, Commitments and Practices of a Diverse Congregation.* San Francisco: Jossey-Bass, 2007.

DeYmaz, Mark, and Harry Li. *Leading a Healthy Multi-Ethnic Church: Seven Common Challenges and How to Overcome Them.* Grand Rapids: Zondervan, 2010.

DeYoung, Curtiss P., et al. *United by Faith: The Multiracial Congregation as an Answer to the Problem of Race*. New York: Oxford University Press, 2003.

Dias, Elizabeth, and Ruth Graham. "The Growing Religious Fervor in the American Right: 'This Is a Jesus Movement.'" *New York Times*, Apr. 11, 2022. https://www.nytimes.com/2022/04/06/us/christian-right-wing-politics.html.

Dorsey, David A. *The Literary Structure of the Old Testament: A Commentary on Genesis–Malachi*. Grand Rapids: Baker Academic, 1999.

Doyle, Glennon. "Queer Freedom: How Can We Be Both Held and Free?" *We Can Do Hard Things*. https://www.audacy.com/1043jams/topic/glennon-doyle.

Dreher, Rod. *The Benedict Option: A Strategy for Christians in a Post-Christian Nation*. New York: Sentinel, 2018.

———. "The Great Christian Sorting: Now Is the Time to Find a Church and a Spirituality Built on a Solid Rock." *American Conservative*, June 28, 2020. https://www.theamericanconservative.com/dreher/the-great-christian-sorting-orthodox-church.

Dubner, Stephen J. "The U.S. Is Just Different—So Let's Stop Pretending We're Not." *Freakonomics Radio*, July 14, 2021. Produced by Brent Katz. https://freakonomics.com/podcast/american-culture-1/.

Dunn, James D. G. *The Theology of Paul the Apostle*. Grand Rapids: Eerdmans, 1998.

Dyck, Bruno, and Elden Wiebe. "Salvation, Theology and Organizational Practices Across the Centuries." *Organization* 19.3 (2012) 299–324. https://doi.org/10.1177/1350508412437073.

Emerson, Michael O., and Christian Smith. *Divided by Faith: Evangelical Religion and the Problem of Race in America*. New York: Oxford University Press, 2000.

Enns, Peter, and Jared Byas. "Xavier Pickett: So When Did White Christian America Lose Its Mind?" *Bible For Normal People*, Feb. 25, 2019. Podcast, 54:00. https://thebiblefornormalpeople.com/so-when-did-white-christian-america-lose-its-mind/.

Ephrata Cloister. "History: Historic Ephrata Cloister; A Unique 18th-Century Monastic Settlement." https://ephratacloister.org/about/history/.

Ferguson, Sinclair. "The Goal of Doing Theology." *TableTalk*, Feb. 2018. https://tabletalkmagazine.com/article/2018/02/the-goal-of-doing-theology/.

Figart, Thomas. *A Biblical Perspective on the Race Problem*. Grand Rapids: Baker, 1973.

Frame, Randy. "Violence Against Abortion Clinics Escalates Despite the Opposition of Prolife Leaders." *Christianity Today*, Feb. 1, 1985. https://www.christianitytoday.com/1985/02/violence-against-abortion-clinics-escalates-despite/.

Francis. *Fratelli Tutti*. Encyclical letter. Vatican website. Oct. 3, 2020. https://www.vatican.va/content/francesco/en/encyclicals/documents/papa-francesco_20201003_enciclica-fratelli-tutti.html.

Freeman, Stephen. "The Sins of a Nation." *Glory to God for All Things* (blog), June 4, 2020. https://blogs.ancientfaith.com/glory2godforallthings/2020/06/04/the-sins-of-a-nation-3/.

French, David, and Curtis Chang. "Liberty University and the Reality of Institutional Sin." *Good Faith*, Nov. 20, 2021. https://good-faith.simplecast.com/episodes/liberty-university-and-the-reality-of-institutional-sin.

Garces-Foley, Kathleen. "New Opportunities and New Values: The Emergence of the Multicultural Church." *Annals of the American Academy of Political and Social Science* 612.1 (2007) 209–24. https://doi.org/10.1177%2F0002716207301068.

———. "Multiethnic Congregations." In *Racism*, edited by Robert B. Kruschwitz, 62–69. Christian Reflection: A Series in Faith and Ethics. Waco, TX: Center for Christian Ethics at Baylor University, 2010. https://www.baylor.edu/content/services/document.php/110977.pdf.

Gebara, Ivone. *Out of the Depths: Women's Experience of Evil and Salvation*. Minneapolis: Fortress, 2002.

Graham, Michael, and Skyler Flowers. "The Six Way Fracturing of Evangelicalism." *Mere Orthodoxy*, June 7, 2021. https://mereorthodoxy.com/six-way-fracturing-evangelicalism/.

Gramlich, John. "Far More Americans Say There Are Strong Conflicts Between Partisans Than Between Other Groups in Society." *Pew Research*, Dec. 19, 2017. https://www.pewresearch.org/fact-tank/2017/12/19/far-more-americans-say-there-are-strong-conflicts-between-partisans-than-between-other-groups-in-society/.

Green, Emma. "The Crisis of American Christianity, Viewed from Great Britain: The Theologian N. T. Wright Is Unfazed by the Faith's Politicization in the U.S." *Atlantic*, Dec. 1, 2019. https://www.theatlantic.com/politics/archive/2019/12/nt-wright-american-evangelicals-and-trump/602749/.

Greer, Peter, and Chris Horst. *Entrepreneurship for Human Flourishing*. Washington, DC: AEI, 2014.

———. *Mission Drift: The Unspoken Crisis Facing Leaders, Charities and Churches*. Minneapolis: Bethany House, 2014.

Griswold, Eliza. "Silence Is Not Spiritual: The Evangelical #MeToo Movement." *New Yorker*, June 15, 2018. https://www.newyorker.com/news/on-religion/silence-is-not-spiritual-the-evangelical-metoo-movement.

Gross, Jörg, and Carsten K. W. de Dreu. "Individual Solutions to Shared Problems Create a Modern Tragedy of the Commons." *Science Advances* 5.4 (Apr. 2019). https://doi.org/10.1126/sciadv.aau7296.

Grylls, Bear, host. *Running Wild with Bear Grylls*. Season 3, episode 4, "Shaquille O'Neal." Aired Aug. 29, 2016. https://www.amazon.com/gp/video/detail/B084ZYR8HL/ref=atv_dp_share_cu_r.

Halfbrick. *Fruit Ninja Classic*. Halfbrick Studios, 2010. https://www.halfbrick.com/games/fruit-ninja-classic.

Halloran, Michael J. "African American Health and Posttraumatic Slave Syndrome: A Terror Management Theory Account." *Journal of Black Studies* 50.1 (2019) 45–65. https://journals.sagepub.com/doi/full/10.1177/0021934718803737.

Hao, Karen. "Troll Farms Reached 140 Million Americans a Month on Facebook Before 2020 Election, Internal Report Shows." *MIT Technology Review*, Sept. 16, 2021. https://www.technologyreview.com/2021/09/16/1035851/facebook-troll-farms-report-us-2020-election/.

Harrill, J. Albert. "Slavery." In *Dictionary of New Testament Background: A Compendium of Contemporary Biblical Scholarship*, 1124–27. Downers Grove, IL: InterVarsity, 2000.

Hart, Drew G. I. *Trouble I've Seen: Changing the Way the Church Views Racism*. Harrisonburg, VA: Herald, 2016.

———. *Who Will Be A Witness? Igniting Activism for God's Justice, Love, and Deliverance*. Harrisonburg, VA: Herald, 2020.

Havel, Vaclav. *Disturbing the Peace: A Conversation with Karel Hvizdala*. Translated by Paul Wilson. New York: Knopf, 1990.

Haven, Cynthia. "Stalin Killed Millions: A Stanford Historian Answers the Question, Was It Genocide?" *Stanford Report*, Sept. 23, 2010. https://news.stanford.edu/stories/2010/09/naimark-stalin-genocide-092310.

Hendriksen, William, and Simon J. Kistemaker. *Exposition of Galatians*. New Testament Commentary 8. Grand Rapids: Baker, 2001.

Heschel, Abraham Joshua. *God in Search of Man: A Philosophy of Judaism*. New York: Farrar, Straus & Giroux, 1983.

Higdon, Hal. "Marathon Training: Novice 1." https://www.halhigdon.com/training-programs/marathon-training/novice-1-marathon/.

Hill, Wesley. *Spiritual Friendship: Finding Love in the Church as a Celibate Gay Christian*. Grand Rapids: Brazos, 2015.

———. *Washed and Waiting: Reflections on Christian Faithfulness and Spirituality*. Expand. ed. Grand Rapids: Zondervan, 2016.

Hillenbrand, Laura. *Unbroken: A World War II Story of Survival, Resilience and Redemption*. New York: Random House, 2014.

Hirsch, Alan. *The Forgotten Ways: Reactivating Apostolic Movements*. 2nd ed. Grand Rapids: Brazos, 2016.

Hirsch, Alan, and Mark Nelson. *Reframation: Seeing God, People, and Mission Through Reenchanted Frames*. San Bernardino: 100Movements, 2019.

Holmes, Barbara A. *Joy Unspeakable: Contemplative Practices of the Black Church*. 2nd ed. Minneapolis: Fortress, 2017.

Hooker, Morna. *Not Ashamed of the Gospel: New Testament Interpretations of the Death of Christ*. Grand Rapids: Eerdmans, 1994.

Howell, Brian, and Janell Paris. *Introducing Cultural Anthropology: A Christian Perspective*. Grand Rapids: Baker Academic, 2010.

Hunter, James Davison. *To Change the World: The Irony, Tragedy and Possibility of Christianity in the Late Modern World*. New York: Oxford University Press, 2010.

Hurley, Lawrence. "Trump's Justices Decisive in Long Campaign to Overturn Roe v. Wade." *Reuters*, June 24, 2022.

James, Carolyn Custis. *Half the Church: Recapturing God's Global Vision for Women*. Grand Rapids: Zondervan, 2010.

Jenkins, Philip. *The Next Christendom: The Coming of Global Christianity*. New York: Oxford University Press, 2002.

Jha, Sandhya Rani. *Transforming Communities: How People Like You Are Healing Their Neighborhoods*. St. Louis: Chalice, 2017.

Jolie, Angelina, dir. *Unbroken*. Beverly Hills, CA: 3 Arts Entertainment, 2014.

Keller, Timothy, and Katherine Leary Alsdorf. *Every Good Endeavor: Connecting Your Work To God's Work*. New York: Dutton, 2012.

Kendi, Ibram X. *Stamped From the Beginning: The Definitive History of Racist Ideas in America*. New York: Bold Type, 2016.

Kime, Joel. "Is 1 Corinthians 6:9–11 Really About Homosexuality?" *Engaging Scripture* (blog), Apr. 16, 2014. https://joelkime.com/2014/04/16/is-1-corinthians-6_9–11-really-about-homosexuality/.

King, Jonathan. *The Beauty of the Lord: Theology as Aesthetics*. Bellingham, WA: Lexham, 2018.

King, Martin Luther, Jr. "Dr. Martin Luther King's Visit to Cornell College." News Center, Cornell College. https://news.cornellcollege.edu/dr-martin-luther-kings-visit-to-cornell-college/.

Koch, Richard. "Is Individualism Good or Bad?" *HuffPost*, Jan. 23, 2014. https://www.huffpost.com/entry/is-individualism-good-or-_b_4056305.

Koehler, Ludwig, et al. *The Hebrew and Aramaic Lexicon of the Old Testament*. 5 vols. Leiden: Brill, 1994–2000. Logos.

Kotz, Deborah. "University of Maryland School of Medicine Faculty Scientists and Clinicians Perform Historic First Successful Transplant of Porcine Heart into Adult Human with End-Stage Heart Disease." University of Maryland School of Medicine, Jan. 10, 2022. https://www.medschool.umaryland.edu/news/2022/University-of-Maryland-School-of-Medicine-Faculty-Scientists-and-Clinicians-Perform-Historic-First-Successful-Transplant-of-Porcine-Heart-into-Adult-Human-with-End-Stage-Heart-Disease.html.

Kranz, Jeffrey. "All the 'One Another' Commands in the NT." *Overview Bible*, Mar. 9, 2014. https://overviewbible.com/one-another-infographic/.

Kristof, Nicholas D., and Sheryl WuDunn. *Half the Sky: Turning Oppression into Opportunity for Women Worldwide*. New York: Alfred A. Knopf, 2009.

Ladd, George Eldon. *The Gospel of the Kingdom: Scriptural Studies in the Kingdom of God*. Grand Rapids: Eerdmans, 1959.

Larson, Frances. "ISIS Beheadings: Why We're Too Horrified to Watch, Too Fascinated to Turn Away." *CNN*, Jan. 13, 2015. https://www.cnn.com/2015/01/13/opinion/beheadings-history/index.html.

LaSor, William S., et al. *Old Testament Survey: The Message, Form, and Background of the Old Testament*. 2nd ed. Grand Rapids: Eerdmans, 1996.

Ledbetter, Bernice M., et al. *Reviewing Leadership: A Christian Evaluation of Current Approaches*. 2nd ed. Grand Rapids: Baker Academic, 2016.

Lederleitner, Mary T. *Women in God's Mission: Accepting the Invitation to Serve and Lead*. Downers Grove, IL: InterVarsity, 2018.

Liu, Amy, and Alan Berube. "Big Cities Aren't Dividing America: They Hold the Key to Our Collective Future." *Brookings*, Nov. 9, 2021. https://www.brookings.edu/blog/the-avenue/2021/11/09/big-cities-arent-dividing-america-they-hold-the-key-to-our-collective-future/.

Live. "Operation Spirit (The Tyranny of Tradition) (Live at the Roxy)." Track 26 on *Mental Jewelry*. 25th anniv. ed. UMG Recordings, 2017.

Louw, Johannes P., and Eugene Albert Nida, eds. *Greek-English Lexicon of the New Testament: Based on Semantic Domains*. 2nd ed. New York: United Bible Societies, 1996.

Marsden, George M. *Fundamentalism and American Culture*. 2nd ed. New York: Oxford University Press, 2006.

McGowan, Andrew B. *Ancient Christian Worship: Early Church Practices in Social, Historical, and Theological Perspective*. Grand Rapids: Baker Academic, 2014.

McKnight, Scot. *A Fellowship of Differents: Showing the World God's Design for Life Together*. Grand Rapids: Zondervan, 2014.

———. *The Letter to the Colossians*. New International Commentary on the New Testament. Grand Rapids: Eerdmans, 2018.

McKnight, Scot, and Laura Barringer. *A Church Called Tov: Forming a Goodness Culture That Resists Abuses of Power and Promotes Healing*. Carol Stream, IL: Tyndale Elevate, 2020.

McWhorter, Matthew R. "Aquinas on God's Relation to the World." *New Blackfriars* 94.1049 (2013) 3–19. https://doi.org/10.1111/j.1741-2005.2012.01483.x.

Merriam-Webster Dictionary. "Together." 11th ed. Springfield, MA: Merriam Webster, 2003. https://www.merriam-webster.com/dictionary/together.
Meta. "Introducing Meta: A Social Technology Company." Meta, Oct. 28, 2021. https://about.fb.com/news/2021/10/facebook-company-is-now-meta/.
me too. "You Are Not Alone." https://metoomvmt.org/.
Miller, David W. *God At Work: The History and Promise of the Faith at Work Movement*. New York: Oxford University Press, 2007.
Miller, Matthew M. F. "The Radical Individualism Raging Throughout America." *Shondaland*, Nov. 20, 2020. https://www.shondaland.com/act/news-politics/a34729330/the-radical-individualism-raging-throughout-america/.
Moore, Osheta. *Dear White Peacemakers: Dismantling Racism with Grit and Grace*. Harrisonburg, VA: Herald, 2021.
Moreland, J. P. *Finding Quiet: My Story of Overcoming Anxiety and the Practices That Brought Peace*. Grand Rapids: Zondervan, 2019.
Moreland, J. P., and William Lane Craig. *Philosophical Foundations for a Christian Worldview*. Downers Grove, IL: InterVarsity, 2003.
Morrison, Latasha. *Be the Bridge: Pursuing God's Heart for Racial Reconciliation*. Colorado Springs: Waterbrook, 2019.
Mundey, Peter. *Sacred Consumption: The Religions of Christianity and Consumerism in America*. Lanham, MD: Lexington, 2023.
National Human Genome Research Institute. "Genetics v. Genomics Fact Sheet." Last updated Sept. 7, 2018. https://www.genome.gov/about-genomics/fact-sheets/Genetics-vs-Genomics.
Newbigin, Lesslie. *The Gospel in a Pluralist Society*. Grand Rapids: Eerdmans, 1989.
Niebuhr, H. Richard. *Christ and Culture*. New York: Harper, 1956.
———. "The Grace of Doing Nothing." *Christian Century*, Mar. 23, 1932.
Niringiye, David Zac. *The Church: God's Pilgrim People*. Downers Grove, IL: InterVarsity, 2015.
Noll, Mark A. *America's God: From Jonathan Edwards to Abraham Lincoln*. New York: Oxford, 2002.
———. *A History of Christianity in the United States and Canada*. 2nd ed. Grand Rapids: Eerdmans, 2019.
Oden, Thomas C. *Systematic Theology: Life in the Spirit*. Vol. 3. Peabody, MA: Hendrickson, 2006.
Orr, James, et al. *The Fundamentals: A Testimony to the Truth*. Chicago: Testimony, 1910. https://digitalcommons.biola.edu/the-fundamentals/1.
Overgaard, Christian Staal Bruun, and Gina M. Masullo. "Finding Common Ground: Habits That May Help." *Center for Media Engagement*, Aug. 30, 2020. https://mediaengagement.org/research/finding-common-ground/.
Ozenc, Kursat, and Margaret Hagan. *Rituals for Work: 50 Ways to Create Engagement, Shared Purpose and a Culture That Can Adapt to Change*. Hoboken, NJ: Wiley, 2019.
Painter, Nell Irvin. *The History of White People*. New York: W. W. Norton, 2010.
Park, Andrew Sung. *The Wounded Heart of God: The Asian Concept of Han and the Christian Doctrine of Sin*. Nashville: Abingdon, 1993.
Patagonia. "B Lab." 2024. https://www.patagonia.com/b-lab.html.

Patriot News. "The End of Alabama 'Inbetween'? 2016 Is a Chance to Retired a Tired Stereotype." *Patriot News*, Apr. 11, 2016. https://www.pennlive.com/opinion/2016/04/alabama_inbetween_2016_is_a_ch.html.

Paulsen, Gary. *Hatchet*. New York: Simon & Schuster, 1987.

Perkins, John M. *Beyond Charity: The Call to Christian Community Development*. Grand Rapids: Baker, 1993.

Perkins, John M., and Karen Waddles. *He Calls Me Friend: The Healing Power of Friendship in a Lonely World*. Chicago: Moody, 2019.

Perrin, Nicholas. *The Kingdom of God: A Biblical Theology*. Grand Rapids: Zondervan, 2019.

Persons, Stow. *Socialism and American Life*. Vol. 1. Princeton: Princeton University Press, 2015.

Pew Research Center. "Political Polarization in the American Public: How Increasing Ideological Uniformity and Partisan Antipathy Affect Politics, Compromise and Everyday Life." June 12, 2014. https://www.pewresearch.org/politics/2014/06/12/political-polarization-in-the-american-public/.

Pianigiani, Gaia, and Jack Ewing. "Days May Be Numbered for World's Oldest Bank." *New York Times*, Aug. 17, 2021. https://www.nytimes.com/2021/08/17/business/days-may-be-numbered-for-the-worlds-oldest-bank.html.

Poirier, Agnes. "Coffee and Revolution." *Guardian*, Apr. 11, 2008. https://www.theguardian.com/travel/2008/apr/12/paris.may1968.

Pollack, Susan. "The Idea of the Beloved Community." *Psychology Today*, Jan. 13, 2023. https://www.psychologytoday.com/us/blog/the-art-of-now/202301/the-idea-of-the-beloved-community.

Powery, Emerson B., and Rodney S. Sadler Jr. *The Genesis of Liberation: Biblical Interpretation in the Antebellum Narratives of the Enslaved*. Louisville: Westminster John Knox, 2016.

Rah, Soong-Chan. *Prophetic Lament: A Call for Justice in Troubled Times*. Downers Grove, IL: InterVarsity, 2015.

Rauschenbusch, Walter. *A Theology for the Social Gospel*. Eastford, CT: Martino, 2011.

Reuters. "Facebook Says Took Down 1.3 Billion Fake Accounts in Oct–Dec." Mar. 22, 2021. https://www.reuters.com/article/facebook-misinformation-int/facebook-says-took-down-1-3-billion-fake-accounts-in-oct-dec-idUSKBN2BE12M.

Rivera, Bridget Eileen. *Heavy Burdens: Seven Ways LGBTQ Christians Experience Harm in the Church*. Grand Rapids: Brazos, 2021.

Rothstein, Richard. *The Color of Law: A Forgotten History of How Our Government Segregated America*. New York: Liveright, 2017.

Rotundi, Jessica Pearce. "How Coffee Fueled Revolutions—And Revolutionary Ideas." *History*, Feb. 11, 2020. https://www.history.com/news/coffee-houses-revolutions.

Rusakoff, Dale. "In Pa. Governor's Race, a Democratic Divide." *Washington Post*, Apr. 3, 2002. https://www.washingtonpost.com/archive/politics/2002/04/03/in-pa-governors-race-a-democratic-divide/a0ff8a12-bb13-4445-b4de-b9e6e42352d8/.

Rusaw, A. Carol. "All God's Children: Leading Diversity in Churches as Organizations." *Leadership Quarterly* 7.2 (1996) 229–41.

Rutledge, Fleming. *The Crucifixion: Understanding the Death of Jesus Christ*. Grand Rapids: Eerdmans, 2017.

Sacks, Jonathan. *Morality: Restoring the Common Good in Divided Times*. New York: Basic, 2020.

Salley, Columbus, and Ronald Behm. *Your God Is Too White*. Downers Grove, IL: InterVarsity, 1970.

Sanders, E. P. *Paul and Palestinian Judaism: A Comparison of Patterns of Religion*. Philadelphia: Fortress, 1977.

Schmemann, Alexander. *For the Life of the World: Sacraments and Orthodoxy*. Yonkers, NY: SVSP, 2018.

Schur, Michael, dir. *The Good Place*. Los Angeles, CA: Fremulon Studios, 2018. https://www.nbc.com/the-good-place.

Schwanda, Tom. "'To Gaze on the Beauty of the Lord': Evangelical Resistance and Retrieval of Contemplation." In *Embracing Contemplation: Reclaiming a Christian Spiritual Practice*, edited by John H. Coe and Kyle C. Strobel, 95–117. Downers Grove, IL: IVP Academic, 2019.

Scriven, Charles. *The Transformation of Culture: Christian Social Ethics After H. Richard Niebuhr*. Scottdale, PA: Herald, 1988.

Seeds. "Seeds Intro Video." Produced by Five Thirteen Media. Apr. 14, 2023. Vimeo, 1:02. https://vimeo.com/817714997.

Seigler, M. G. "Facebook Is Too Big, Fail." *Medium*, Oct. 4, 2021. https://500ish.com/facebook-is-too-big-fail-eb8c143a9afc.

Seligman, Adam B., et al. *Ritual and Its Consequences: An Essay on the Limits of Sincerity*. New York: Oxford University Press, 2008.

Shellnut, Kate. "Biggest Mennonite Conference Leaves Denomination." *Christianity Today*, Jan. 2, 2018. https://www.christianitytoday.com/news/2018/january/biggest-mennonite-conference-leaves-denomination.html.

Sherman, Amy L. *Kingdom Calling: Vocational Stewardship For the Common Good*. Downers Grove, IL: InterVarsity, 2011.

Shoemakers Academy. "Online Footwear Courses: Break into the Shoe Business." https://www.sneakerfactory.net/.

Small Business Trends. "Small Business Statistics." *Small Business Trends*, July 9, 2021. https://smallbiztrends.com/tag/small-business-statistics/.

Soanes, Catherine, and Angus Stevenson, eds. "Gemeinschaft." *Concise Oxford English Dictionary*. Oxford: Oxford University Press, 2004.

Sørensen, Bent Meier, et al. "Theology and Organization." *Organization* 19.3 (May 2012) 267–79.

Stroopies. "We Are About So Much More Than Making Cookies!" https://www.stroopies.com/.

Sweeney, Douglas A. *The American Evangelical Story: A History of the Movement*. Grand Rapids: Baker Academic, 2005.

Sweet, Leonard. *From Tablet to Table: Where Community Is Formed and Identity Is Found*. Colorado Springs: Navigators, 2014.

Thomas á Kempis. *The Imitation of Christ*. In *The Treasury of Christian Spiritual Classics*, 433–554. Nashville: Thomas Nelson, 1994.

Thurman, Howard. *Disciplines of the Spirit*. Richmond, IN: Friends United, 1963.

Tigay, Jeffrey H. *Deuteronomy*. JPS Torah Commentary. Philadelphia: Jewish Publication Society, 1996.

Tisby, Jemar. *The Color of Compromise*. Grand Rapids: Zondervan, 2019.

———. *How to Fight Racism: Courageous Christianity and the Journey Toward Racial Justice*. Grand Rapids: Zondervan, 2021.

Tozer, A. W. *The Knowledge of the Holy: The Attributes of God; Their Meaning in the Christian Life*. Lincoln, NE: Back to the Bible, 1961.

Treat, Jeremy. *Seek First: How the Kingdom of God Changes Everything*. Grand Rapids: Zondervan, 2019.

Vadukul, Alex. "Aleksander Doba, Who Kayaked Across the Atlantic, Dies at 74." *New York Times*, Mar. 11, 2021. https://www.nytimes.com/2021/03/11/world/europe/aleksander-doba-dead.html.

Vernimmen, Tim. "Why Do Humans Embrace Rituals? Disease and Danger May Be at the Root of the Behaviors." *National Geographic*, Jan. 12, 2021. https://www.nationalgeographic.com/science/2021/01/why-do-humans-embrace-rituals-disease-and-danger-may-be-at-the-root/.

Volf, Miroslav. *After Our Likeness: The Church as the Image of the Trinity*. Grand Rapids: Eerdmans, 1998.

———. *Exclusion and Embrace: A Theological Exploration of Identity, Otherness, and Reconciliation*. Nashville: Abingdon, 1996.

Volf, Miroslav, and Matthew Croasmun. *For the Life of the World: Theology That Makes a Difference*. Grand Rapids: Brazos, 2019.

Vroegop, Mark. *Weep with Me: How Lament Opens a Door for Racial Reconciliation*. Wheaton: Crossway, 2020.

Walker, Carter. "Could Lancaster County One Day Vote Democrat? Here Is What Recent Election Data Show." *LNP/LancasterOnline*, May 22, 2020. https://lancasteronline.com/news/local/could-lancaster-county-one-day-vote-democrat-here-is-what-recent-election-data-show/article_6f51326e-32fd-11ea-97be-73bc808d8337.html.

Wallis, Jim. *God's Politics: Why the Right Gets It Wrong and the Left Doesn't Get It*. San Francisco: Harper, 2005.

Warren, Tish Harrison. "7 Thoughtful Reader Responses on Ending Online Church." *New York Times*, Feb. 6, 2022. https://www.nytimes.com/2022/02/06/opinion/online-church-services-readers.html.

———. "Churches Should Drop Their Online Services." *New York Times*, Jan. 30, 2022.

Webber, Robert. *Ancient-Future Worship: Proclaiming and Enacting God's Narrative*. Grand Rapids: Baker, 2008.

Welch, Skot, et al. *Plantation Jesus: Race, Faith, and a New Way Forward*. Harrisonburg, VA: Herald, 2018.

Weltman, Barbara. "Sole Proprietorships Continue to Increase in Numbers." *Big Ideas For Small Business*, May 30, 2019. https://bigideasforsmallbusiness.com/sole-proprietorships-continue-to-increase-in-numbers/.

Wesley, John. *A Plain Account of Christian Perfection*. In *Thoughts, Addresses, Prayers, Letters*, 366–446. The Works of John Wesley 11. Edited by Thomas Jackson. The Wesley Center Online. http://wesley.nnu.edu/john-wesley/a-plain-account-of-christian-perfection/.

Wie-Skillern, Jane, and Nora Silver. "Four Network Principles for Collaboration Success." *Foundation Review* 5.1 (2013) 121–29. https://doi.org/10.4087/FOUNDATIONREVIEW-D-12-00018.1.

Willard, Dallas. *The Divine Conspiracy: Rediscovering Our Hidden Life in God*. San Francisco: Harper, 1998.

Williams, Reggie L. *Bonhoeffer's Black Jesus: Harlem Renaissance Theology and an Ethic of Resistance*. Waco: Baylor University Press, 2014.

Wilson-Hartgrove, Jonathan. *Reconstructing the Gospel: Finding Freedom from Slaveholder Religion*. Downers Grove, IL: InterVarsity, 2018.

Wiseman, Donald J. *1 and 2 Kings: An Introduction and Commentary*. Tyndale Old Testament Commentaries 9. Downers Grove, IL: InterVarsity, 1993.

Witt, Shawn, et al., prods. *Alone*. Season 1. Jun–Aug. 2015, on History. https://play.history.com/shows/alone.

Wright, Christopher J. H. *The Mission of God: Unlocking the Bible's Grand Narrative*. Downers Grove, IL: IVP Academic, 2006.

Wright, H. Norman and Wes Roberts. *Before You Say "I Do": A Marriage Preparation Guide for Couples*. Eugene, OR: Harvest House, 2019.

Wright, N. T. *The Day the Revolution Began: Reconsidering the Meaning of Jesus's Crucifixion*. New York: HarperOne, 2016.

———. *God and the Pandemic: A Christian Reflection on the Coronavirus and Its Aftermath*. Grand Rapids: Zondervan, 2020.

———. *What Saint Paul Really Said*. Grand Rapids: Eerdmans, 1997.

Yancey, George. *Beyond Racial Division: A Unifying Alternative to Colorblindness and Antiracism*. Downers Grove, IL: InterVarsity, 2022.

———. *One Body, One Spirit: Principles of Successful Multi-Racial Church*. Downers Grove, IL: InterVarsity, 2003.

Yoder, John Howard. *The Politics of Jesus*. Grand Rapids: Eerdmans, 1994.

Young, William P. *The Shack*. Newbury Park, CA: Windblown, 2007.

Zemeckis, Robert, dir. *Cast Away*. Los Angelas, CA: Twentieth Century Fox, 2000. https://www.amcplus.com/movies/cast-away--1062437.

www.ingramcontent.com/pod-product-compliance
Lightning Source LLC
Chambersburg PA
CBHW071330190426
43193CB00041B/1053